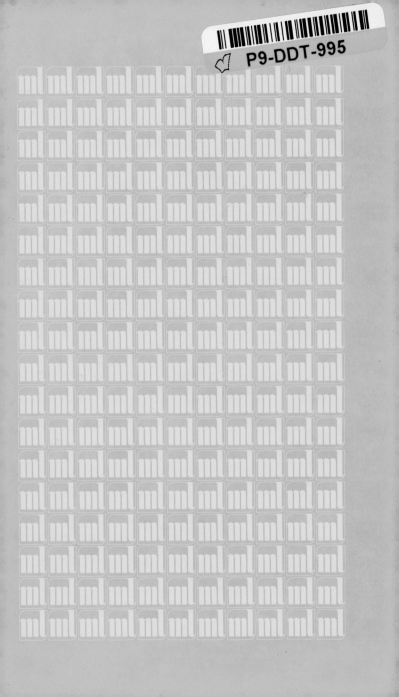

THE COMPLETE PLAYS
OF JEAN RACINE

I

JEAN RACINE

❦❦❦

COMPLETE PLAYS

*Translated into English Verse and with a
Foreword and Notes by*

SAMUEL SOLOMON

Introduction by Katherine Wheatley

[IN TWO VOLUMES]

VOLUME I

THE MODERN LIBRARY • NEW YORK

To
Jonathan, my son,
who encouraged me
to persevere

CONTENTS

INTRODUCTION
to Volume I

Samuel Solomon's translations of Racine's complete dramatic works are a splendid mutation in translation of Racine, a mutation in the concept of the relation of the language used by the translator to the language of the original, and a mutation in the concept of the relation of the translator to the author translated.

Whether he was born with it or acquired it, Mr. Solomon has the same aesthetic as Racine, *la bienséance*, in the broadest sense of the term, of the age of taste of French classicism. Because he completely understands the aesthetic of the author he is translating, Mr. Solomon's translations are superb. And this may be said of each and every play as a whole, although each one falls short of perfection, of course, in some details. Not a few lines may fall below the level of *good*, even. But as a whole each play comes close enough to perfection for anyone who knows Racine well to say that Racine has found his translator and that the untranslatable has been translated for the first time in the three hundred years which have gone by since the spectators at the Hôtel de Bourgogne witnessed the miracle of *Andromaque*, and the third *great* dramatic poet of France's golden age was revealed to the public—the great tragic poet of the Sun King and of the age of mature French classicism. Since that memorable day Racine's fortunes and reputation in France have had their ups and downs; however, with a long line of discerning critics he has been acclaimed a great tragic poet and a great living dramatist who belongs in the theatre, as opposed to the study or the classroom.

Until now Racine has been inaccessible to the English-speaking world, except for the few who are able to read him in the original.

Not everybody who reads the French language with ease is included among those few who are able to read Racine, since to do
so one must have a special reading technique.

Despite his small vocabulary, consisting largely of simple
words used in ordinary speech, his almost modern syntax, and
the rapid and easy flow of his Alexandrines, the precision and
density of his style constitute one barrier, but not the most formidable one. The essential requisite for reading Racine is dramatic
imagination. A reader must be able to hear in his imagination
the tones that give affective meaning to the lines of Racinian
dialogue.

A translator must be able to do even more. He must be able
to read the original French with imagination, and he must in
addition be able to hear those tones of his own language that
give it affective value, finding corresponding patterns in which to
transpose Racine's French. He must also realize that style in the
aesthetic of the fitness of things is not something added to the
dialogue (ornamentation, imagery, "splendid diction"). Style
must be self-effacing in order to perform its proper function: to
make perceptible the drama, the struggle, the clash of character,
interests, motives moving toward a central crisis (*noeud*) through
crescendo after crescendo of emotion and, having reached that
central crisis, moving on, still in crescendo, to the final eruption
in the act of violence that brings the action to a definitive end.

The principal function of Racine's style is to project this drama;
poetry is strictly subordinated to this function, according to the
principle of propriety or appropriateness. According to the same
principle, nothing but the dramatic is appropriate to the dramatic
genre. All irrelevant and inert matter must be eliminated.*

According to the doctrine of the fitness of things, of internal
harmony, Racine's style and versification vary with the speaker,
the moment at which he speaks, the person to whom he speaks,

---

* At this point I should like to offer a suggestion to English readers; i.e., that
they would do well not to look to the neo-classical age in England for an aesthetic
akin to that of Racine and Boileau, Boileau as he is seen today, the Boileau who
translated and interpreted Longinus and who praised La Fontaine for the *je ne
sais quoi* that is the mark of genius. They might find something much closer to
the aesthetic of French classicism in Coleridge. Paradoxical as this may seem, the
similarity can be explained as a matter of similar background and training in the
study of the literature of classical antiquity in minds of comparable caliber and
similar bent.

and the momentum of all that has gone before. Mr. Solomon interprets before he translates because he is aware that in a tight and complex form like the Racinian genre, every word has its function in the structure of the whole, and even the placement of a word or phrase may be vital. He interprets deeply the nexus of psychological currents and the complex emotions and their hidden springs in Racine's personages; he hears their tones.

He is deaf to the confusing medley of the voices of English critics around him, with their sorry pronouncements on Racine's shortcomings as a poet. He takes the step necessary to make Racine come alive in English, a step no translator has, to my knowledge, taken before him. Mr. Solomon uses the English language as Racine uses the French. He imitates Racine's style. And he brings to life something that has never before been perceptible in English translations: the dramatic movement of psychological events occurring in the minds of the speakers and conveyed to the spectator, who is also a listener, by the style of the dialogue itself.

He does not decide a priori on a style or a verse form and apply it indiscriminately everywhere, as translators today apparently do, and as all adapters and translators of the past have done, as far as I know. He varies the style as Racine does. This too is in accordance with the doctrine of *la bienséance*.

Racine created his tragedies deliberately, it must be assumed, but, guided by his own aesthetic principles, from subject matter varying greatly in nature from play to play. The style and the versification vary fittingly. Into each he puts his own tragic vision, and therefore the tragic in one play differs from the tragic in another, according to the subject treated. (See Raymond Picard's masterly synthesis of all the essential elements in each tragedy in his Introductions, in the *Pléiade* Edition of Racine.)

Since *Andromaque* represents a mutation in Racine's style just as Mr. Solomon's translations represent a mutation in translations of Racine, it seems fitting to center my remarks on the translations in this volume around that particular play. The Racinian style of dialogue first appeared there. (See Raymond Picard's Introduction to *Alexandre*, in the *Pléiade* edition of Racine.) The tragedy itself is a new genre, the Racinian genre, par excellence. *Andromaque* is a new form of crisis-tragedy, itself a form that developed in seventeenth-century France because the public preferred it to panoramic drama, as noted by Jacques Scherer. The subject is love, viewed as a powerful, amoral, primitive instinct that paralyzes the will and beguiles the reason of its victims (according to Paul Bénichou), overriding obligations to the state and to the society of individuals with whom the tragic personages are associated and, in the end, overriding another powerful instinct, that of self-preservation:

CLÉONE (*The voice of reason*)
Vous vous perdez, madame, et vous devez songer . . .

HERMIONE
Que je me perde ou non, je songe à me venger. (verses 1255–56)

Andromaque may be called the tragedy of the narrow room, for the destined and the doomed face one another in a narrow room where fortune or the destiny of their own tragic weakness has brought them together and is keeping them. They must break away from one another or die before evening comes, for the nature of the emotional tension between them makes death or madness the inevitable end, unless their wills are strong enough to remove them from the circle of doom. The lives of three tragic personages, Oreste, Hermione, and Pyrrhus, are hopelessly enmeshed, and all three lives are enmeshed with that of a fourth personage, Andromaque, who is not living in the present but in the past.

In *Andromaque*, in *Bajazet*, and in certain scenes of all the tragedies after *Andromaque*, when two tragic personages meet and talk, there is crescendo of emotional tension. They talk at cross-purposes, trying to deceive each other or deceiving themselves. The dialogue is a fragmentary and imperfect reflection of the complex emotions that are driving them, but the emotional implications are clear because of the style. Under the circumstances the characters may not wish to be explicit, but they could not be so even if they wished because they are in the grip of emotion. Their true feelings and motives, hidden by their words, are made clear to the spectator (the listener), and then inadvertently revealed to the interlocutor. In *la chaleur du théâtre*, they do not converse with each other; they react to a protest that bursts out too quickly to be reasoned, and reveals behind the pretext, expressed by the words, a secret motive; they react to a word that stings, to a tone that chills words intended to appear warm, or to a warmth that colors a speaker's voice despite the speaker's effort to appear cold, even to a revealing silence. They look *at* each other and speak *to* each other. The unloved scans the beloved's face in order to surprise the truth in the revelatory, involuntary gesture: a shadow that flits unbidden across that face, and in the face, Racine's personages watch especially the eyes, the involuntary veiling with the eyelids of what is within,* an absent look, an involuntary movement of eyes following thoughts that are elsewhere.

All of this drama of the mind that can be put into words and suggested by words is conveyed by the style of Racinian dialogue. Racine imitates emotional speech (Le Bidois). An observer of emotional speech in both French and English knows that it has its own syntax, its own sentence structure, its own grammar, its own pitch patterns, different emotions manifesting themselves in different arrangements of these elements, and that in the expression of emotion the two languages come closer to one another than in the expression of cool, logical thought.

Violent emotion expresses itself in short, disconnected sentences. There is no descriptive element. Brevity and force are the essential qualities. Verbs and pronouns are all-important. Descriptive adjectives and picturesque nouns are banished, as are adverbs. Racine's Alexandrines have the sentence structure of emotional speech, as noted by Le Bidois: no logical connectives, no connectives at all, no logical subordination in long complex sentences; simple sentences unconnected except by the order in which they follow one another; very few inversions.

Racine's favorite figures of speech are "figures of thought," not "figures of words." They are *irony*, which indicates "tension between speakers" (D'Aubignac), and *interrogation*, which shows "agitation of mind" (D'Aubignac). Racine's questions convey many emotions. Most characteristic is the question that conveys a violent, spontaneous, immediate reaction of one person to something said by another. The question itself is often a vehicle for bitter irony. The Racinian question is never the rhetorical question of an orator haranguing a crowd. Two figures of syntax

---

* Compare with George Meredith: "Her eyes were guilty gates that let him in / By shutting, all too zealous for their sin."

appear frequently, ellipsis and syllepsis. These two figures are rhetorical only because they have been listed by grammarians in their analyses of Latin poetry. They do not *sound* rhetorical in Racine's poetry. Emotional speech has gaps in it and no speaker violently moved pays meticulous attention to rules of agreement and reference of pronouns. This type of dramatic dialogue, most constant and most frenetic in *Andromaque*, occurs in all Racinian tragedy in the "confrontation" scenes, in the private lives of emperors and kings.

The rhythm of the Alexandrine does not exist without emotion to create it. Twelve syllables on the printed page with a pause in the middle and at the end do not constitute an Alexandrine. The stresses of the Alexandrine fall at the end of a syntactic group. There is no word stress, only group stress. The break at the sixth syllable, or at the end may be slight or strongly marked. The number, placement, and force of the stresses in a line vary with the emotion of the speaker; the tempo may be hurried or slow.

There are tirades in Racine, but there are also very short speeches. A speech may be only a part of an Alexandrine. It may be only one strongly stressed word with the pitch pattern of a strong emotion. Néron says to Narcisse, "It's happened at last! Néron is in love!"—Narcisse's shock and surprise are expressed in a single word, "*Vous!*" Almost everybody is aware that the English pronoun, *you*, may convey various strong emotions, each one having its own intonation.

Racine's Alexandrines are focused on the word having the highest emotional charge or the heaviest semantic load. For example, Iphigénie accuses Eriphile of being secretly in love with Achille. Eriphile protests, too vehemently. Iphigénie interrupts her in the middle of a sentence and the middle of an Alexandrine. She repeats her accusation furiously: "*...Oui, vous l'aimez, perfide.*" The interruption itself indicates a spontaneous outburst. All the emphasis is on the verb *aimez*. The second syllable would have the abnormal rise in pitch of special emphasis. It should translate itself into English thus: "Yes, you *love* him, ——," the abusive epithet being the only problem, since we do not use adjectives as nouns or epithets of this type. Mr. Solomon translates: "Yes, you *love* him, traitress." But I know of no one else who does. Charles Johnson lengthens the line out thus: "Eriphile, you love that dreadful man."* This is no longer a woman in love, angrily giving the lie to a hypocritical rival. Johnson's Iphigénie is reciting poetry, as his age saw poetry. He is what F. Y. Eccles called one of the "romantic cobblers," who patched up Racine for the English theatre in the early eighteenth century. Without exception, these inferior dramatists and poetasters printed off on their grotesque imitations of Racine a cliché of style, which they identified with the English language itself.†

It is, strictly speaking, impossible to imitate the rhythm of the Alexandrine in English because of the difference between the dynamics of spoken French and the dynamics of spoken English. The tremendous relative force of the stressed syllable in English often causes English dramatic poetry to fall into a thumping pentameter or tetrameter, whether in blank verse or in the heroic couplet. The line from Charles Johnson's *The Victim*, quoted above, is a good example. But Charles Johnson scarcely deserves the name of poet at all; still less that of dramatist. Whether because of the fetish for adjective-noun combinations (both words having the strongest sentence stress) or because Johnson felt the need for a rhythm marked by strong regularly recurring accents alternating with very weakly stressed syllables, this line falls into a thumping beat that deadens its dramatic force. But this is not good English poetry.

Fine English poets use the gradations of sentence stress (or sense stress) to give their poetry a subtler dynamics. Thus in Shakespeare's most dramatic lines, sequences of monosyllabic words with some degree of sentence stress subdue the ictus, while phrasing and emotional intonations of special emphasis follow the patterns of speech. Two lines spoken by Juliet at highly dramatic moments will serve to illustrate: (1) "If all else fail, myself have power to die." (2) "My dismal scene I needs must act alone." There is no regular alternation of completely unstressed syllables with syllables having the highest degree of sentence stress. In the first line, the special emphasis on the second syllable of *myself* gives that syllable the highest pitch in the line. Thus, Shakespearean

---

The Victim, Charles Johnson (London), 1714, p. 22.

† John Dryden apparently is chiefly responsible for creating the cliché and for confusing it with the English language itself, considered as independent of writers using it. See *The Name and Nature of Poetry*, A. E. Housman (New York: The Macmillan Co.), 1933.

blank verse, at times, and particularly when it is most dramatic, approaches the rhythm of Racine's Alexandrines. In Shakespeare's blank verse, as in the Alexandrine, the syllable count is fixed, the rhythm free. An examination of samples of his blank verse shows that with remarkable frequency the lines have ten syllables with a stress on the tenth, or eleven syllables, the tenth being stressed and the eleventh unstressed.

A translator, by following such a pattern in his blank verse, can come as close as possible to achieving in English the effect of Racine's Alexandrines. That is the verse form Mr. Solomon uses for the most part; he does, however, introduce rhyme in some scenes—a dangerous thing to do—but he carries it off well. Rhyme and alliteration are far more obtrusive in English than in French because of the strong ictus in English. Both rhyme and alliteration found in Racine are a muted obligato. By using the proper gradations of sentence stress, the proper phrasing, and the pitch patterns of emotional intonation, Mr. Solomon subdues the thumping meter, the clang of rhyme, and the drumbeat of alliteration.

He uses rhyme only occasionally, when it seems appropriate to him. His rhymes are for the most part free from the usual faults of English translations of Racine into the heroic couplet. These faults are to be found in Robert Lowell's *Phaedra*, as well as in Thomas Otway's *Titus and Berenice*. English poets with whom rhyming is not second nature pad their couplets by inserting a whole inert line—deadly to Racinian drama—or by placing an inert phrase at the end of a line for the sake of rhyme. Worst of all, they allow the rhyme to run away with the meaning.

> *Mais lorsqu'on la [la rime] néglige, elle devient rebelle,*
> *Et pour la rattraper, le sens court après elle.*

That is the way Boileau puts it. As an example of this fault, a couplet might be taken from Lowell's version of Phaedra's delirious description of Hippolytus as compared with Theseus: "What am I saying? Theseus is not dead./He lives in you. He speaks, *he's taller by a head*."* Such rhymes occur frequently in Lowell's *Phaedra*. Indeed, rhyme takes the bit in its teeth so often

---

*Racine, "Phaedra," Robert Lowell, trans., Eric Bentley, ed., *Classic Theatre,* Vol. IV (New York: Doubleday & Co., Inc.), 1961.

that we get the impression that rhyme was an active influence in shaping Mr. Lowell's version of the tragic couple. On the other hand, Mr. Solomon uses rhyme with discretion and propriety.

Mr. Solomon's *Andromache* is certainly among the most brilliant of his versions, if not *the* most brilliant. Racine has the gift of imaginative *dédoublement*, or what Coleridge calls simply, "imagination," I believe. He creates complex characters who speak with their own voices, voices charged with emotion, yet each having its own tone (e.g., the morbid intensity of Oreste, who has yielded to the human bondage of an incurable love; the deep sincerity of Pyrrhus, now erupting into violence, his fatal flaw, now returning to tenderness and compassion). Mr. Solomon hears these tones. He realizes that true "unity of tone" is the emotional tone of a speech which fuses disparate elements of style and creates poetic magic. The secret of the "electric current" that runs through Racine's most simple lines is not, I believe, in the sounds of the words themselves, apart from their psychological implications, as the apostles of "pure poetry" seem to think. This secret is, it seems to me, what Coleridge called a "visionary state" of the poet's imagination—"A state which spreads its influence and coloring over all . . . and in which 'The simplest, and the most familiar things/Gain a strange power of spreading awe around them'."

Mr. Solomon's ear is attuned to all the tones of Racine's dialogue. He is always aware that he must translate emotional tone above everything else. He is absolutely faithful to Racine's text—his lines even have the same numbers as Racine's. But he realizes that in order to be most faithful, both to Racine and to the English language, he must sometimes make daring translations of certain words or phrases. Because he realizes that he is translating emotion, not meaning for the intellect, and because he realizes that *words* are not *units* of meaning either emotional or intellectual, he goes so far, for instance, as to translate the epithet "cruel" as "dearest." He is careful to explain in footnotes his reasons for making such apparently drastic changes. In the scene in which "cruel" is thus rendered, he achieves a valid interpretation which, in my opinion, brings to life and gives meaning to a scene often condemned and variously interpreted by critics.

It must be obvious from what I have said of the dialogue of

Andromaque that almost nothing can be plucked from its context
and quoted without losing most of its meaning. Nothing but a
detailed and minute analysis of the most dramatic scenes can even
begin to show Racine's art. Critics who quote his lines out of
context and compare them with lines from other poets do Racine
a great injustice. The fact that nothing is detachable is evidence
of Racine's mastery of his art.

There is, however, one famous quotation from *Andromaque*:
"Qui te l'a dit?"—it is quoted, of course, by people who know
the context. This quotation of four syllables forms the first part
of an Alexandrine and ends a ten-line speech of Hermione addressed to Oreste at the mortal moment of this tragedy of many
ironies; this is the final ironic reversal of the action, the final
perfidy of the blindness and unreason of love. The last two
Alexandrines of Hermione's speech are: *"Pourquoi l'assassiner?
Qu'a-t-il fait? A quel titre?/Qui te l'a dit?"* [1242–3]. This is typical
Racinian dialogue when emotion is violent. What is especially
noteworthy about the four-syllable quotation is its brevity and
force, a force due, in large measure, to the familiar everyday
language. This speech illustrates what Le Bidois notes as typical
of Racine's style, the art *"de faire sortir le tragique du familier."*

Let us see how contemporary translators render this famous
third of a line. Mr. Solomon has: "Who told you to?" That is
exactly right. George Dillon translates: "Who told you so?"—
a complete contresens. Mr. Dillon tells us in his Introduction* that
his aim is to make a *literal* translation. Apparently by *literal* he
means "word for word." Here he translates a sentence according
to a rule one might find in a modern grammar based on the translation of isolated sentences. He fails to consider what the pronoun
le replaces here, i.e., *"d'assassiner Pyrrhus."* Professor Kenneth
Muir has: "Who set you on?"—that is right for meaning and for
brevity, but wrong for emotional force, since "to set on" is a
livresque expression not likely to be heard in emotional *speech*.
It is puzzling that Professor Muir should feel the need to elevate
the tone of Racine's dialogue. In describing Racine's style, he
repeats a cliché of English criticism: Racine's speeches are long.

---

* Racine, *Three Plays of Racine,* George Dillon, trans., Phoenix Books
(Chicago: Univ. of Chicago Press), 1961.

They are rhetorical. They are *never colloquial* (italics mine).* Yet when he meets the colloquial face-to-face, in translating he makes it literary and stilted.

Mr. Solomon's sense of fitness and his discriminating taste are strikingly illustrated in his translation of Act III, Scene 8, of *Britannicus*. This is not typical Racinian dialogue. Racine uses sticomythia here and only occasionally in a few other plays. This type of dialogue is most fitting for this particular scene, a duel in words between two young rivals-in-love. Britannicus, the courageous and the pure of heart, faces the young monster Nero, who enjoys the power that was his rival's birthright. Here, even the prominent clang of English rhyme would be quite appropriate. Mr. Solomon uses rhyme here and the rhyme is like the clash of swords. Here is a bit of the French:

NÉRON

Rome ne porte point ses regards curieux
Jusque dans des secrets que je cache à ses yeux.
Imitez son respect.

BRITANNICUS

On sait ce qu'elle en pense.

NÉRON

Elle se tait du moins; imitez son silence.

BRITANNICUS

Ainsi Néron commence à ne se plus forcer.

NÉRON

Néron de vos discours commence à se lasser.

Mr. Solomon translates:

NERO

The Empire casts no curious glances, Sir,
Into the secrets that I hide from her.
Follow her respect.

* Racine, *Five Plays*, Kennith Muir, trans., Mermaid Drama (New York: Hill & Wang, Inc.), 1960, p. xiv.

BRITANNICUS

Her respect is hollow.

NERO

She holds her tongue at least: her silence follow.

BRITANNICUS

Nero begins thus to grow out of reach.

NERO

Nero begins to weary of your speech.

Another translator of our century, Dr. Lacy Lockert, tells us in his Translator's Foreword that the heroic couplet of the neoclassical period is disagreeable to modern ears because of the very prominent rhyme, which he describes as "heavily clashing." He proposes to remedy this defect by placing pauses in the middle of the lines instead of at the end, or by using imperfect rhymes. He applies this principle everywhere. Here is his translation of the same lines:*

NERO

Rome never pries with curious glance too deep
Into the secrets that I choose to keep
From her. Imitate her respect.

BRITANNICUS

                                    Her thought
Hereof we know.

NERO (*Fiercely*)

                    At least she sayeth naught.
Imitate her in that.

BRITANNICUS

                    So Nero now
Doth curb himself no more!

* *The Best Plays of Racine*, Dr. Lacy Lockert, trans. (Princeton, N.J.: Princeton Univ. Press), 1936, p. 158.

NERO

> Nero doth grow
Tired of thy talking.

To praise Mr. Solomon just for having translated the *complete* dramatic works of Racine (Mr. Solomon includes also the prefaces and dedicatory epistles) would be to place him on a level with Robert Bruce Boswell, whose "metrical versions" of all the plays appeared in the Bohn Classical Library in the nineteenth century. Boswell could not read French or write English with any precision. No one could get the faintest idea of what Racine is like from reading Boswell. Indeed, he is even extremely difficult to follow.

Mr. Solomon's versions read rapidly and leave an emotional impact. They are accurate and close enough to be used in English classes where the "*explication de texte*" method is used. But everybody should read them first as "escape" literature, for that is what they are. They take us for an hour or so out of the world of raw reality and trivial humdrum existence into a dreamworld— a dreamworld which is not the bizarre fancy of an individual, but life itself, transfigured by a great imaginative genius.

Reading the prefaces along with the plays, and particularly the little farce, *The Litigants*, with Racine's prefatory remarks, we see a new aspect of Racine, his malicious wit. In the farce itself he satirizes an aspect of the society of his time—not without analogy to our own. In his prefatory remarks he gives us a Molièresque satire of a psychological type. Here it is the "rules critic" at a performance of a farce, i.e., the intellectual snob witnessing entertainment of a low order.

Then too Mr. Solomon gives us the dedicatory epistles. One that should prove particularly arresting is the dedication of *Andromache* to Henrietta of England. Raymond Picard suggests that Henrietta is the image of the ideal spectator for whom Racine wrote. Henrietta sponsored the first performance of *Andromaque*. That was a private performance which took place on November 17, 1667, in the Queen's suite. The Queen and the King himself were present, together with a select group of courtiers. The best sort of advance publicity for a play at the time was to have it talked about in the salons (Pierre Mélèse). Doubtless *Andromaque* had been read and talked about in Henrietta's circle. The private performance was a glorious preview. The public flocked to the play at the Hôtel de Bourgogne. It had a long run. Public interest was great and enduring. Racine had his public.

Mr. Solomon's versions are eminently suited for performance in the theatre. *Andromaque* would be admirably suited to television. Let us hope that the theatrical illusion will bring this great play completely to life in the American theatre and that others of Racine's plays may follow, now that they have been adequately translated into English.

I owe a great debt to the many French critics who have illumined Racine and enriched my enjoyment of reading him. In this Introduction I have referred frequently to Raymond Picard. I am greatly indebted to Professor Picard. In his Introductions to the plays in the *Pléiade* edition of Racine, drama criticism has at last become what it should be. It is no longer analysis, separating plot and characters, describing characters as portraits in a picture gallery, and reducing action to a dull summary. It is a synthesis of all the elements of the tragedies, showing them moving through time to an end. Together with Professor Picard's notes, these Introductions constitute an *analyse de texte* which is invaluable for an understanding of the sense of the tragic in Racine. I am also greatly indebted to Professor Picard for giving me an opportunity to discuss with him my plan for this Introduction, and to talk with him about current productions of Racine and Molière at the *Comédie-Française*.

Other books which have been most helpful to me are: Paul Bénichou, *Morales du grand siècle*, Paris, 1948; Georges Le Bidois, *De l'Action dans la Tragédie de Racine*, Paris, 1900; Thierry Maulnier, *Racine*, Paris, 1947; Pierre Mélèse, *Le Théâtre et le Public sous Louis XIV*, Paris, 1934; Jacques Scherer, *La Dramaturgie Classique en France*, Paris, 1964. Many critics and scholars not mentioned in the Introduction have contributed to an understanding of Racine and his times: E. B. O. Borgerhoff, Jules Brody, Ferdinand Brunetière, Ferdinand Brunot, Sister Marie Philip Haley, R. C. Knight, Jules Le Maître, Georges Lote, Georges May, Gustave Michaut, Daniel Mornet, Raymond Picard (*La Carrière de Jean Racine*), and many others.

In my remarks about the dramatic qualities of Racine's dialogue and in my comments on Charles Johnson's adaptations I have sometimes paraphrased passages from my book, *Racine and English Classicism*, and I have quoted a few sentences verbatim. These borrowings were made with the permission of the University of Texas Press.

KATHERINE E. WHEATLEY

FOREWORD

It has been a labour of love translating Racine's *théâtre complet*. Undoubtedly one of the world's greatest poet dramatists, Racine has been a favourite author, ever since my school days, and one of my long-standing ambitions has been to bring as much of his genius as possible to the attention of the ordinary discriminating reader and spectator in the English-speaking world, whose knowledge of French is inadequate to savour him straightaway in the original. The difficulties of the task are immense, as Racine the playwright is one of those great artists who, with a remarkably restricted vocabulary, uses a great number of the technical resources open to a poet —alliteration, assonance, internal rhymes, subtle repetition, vowel music, etc.—to achieve his maximum dramatic effect. It is therefore essential if a translator is even to attempt to do him justice, that he pay particular attention to Racine's style; how far the versions that follow have succeeded is for the reader alone to judge, but at least he may be sure that any failure on the translator's part is not due to lack of appreciation of the original.

I have sought, within the genius of the English language, to be as faithful as possible to the French, considering it an impertinence, as some translators of Racine, eminent in other spheres, have done, radically to alter the original of even a masterpiece like *Phèdre*, in order to express their own personalities in the guise of Racine. Where the requirements of English verse have forced me, here and there, to take liberties with the literal text, I have striven to ensure that such liberties served but to fortify the spirit of the original. Only where, in *Esther* and *Athalie*, Racine has clearly been citing the Bible, I have preferred to adhere, as far as possible, to the revised English version, with its own hallowed tradition, rather than the literal French text.

The question of metre was one of importance but offered, I think, no real choice. It seemed to be inevitable that the French classical Alexandrines in which the masterpieces of the French classical stage were written should, despite the blandishments of novel metrical experiments favoured by some, find their natural counterpart in the iambic pentameters (varied occasionally, as in Shakespeare, with lines of eleven syllables and very rarely with more than eleven or less than ten), in which the verse masterpieces of the English stage are for the most part composed.

The question of rhyme was more difficult. As Racine is rhymed throughout, it seemed clear that totally unrhymed verse would not have the full flavour of Racine. On the other hand, to rhyme throughout a full-length tragedy, in a strongly accented language like English, would, in my opinion, prove too monotonous, and the fact that there is not a single tragic masterpiece in the English language which is rhymed throughout merely emphasises the point. I have therefore, in the eleven tragedies, mingled rhymed with unrhymed verse, using rhyme to drive home psychological points in which Racine abounds, or to mark passages of tension. Where the tension swells to breaking-point I have generally returned to unrhymed verse, as in some of Roxana's rages, Clytemnestra's great imprecations, and some of Phaedra's paroxysms.

To vindicate this mingling of rhymed with unrhymed verse, I have the high example of Shakespeare himself, who, even in his greatest tragedies, like *King Lear*, mixes rhymes not only with blank verse, but with prose.* In the case of *Les Plaideurs*, Racine's sole comedy (*The Litigants*), I have rhymed throughout as in the original, since in a satire or comedy, rhymes in English, even tenuous or ingenious rhymes, merely add to the fun, as a number of English comic masterpieces have shown.

For the purpose of my work I have relied chiefly on the following editions of Racine, which have taken the 1697 edition (the last in Racine's lifetime) as the definitive text: Paul Mesnard (*Les Grands Écrivains de la France, Hachette, Nouvelle Édition*); Gustave Lanson (*Théâtre Choisi de Racine, Hachette*, 1922, based on the *Mesnard Edition*) and Raymond Picard (*Pléiade Édition, Gallimard*, 1950).

---

* More recently, T. S. Eliot, in *Murder in the Cathedral*, his most effective play, mixes rhymed with unrhymed verse.

In the course of my labours I have been indebted to a number of readers and friends in Britain and in the United States for valuable suggestions. In Britain, above all, I am happy to acknowledge my debt to my son, Jonathan, whose relentless zeal backed by his formidable classical training in exposing weaknesses was of inestimable service in my revision of the preliminary versions of *Phèdre* and *Iphigénie*. I am further, most grateful to Dr. R. A. Sayce of Worcester College, Oxford, for several constructive criticisms on reading my versions of *Athalie, Phèdre, Britannicus* and *Les Plaideurs*. I must also thank Professor J. P. Collas of Queen Mary College, London, and Mrs. Claudine Libovitz-Henry for their very kind co-operation in clearing up a number of ambiguous points in the French.

In the United States, apart from the many friends whom I have consulted on American usage, I am particularly indebted to Mr. Eric Bentley of New York, and above all to Dr. Katherine E. Wheatley, Professor Emeritus of the University of Texas, Austin, Texas. Mr. Bentley indeed would appear to be the sponsor (not to say the *guru*) of Racine translators, for I am by no means the first—or even the second—who has publicly acknowledged his debt to Eric Bentley's encouragement and support.

As for Miss Wheatley, my debt to her is inestimable. Not only have I found her book *Racine and English Classicism* (University of Texas Press, 1956) a *sine qua non* for any English-speaking lover of Racine, most helpful in my final revision, but I am enormously indebted to her for her kindness and indefatigable industry in going through all the plays and offering me throughout the constructive suggestions of her expert mind. Her willingness therefore to write an introduction to the work with which she is thoroughly familiar merely crowns my deep obligation to her.

Lastly, but most dearly, I must thank my wife for her exemplary patience, both in Britain and the United States, in putting up with Racine at all hours of the day (and night) for more than a quarter of a century, first in French alone, and latterly in English as well as French! That she can still enjoy a performance of Racine in French (and even in English) is a tribute to his enduring stature.

London, September 16, 1966   S.S.

TRANSLATOR'S NOTE
A Biographical Appreciation

Jean Racine was born at La Ferté Milon, not very far from Paris, and was baptised on December 22, 1639. He was the first child of Jean Racine and his wife, Jeanne Sconin, middle-class parents, with respected connections in both the religious and secular worlds. His mother died on January 28, 1641, shortly after having given birth to his sister Marie, for whom the poet always had a deep affection. Their father died two years later, three months after a second marriage. The two little orphans were reared separately, Marie by their maternal grandfather Pierre Sconin, Racine by his paternal grandmother Marie (Desmoulins) Racine, who after her husband's death, in 1649, retired to the Jansenist retreat at Port-Royal to which her family had long been attached. At Port-Royal her daughter Agnes, Racine's aunt, was to be Abbess from 1690 to her death in 1700, the year after Racine himself died.

Racine's life may be divided into three periods—his education and adolescence, the period of his ten secular plays, and the final period from 1677, the year of his marriage and of his appointment with Boileau as Historiographer-Royal, to his death in 1699. It was during this final period when Racine had, for emotional reasons, retired from the theatre, after the relative failure of *Phèdre* in 1677, that his last two plays, based on the Bible, were, at the express instance of Madame de Maintenon and Louis XIV, composed for performance by the schoolgirls of Saint-Cyr, an institution founded by Madame de Maintenon. Neither of these plays (*Esther*, 1689, and *Athalie*, 1691) was performed before the general public in Racine's lifetime.

Although Racine, prior to his boyhood sojourn at Port-Royal, was educated at the Collège de Beauvais and after Port-Royal at the Collège d'Harcourt in Paris, it was the vital period between 1655 and 1658, which he spent at Port-Royal (*école des Granges*) under the great Jansenist teachers Lancelot and Nicole, Antoine Le Maistre and Hamon, that was to leave the greatest imprint on his mind and heart. It was significant of the great influence of Monsieur Hamon who, with Lancelot, taught him Greek, that Racine in his final testament should express the wish to be buried at the foot of Hamon's grave. For the gentle Hamon personified the two greatest factors that fused to form the chief dynamic of Racine's dramatic genius: the Jansenist religious philosophy that man is predestined, through his passions, to damnation in the absence of divine grace, and the Hellenic perception of beauty and perfection of form, radiant against the dark background of Greek pessimism.

After finishing his formal education at the Collège d'Harcourt, Racine attached himself to his cousin Nicolas Vitart, who was an official in the Paris mansion of the Jansenist Duc de Luynes. In Paris, Racine made friends with a number of wits and poets, including La Fontaine and Le Vasseur, a young society *abbé*, who was later to introduce him to Boileau; in their company he was constantly scribbling verses, but it was not till 1660 that Racine may be said to have "arrived" on the literary stage when his ode *La Nymphe de la Seine*, composed in celebration of Louis XIV's marriage, won the approval of Perrault and Chapelain— the latter at that time the doyen of the French Parnassus—as well as a prize of a hundred louis from the King. The same year he wrote his first play, *Amasie*, which only just failed to be performed at the Théâtre du Marais, and has been lost to posterity. In the following year he began a tragedy on the loves of Ovid for the rival Hôtel de Bourgogne, which was never finished and is likewise lost.

This commerce with the theatre alarmed his pious relatives at Port-Royal and Racine was induced, both by their pressure and the necessity to earn his living, to accept the invitation of his maternal uncle, Antoine Sconin, Vicar-General at Uzès, to try his luck with the Church in the South. But in spite of his theological studies and a good many representations in appropriate quarters, no benefice came his way, and Racine returned to Paris in 1663 with his pocket as empty as when he had left, except for the draft of his first extant play, *La Thébaïde*, which, encouraged by Molière, he completed in Paris in December, 1663.

* * * * * * * * *

La Thébaïde, or *Les Frères Ennemis*, was first performed on June 20, 1664, by Molière's Company. It is based on Euripides' *Phoenician Women*, and owes something also to Rotrou's *Antigone*. It is the story of the fratricidal quarrel of the sons of Oedipus, and is by no means a masterpiece. But to students of Racine, it is a fascinating nursery of many features of his genius that were to find fruition in the subsequent masterpieces. It enjoyed a moderate contemporary success.

Racine's second play, *Alexandre Le Grand* (1665), was a great contemporary success. It deals with the historical episode of Alexander's magnanimity towards his defeated enemy Porus, the Indian King, recorded in Quintus Curtius and Justin. It has many beauties, but is irreparably disfigured in the eyes of posterity by the language of gallantry that infects even the main protagonists, Alexander and Porus themselves.

The performance of this play was to lead to a breach in the good relations between Molière and Racine. The play was first given by Racine to Molière at the Palais-Royal, but Racine was soon dissatisfied by the inferiority, in his opinion, of Molière's Company in tragic rôles when compared with the artistes of the leading Hôtel de Bourgogne.* So within a fortnight of the première, *Alexandre*, unknown to Molière, was also presented by the Hôtel de Bourgogne, enticed by the superiority of Racine's play to Boyer's play on the same theme, which they were contemporaneously presenting in competition with the Palais-Royal. Subsequently all Racine's plays, until he retired from the theatre after *Phèdre*, were given at the Hôtel de Bourgogne.

Racine meanwhile had fallen in love with the beautiful actress, Mademoiselle Marquise du Parc, who had also inspired

---

* Racine's opinion, recorded by his son Louis in his *Mémoires sur la vie de Jean Racine*, appears to have been endorsed by the public, for while performances of the play at both theatres continued for a while, at the Palais-Royal, where the première had been given under the highest auspices, in the presence of Monsieur, the King's brother and Madame (Henrietta of England, to whom Racine was to dedicate his next play, *Andromaque*), the receipts declined and performances ceased, while the rival performances at the Hôtel de Bourgogne prevailed.

Corneille's verses, *A Marquise*. She had created the rôle of Axiane
in *Alexandre*, and as a result of her liaison with Racine, followed
him to the Hôtel de Bourgogne where, under his personal
direction, she was to create the title role of his next play,
Andromaque.

But even before *Andromaque*, the spectacular success of which
recalled that of *Le Cid* a generation earlier, *Alexandre* had succeeded in souring also the relations between Racine and Corneille.
Racine had hopefully shown the manuscript of *Alexandre* to his
great predecessor before its performance. Corneille had con-
descended to praise the versification, but advised Racine to keep
off drama, as his poetic talent lay elsewhere. The subsequent
popular success of *Alexandre* could therefore only serve further
to estrange the two greatest tragic playwrights of France, an
estrangement that was only to be reconciled by death, with
Racine's generous tribute at the Académie Française to the
departed Corneille.

With the performance of *Andromaque* (November, 1667), it was
clear that a tragic genius of the highest order had arrived. The
construction of the play is perfect, perhaps too perfect. After the
masterly exposition in the first scene, the play is carried forward
to the third-act climax and its denouement in the last act, solely
by the conflicting emotions of the four chief characters, three of
them, Orestes, Hermione and Pyrrhus, obsessed by that "love"
which La Rochefoucauld likened to a fever sometimes nearer to
hate than to affection, and the fourth, Andromache, in noble
contrast, wedded to the memory of her dead Hector. The psychological ruthlessness with which Racine lays bare the heart of
Hermione, not without a touch of tenderness, makes of her one
of the greatest creations in dramatic literature.

Racine's fourth play, *Les Plaideurs* (1668), was his only comedy.
It is a satiric farce ridiculing the absurdities of Bench, Bar and
fanatical litigants. Racine, as a dilettante litigant, had just lost a
case, as he hints to us in his note To the Reader, and so was in
the right mood to deploy his considerable satiric talents at the
expense of the law, egged on, as he was, by his friends Boileau,
La Fontaine, Chapelle and Furetière. Based partly on the *Wasps*
of Aristophanes, *Les Plaideurs* has held the stage throughout the
centuries, being performed with delight even by English school-

boys today. Its first performance in Paris, however, was precarious, doubtless because the audience hesitated to relish Racine's impudent sallies at the high dignity of the Bench and Bar, not to mention the lesser aristocracy. It was not until the King burst out laughing at Versailles, that Paris felt itself free to giggle, a point which Racine did not let pass in his note To the Reader, where he mockingly observes that "those who had imagined it to be disreputable to laugh in Paris, were perhaps compelled to laugh at Versailles to save their reputations."

While the Parisian public were laughing at *Les Plaideurs*, tragedy struck Racine in his personal life. His mistress, Mlle. du Parc, like Andromache, the rôle she created, a widow devoted to her children, died in childbirth in circumstances which a decade later (in 1680, when Racine had already retired from the theatre) inspired the accusation by La Voisin, the notorious poisoner, that Racine had poisoned his mistress. The authorities did not consider La Voisin's statement reliable enough to proceed against the poet, and we have a contemporary picture of Racine's grief at Mlle. du Parc's funeral in December, 1668. But even though Racine may not have been legally responsible for his mistress's death, a sensitive nature like his could not escape his moral involvement, and the utter desolation of Phaedra's remorse at her illicit love in his most famous play, composed at a time when he was beginning to weary of the competitive world, draws its profundity from the very heart of Racine. This sense of remorse was heightened by another unhappy episode occurring in this period of Racine's life. Stung by the polemic of Nicole, his former mentor at Port-Royal, against Desmarets de Saint-Sorlin, a playwright like himself, Racine felt personally implicated when Nicole wrote that "a dramatic poet is a public poisoner, not of the bodies but of the souls of the faithful, who should consider himself guilty of an infinite number of spiritual murders." Wounded to the quick, Racine retorted in a wickedly witty letter (January, 1666), sparing neither the living nor the dead. This infuriated Port-Royal who found further champions in Barbier d'Aucour and Du Bois. Racine, now thoroughly roused, composed a rejoinder even wittier and more wicked than the first. But the wise counsels of Boileau, who was to become his good friend, prevented him from publishing it. Boileau convinced Racine that while the letter proved the qualities of the author's mind, it cast doubt on those of his heart.

Racine later made honourable amends for this youthful aberration towards Port-Royal, when he declared publicly in the French Academy (to which he was elected in 1673) that this was an episode in his life he would have dearly erased, and of which he could not think without remorse. Complete reconciliation with the Jansenists was effected in 1677, when Boileau took a copy of *Phèdre* (Racine's sacrificial offering to Port-Royal) to the great Arnauld, Port-Royal's spiritual leader, who found it "perfectly beautiful—and entirely Christian in inspiration." Thereafter, Racine threw himself in tears at Arnauld's feet and to the end of his life remained courageously faithful to Port-Royal, despite the frowns of the royal master to whom he was so devoted, and to whom the unorthodox views of the Jansenists were anathema.

But between the death of Mlle. du Parc and his final reconciliation with Port-Royal lay an interval of eight years, chequered with Racine's passion for La Champmeslé, and productive of six more tragic masterpieces.

The first of these was *Britannicus*, Racine's fifth play (1669), which Voltaire, following Racine's own hint in his Preface, considered "the play for connoisseurs." It took some time to establish itself with the general public, but by 1676, as Racine records in his second Preface, it was the most popular of his plays, all of which, except for *Phèdre*, *Esther* and *Athalie*, had already appeared. Its reputation has been maintained throughout the centuries and today its thoroughly contemporary theme of an "Oedipus complex" tussle between the domineering Agrippina and her imperial son, the "budding monster" Nero, makes it, despite its milieu in ancient Rome, the most modern of Racine's plays. In particular, his portrayal of Agrippina is one of the most accomplished in his gallery of master portraits; and a fine actress in the rôle has been seen to sweep a modern audience off its feet. The young Nero is also depicted with considerable dramatic skill, while the figure of Burrhus, the Emperor's wise counsellor, was one of Boileau's favourite characters. The great scenes in the fourth act where Nero feigns surrender to his mother's expostulations; has his murderous intent deeply shaken by the high sincerity of Burrhus;

and is finally seduced into murder by Narcissus, his evil genius, makes of the act one of the finest in Racine.

Britannicus was followed (1670) by *Bérénice*, his simplest and most enchanting play. The historical theme, the parting of the great lovers, Titus, Emperor of Rome, and Berenice, Queen of Palestine, for reasons of State, was, according to a well-authenticated tradition,* suggested to both Corneille and Racine by Louis XIV's young sister-in-law, Henrietta, Duchess of Orleans (tragic daughter of the ill-starred King Charles I), who was to die suddenly before either play could appear.

It was an unfair competition, as Corneille, now ageing and never preeminent in the portrayal of love, was sure to be outclassed by "*le tendre Racine*," who certainly deserves that title in this play where the passion of sexual love is for once depicted in its tenderest, saddest hues.

It is significant, as Voltaire records in the following century, that Frederick the Great, who, like Titus, had personal experience of the peremptory duty demanded of a ruler by the State, should have been in tears at a mere reading of the play. In our own times, the dilemma posed in the play (resolved differently by a British Sovereign, Edward VIII, who reluctantly abdicated his imperial throne rather than renounce his love) has been of such enduring validity, that young ladies in London have been seen to walk around bewitched for days under the spell of a great performance of the tragedy.

Bérénice, although it pushes the three chief characters, Berenice, Titus and Antiochus (whose disinterested and unrequited love for Berenice adds to her tragic stature), to the brink of suicide, was criticized in Racine's day and even subsequently as being something less than a tragedy, presumably because it ends without actual bloodshed.

As if to make sure that this criticism, at least, would not apply to his next play, *Bajazet*, Racine makes it the most terrible of his

---

* This tradition, supported by the Abbé Dubos, Corneille's nephew Fontenelle, Racine's son Louis, and Voltaire, has been sought to be refuted by Gustave Michaut with elaborate and ingenious, rather than convincing, arguments in his *La Bérénice de Racine* (Paris, 1907). One has only to accept that Boileau did say what both Dubos and Louis Racine say he did, for the whole of Michaut's elaborate edifice to come crashing down. Michaut's analysis of the play itself is far more rewarding.

tragedies, with more corpses (offstage) than even in his initial play *La Thébaïde*, which itself would not have been disowned by the more moderate of the Elizabethans and Jacobeans. *Bajazet*, moreover, is unique in being the only Racine play in which a character (Athalida) actually kills herself *on* the stage, although the deaths on the stage of the mortally wounded Mithridates and the self-empoisoned Phaedra are among the most moving scenes in tragedy.

Bajazet is unique in another respect. It is his only tragedy that deals with almost contemporary events. These took place in the Seraglio at Constantinople only a generation before the date of the play (1672), and the touch of physical violence on stage at the end is in keeping with the whole spirit of violence that pervades the tragedy, the most melodramatic (in the best sense) in Racine. The play (again a masterly exposition) opens with the noose almost literally round the hero's neck, and it is thrilling to watch for the precise moment in the politico-amorous plot when it becomes inevitable that it will be pulled tight. That it should be a woman's (Athalida's) unreasonable jealousy that, setting off Bajazet's obstinate chivalry, makes the whole palace revolution come tumbling down, is typical of one facet of Racine's genius. In Roxana, the passionate Sultana, burning with desire for Bajazet, he has created the most physically obsessed of his three great feminine characters, consumed by the fever of love. The scene in the fourth act, when learning of the mutual love of Bajazet and Athalida, she finds her own passion frustrated and gloats instead, in dusty consolation, on her prospective vengeance —a vision of Bajazet strangled on her orders and his corpse dragged in her presence before Athalida's transfixed eyes, is a rare moment of the darkest beauty in French tragedy.

Bajazet was followed by *Mithridate*, (1673)—Louis XIV's favourite play.* It shows us the great and ageing Mithridates—the one-time terror of Rome—in defeat, both on the political and emotional field, his hatred for Rome being only equalled by his unrequited passion for the young Monima, a passion as obsessive

---

* Dangeau attests this in his Diary (Fontainebleau, Sunday, November 5, 1684). Louis' enthusiasm was shared by the heroic Charles XII of Sweden, who, like Mithridates, had tasted the bitterness of defeat, and by Prince Eugene of Savoy, comrade at arms of Marlborough, Winston Churchill's great ancestor.

and frustrated as that of Orestes or Roxana. Of all the author's successful male portraits (and there are many of them), Mithridates is the most masterly. Supplanted by his sons, there glows in him (for the first time in Racine) that sense of a deeper humiliation that was to burn darkly in Eriphyle (in *Iphigénie*), and was utterly to consume Phaedra—a humiliation, emerging from the author's psyche, out of the ashes of which was to rise, phoenix-like, Racine's own spiritual regeneration.

The première of *Iphigénie en Aulide*, Racine's ninth play, took place in the Orangerie at Versailles in August, 1674, before the assembled court. La Champmeslé was at her best in the title rôle and had the distinguished audience in tears. The first Racine rôle she had "created" was Bérénice. Racine had been enchanted by her performance of Hermione in a revival of *Andromaque*, and thereafter had entrusted to her all his leading feminine rôles up to and including Phèdre—in *Bajazet*, after some hesitation between Roxane and Atalide, she had eventually "created" Atalide. With *Iphigénie*, Racine was at the peak of his popularity as a playwright, and deservedly so. Based on Euripides' tragedy of the same name, it is a most powerful and moving drama in spite of the fact that love, Racine's forte, plays a very secondary rôle: this is perhaps precisely the reason why Voltaire, himself never very convincing with love, thought it Racine's greatest play. The characters of the wily and ambitious Agamemnon, whose father's heart none the less triumphs in the end, the lofty Achilles, who can never for a moment forget that his mother was a goddess, and the tigress-tender Clytemnestra, fighting for her daughter's life, are most vividly drawn. Iphigenia herself is one of the nobler Racine heroines, of whom there are at least as many in his repertoire—Andromache, Berenice, Monima, Esther —as the other more intemperate type, for which he is preeminently renowned. These—Hermione, Roxana, Phaedra—include Eriphyle, whom Racine created in order to effect the semi-happy ending in *Iphigénie*. Although he has incorporated her unfortunate story most skillfully into the main plot and her ordained suicide is the only dark cloud, silver-lined with the tears of deliverance that mark the end of the play, yet one cannot help feeling that Racine has not wholly succeeded in carrying conviction with this creation. On the other hand the versification of the play is exquisite and, there is more fresh air and natural beauty in *Iphigénie*, with its hushed winds and shuddering sea, than in any other Racine play, not excluding *Phèdre*.

Racine's tenth and last secular play, *Phèdre* (his own favourite and, like *Iphigénie*, based on his beloved Euripides), was completed in 1676 and first performed on New Year's Day, 1677. It is by far his most celebrated and popular and, probably, his greatest play, although there are some, even today, who would accord that palm to *Athalie*. However that may be, there can be little question that in the character of Phaedra, Racine, surpassing Euripides, has created the greatest feminine rôle in dramatic literature. Only Shakespeare's Cleopatra, fashioned with equal psychological penetration, broader imaginative flights, but perhaps somewhat less of that utter desolation which is Racine's unique achievement here, is worthy to be set beside it. In contemplating the suicide of Cleopatra, the spectator's pity is mingled with admiration; in contemplating the dying Phaedra, his pity is absolute:

> The venom now has reached my very heart,
> Seizing this failing heart with a strange cold;
> I now can see no more save through a haze,
> Heaven and my husband, whom my presence stains;
> And Death, snuffing the lustre from my eyes,
> Repurifies the sunlight they defiled.

Tortured throughout the play by the sharp spur of illicit passion, to which her heredity had condemned her, and by the deeper prick of true remorse, which Racine had lovingly implanted, she attains in the end an almost chaste serenity as she is released from the torment of life, with the word *pureté* on her lips.*

*   *   *   *   *   *   *   *   *

Phèdre marked the end of Racine's career as a professional dramatist. He had been growing increasingly dissatisfied with his

---

* Several English translations have faithfully ended on "purity," sacrificing what seems even more important to bring out, namely Heaven's absolution, as it were, of the repentant Phaedra, subtly conveyed by Racine in the vowel music of the three caressing *ou*'s in Phèdre's last line: *Et la mort, à mes yeux, dérobant la clarté,/Rend au jour, qu'ils souillaient, toute sa pureté.*

In the version above the long open *i*'s (the most beautiful vowel sound in English) of "repurifies," "sunlight," "defiled," preluded by "my eyes," perhaps achieve this.

mode of life. His liaison with La Champmeslé, which had lasted seven years, must have convinced him of the impermanence of illicit attachments. At first, sharing her favours with her husband, an actor in the same Company, he basked for some time *primus inter pares* among her lovers. Later, in his turn, he found himself supplanted, like Mithridates, by younger (and more aristocratic) rivals, of whom Charles de Sévigné, son of the famous letter writer, was one. By the time she created the rôle of Phèdre (the Comte de Clermont-Tonnerre now her favourite lover), La Champmeslé's relations with Racine were already soured and he had to force her not to omit from Phaedra's speech in the third scene of the third act, lines which she thought were aimed at her*:

> His silence would be vain. I know my baseness,
> Oenone, I'm not like those brazen women
> Who, tasting in their sins a peace serene,
> Dare flaunt a face where not a blush is seen.

His dethronement from the chief place in the regard of his mistress must have been a severe blow to the *amour-propre* of a hypersensitive man like Racine, who never failed to react sharply to any adverse criticism or circumstance, as his Prefaces and Epigrams attest. There is such a deep lyricism in Phaedra's sense of humiliation at her illicit love—a humiliation, as we have seen, already hinted at by Mithridates and Eriphyle as to suggest unmistakably a subjective source, just as the aged Lear's terrible rages against sex rampant seem to surge from the heart of Shakespeare the man, rather than from the mind of Shakespeare the dramatist. Racine's very lack of charity years later towards La Champmeslé, about whom, interested only in her salvation he wrote to his son Jean-Baptiste on May 16, 1698, somewhat unfeelingly, as she lay on her deathbed, shows how deep a scar she had left; and the fact that he mentioned her after her death in a second letter (July 24, 1698), making amends for the first, shows the concern he still felt only a few months before he himself died. Added to the lessons the Champmeslé interlude had taught him, were those that were driven home to him by the virulence

---

* Had La Champmeslé known her Euripides as well as Racine did, she might have been reassured to find the source of these lines in the *Hippolytus* itself!

of his enemies, conspired against him without scruple. This conspiracy led by the Duchesse de Bouillon, the Duc de Nevers, and
the poetess, Madame Deshoulières (who wrote a vicious sonnet
against *Phèdre*), took the form of pitting against Racine the playwright Pradon, who was incited to write a play on the same theme,
as soon as it was known that Racine was writing on the subject
of Euripides' *Hippolytus*. Although Pradon's play *Phèdre et
Hippolyte* (long since forgotten) was performed two days after
Racine's première, the conspirators had taken the precaution of
buying up the seats at the Hôtel de Bourgogne to make sure they
remained largely empty and had taken care to pack the house at
the Hôtel de Guénégaud where Pradon's play thus enjoyed a
synthetic success. The relative failure of the masterpiece that was
to remain his favourite to the end disgusted Racine with the
theatre and its intrigues. Madame Deshoulières' sonnet provoked
a scurrilous rejoinder, and as Racine and Boileau were suspected
of being the authors, they were threatened with physical violence
by their aristocratic enemies. Only the personal intervention of
the great Condé, always partial to Racine, who delighted him
with the recitation of his verse under the trees at Chantilly, saved
the poets from a severe beating. This threat of physical humiliation inflicted by his social superiors was the last straw. Racine,
now morally and physically humiliated, was in despair, as Valincour, who succeeded him and Boileau as Historiographer-Royal
after Boileau's death, attests: "*Je vis Racine au désespoir.*" At this
moment, though at thirty-seven he was still at the height of his
powers, the nostalgia of his innocent childhood at Port-Royal
and the call of his aunt from the Jansenist retreat proved irresistible.

Determined to renounce the world Racine first thought of
becoming a monk, but his wise confessor, cognisant of the poet's
passionate nature, advised a "bourgeois" marriage instead.

Thus on June 1, 1677, he married Catherine de Romanet, aged
twenty-five, a pious orphan of good family with a fair dowry,
rich in the domestic virtues and quite indifferent to her husband's
literary fame. She bore Racine two sons and five daughters and
brought him domestic peace. Although perhaps she did not know,
unless Racine recited the lines to her (for intent on her salvation
she never troubled to read his plays), it was doubtless she who

inspired that most exquisite tribute to conjugal bliss which Racine puts into the mouth of Ahasuerus in *Esther* (however much Mme. de Maintenon may have imagined it was she who had inspired it!), for these are lines that could only have been written by a grateful husband and not by an obliging courtier, however devoted to the King's morganatic wife (the former widow of Scarron, writer of comedies):

> In you alone I find some nameless grace
> That ever fascinates and never stales:
> Sweet virtue's loving charm that brings release.
> In Esther all breathes innocence and peace.
> The darkest shades of care she wafts away,
> And turns my gloomiest days to gleaming day!

Racine's decision to renounce the theatre and to marry was greatly facilitated by the offer to him and Boileau, the same year, of the post of Historiographer-Royal. The appointment, inspired by Madame de Montespan, the King's last mistress before he morganatically married Madame de Maintenon, was on condition that Racine should sever all connections with the theatre (still considered disreputable) and devote all his time to the King's personal exploits. As Historiographer-Royal it, therefore, fell mainly to Racine (in view of Boileau's ill-health) to accompany the King in his campaigns and endure the unaccustomed hardships of the field and the malicious banter of more experienced campaigners and scribblers. The poets' output as Royal Historians, though very pleasing to the King to whom they would read extracts from time to time, has been lost to posterity, the manuscript having been burnt in 1726 in a fire that destroyed the house of their successor, Valincour, at Saint-Cloud. This loss of a work by historians, who were perforce also courtiers, is much easier to bear than Racine's own destruction of his fragment of *Alceste*, the story of Euripides' *Alcestis* that so fascinated him, as his preface to *Iphigénie* attests. This sacrifice was Racine's consummation of his resolve to renounce the secular theatre. It was therefore, in the circumstances, fortunate that the dramatic requirements of Saint-Cyr, Madame de Maintenon's school for daughters of the impoverished nobility, should have given us *Esther* and *Athalie*.

The success of *Esther*, acted by the schoolgirls in full costume before the most exclusive audience in France (January, 1689) was immense. Based on the Book of Esther, in the Old Testament, it is a delightful entertainment in three acts, showing Racine's artistry undiminished. Although in *Esther* Racine's psychological powers have been sublimated, and his characters therefore are much less in the round than in any play since *Andromaque*, there is an unsurpassed purity and charm in the versification. In *Esther*, he has for the first time employed a chorus, and it is his only play where the unities of time and place are very slightly dented; much less so, it is true, than in the *Eumenides* of Aeschylus (the Father of Tragedy), where the scene shifts from Delphi to Athens instead of merely from one part of Ahasuerus' palace to another, and much more time elapses than the couple of days that comprise the action of *Esther*.

As if to make up for the slight liberty he took in *Esther* with the unities, Racine has taken care in *Athalie* (his last play—January, 1691) to confine the action both in time and place almost to the actual period and place of performance. Thus, marking the continuity of the action, the first line of the fifth act rhymes with a line at the end of the fourth act uttered by the same speaker (Shulamith), and in order to bring Athaliah at the end on to the stage (representing the Temple at Jerusalem), Racine is compelled to show us his hero Jehoiada, the High Priest, descending to an unworthy ruse. Yet in spite of this blemish, the loftiness of Racine's conception and the perfection of his execution, together with the beauty of the chorus, make *Athalie* his most sublime play and in the opinion of some, his greatest. To Voltaire—with his limited appreciation, it is true, of Shakespeare and other cultures—*Athalie* was the *chef d'oeuvre de l'esprit humain**, despite Voltaire's incapacity to appreciate the religious devotion, not to say fanaticism, of a character like Jehoiada, the High Priest.

Basing his tragedy on the very sketchy story of Queen Athaliah in the Books of Kings and Chronicles, Racine has built a most imposing dramatic structure in which God Himself is the invisible protagonist; recognized as such by the chief characters,

---

* Voltaire, *Dictionnaire Philosophique*. Also in a letter to Monsieur de Cideville (May 20, 1761), he calls *Athalie* "*le chef d'oeuvre de la belle poésie.*"

Athaliah and Jehoiada. Athaliah is pursued by her dream to fatal courses, much more relentlessly than Clytemnestra in Aeschylus' *Choephori*, who suffers hers—about the serpent—passively: "Hunted I flee, but everywhere it haunts me," cries Athaliah, who is drawn to her doom by her irresistible urge to pry into the secrets of God's Temple. Her character of irresolution, courage, greed, a moment of maternal tenderness and final defiance, is most subtly drawn. Against her is set the monolithic Jehoiada; and only those who have themselves known God-possessed men, of absolutely dedicated faith, can fathom the achievement of Racine in his portrait of the High Priest, whom contemporaries thought to be modelled on the great Arnauld. (He himself, incidentally, preferred *Esther* to *Athalie*, perhaps because, while the play itself was shorter, its pious choruses were longer!) The scene in the third act in *Athalie* when, in prophetic vision, Jehoiada foresees the destruction of Jerusalem and the coming of the Redeemer and senses that his beloved son Zachariah is destined to be murdered by Jehoash, the royal protégé whom, obedient to God's plan, he none the less continues to pilot to the throne, is among the most sublime in dramatic literature. Yet *Athalie*, performed by the schoolgirls of Saint-Cyr, without the splendid trappings of *Esther*, enjoyed but a tepid contemporary success. Racine thought that his dramatic powers may have failed him; only the wise judgment of Boileau could assure him of the contrary; and the first public performance of *Athalie* by the Comédie-Française, on March 3, 1716, was a triumphant endorsement of Boileau's opinion. But perhaps the meagre success of *Athalie*, before Louis XIV and his privileged co-spectators, was due precisely to those portions of the play, thunderously applauded before the French Revolution, where Jehoiada warns the young King Jehoash, before crowning him, of the dangers of absolute power:

> You do not know the wine of absolute power,
> Nor the seductive voice of flatterers.
> They will soon tell you that the holiest laws
> Bind subjects, but must bend before their kings.
>
> Swear on this book, before these witnesses
>
> You will make God judge between King and poor.

Emboldened by the success of *Esther* and the great regard in which he was held by the King, (who would even require him sometimes to sleep in the Royal Bedchamber, to be on hand to read to him, in his hours of insomnia) Racine, through the mouth of Jehoiada, allowed himself the rôle of royal mentor; a rôle unlikely to be relished by the Roi-Soleil. When, some years later, secretly encouraged by Madame de Maintenon, Racine ventured to trespass, in the role of sage, on the political field, his intimate relations with the King were irrevocably compromised.

It was Racine's concern for the common people which proved his undoing. Throughout his plays this esteem for the people (in perfect harmony with his regard for the King, who in Racine's eyes was God's Regent in France) is apparent. Racine's offstage mobs, unlike Shakespeare's mobs onstage, always do justice, or at least uphold the law against the arbitrary will of the ruler.* In *Andromaque*, the mob at the end proclaims the foreign prisoner Andromache, Queen of Epirus, because she has just been lawfully wedded to Pyrrhus, their sovereign, murdered at his bridal altar by Hermione's Greeks, outraged at his marriage to the captive.

In *Britannicus*, the Roman mob, at the close of the play, take under their protection Junia, fleeing for sanctuary to the Vestal Virgins from the lust of Nero, who has just murdered her beloved Britannicus, his rival. Not only do they escort her to the Vestal Virgins, but to ensure her safety, they do not hesitate to kill, in the Emperor's very presence, Narcissus, his evil genius, who, to please Nero, had attempted to lay profane hands on her.

In *Bérénice*, the Roman mob, however cruelly, make it quite clear by their cries offstage, that they do not want the laws of Rome disregarded to satisfy their Emperor's love for Berenice, the foreign queen.

In *Iphigénie* similarly, the common Greek soldiers insist that Agamemnon should not attempt to take advantage of his royal status by evading the divine decree requiring Iphigenia's sacrifice at the altar.

Nor was it merely in his plays that Racine showed his instinctive affinity with the common people. In a letter to Boileau (May 21,

* This theme was first developed in an article in *Contemporary Review* (London), May, 1962.

Facsimile of the second page
of the letter from Racine to his son,
Jean-Baptiste, dated May 16, 1698
(Bibliothèque Nationale)

1692) from the front, after noting the troops at an exhausting parade, Racine wrote: "I might have wished with all my heart that all those I saw had been, all of them, in their cottages and houses with their wives and children and I, in my Rue des Maçons, with my family."

It was therefore in keeping with his fundamental feeling that Racine (as recounted by his younger son, Louis Racine, in his *Mémoires sur la vie de Jean Racine*) should have been led, entirely to his honour, to compose a confidential memorandum for Madame de Maintenon on the miseries of the common people upon whom Louis XIV's wars had weighed heavily. The King came upon Madame de Maintenon, while she was reading it, and insisted on seeing it and knowing the author's name. Louis' pique was evident: "Because he is a great poet, does he fancy himself a minister?" From that moment Racine's credit at court was fundamentally compromised. The subtle displeasure of the King was more than Racine's sensitive heart could bear. Soon after, he took to his bed with an abscess of the liver and, lingering for a year, perhaps with the psalmist's, "Put not your trust in Princes" in mind, he died in his sixtieth year (April 21, 1699).

His final gesture for the freedom of the individual, his testament, desiring to be buried at the foot of Monsieur Hamon's grave, had been made six months before his death. This too came eventually to be thwarted by Louis XIV's arbitrary will, for, following on the demolition of Port-Royal by Louis' anti-Jansenist fiat a few years later, Racine's remains had to be removed from Port-Royal des Champs to the Church of St. Etienne du Mont in Paris, where, together with Pascal's, that other rare spirit of Port-Royal, they now lie.

* * * * * * * * *

Racine's fame, as one of the half-dozen greatest world dramatists, is assured. If his one comedy, *Les Plaideurs*, despite its lasting qualities of gay farce and shrewd satire, cannot compare with Molière's best, nine of his eleven tragedies, that is to say, all except the first two, are each one of them masterpieces in their own right. All nine enjoy the perfection of form of a Greek temple; all, except perhaps for a word or two, are written with consummate taste. No theatre director in his right senses would dare to change a line in Racine's masterpieces, let alone cut out chunks, as is the normal practice with Shakespeare, even in his very greatest plays.

Against the perfect architecture of his tragedies, Racine's characters range, clash and die, compassionately observed by their creator, with unsurpassed psychological insight and emotional intensity. Among his women characters, Hermione and Phaedra stand unexcelled, while any dramatist would be proud to own Andromache, Agrippina, Berenice, Roxana, Monima*, Esther, Athaliah. Of his men characters only Shakespeare's Hamlet, Lear and Macbeth are greater tragic figures than Racine's Mithridates; while Pyrrhus, Nero, Burrhus, Narcissus, Titus, Bajazet, the Vizir Ahmet, Agamemnon, Achilles and Jehoiada are successful portraits by any standard.

To the profundity of his observation Racine has brought all the resources of a unique style. His language, amazing in the poverty of its vocabulary (words like *transports*, *yeux*, *coeur*, *fureurs*, like some clichés of the great Mozart, are forever in currency), is wielded with such artistic mastery, with subtle alliteration and repetition, internal rhymes and assonances, onomatopoeia and vowel music, all attuned like some chamber orchestra to the expression of the dramatic moment that, from the simplest material as it were by magic, the most powerful dramatic effects are achieved. Sometimes, it is true, it is by the *mot juste* that he strikes home, as when Agrippina in *Britannicus* boasts about:

> Le sang de mes aieux qui brille dans Junie (Act I, Scene 2)
> (My forebears' blood, that *sparkles* in her veins.)

But more often it is by a combination of factors, as outlined above, that the most splendid result supervenes. One or two instances taken at random must suffice. Thus in *Bajazet* (Act IV, Scene 5), when Roxana learns through the discovery of Bajazet's letter to Athalida of the deceit practised upon her by Bajazet, who loves Athalida and not her, her rage and mortification are extreme. Immediately she thinks of giving the order for Bajazet's strangulation, which her lord, the Sultan, has left in her hands.

---

* Monima, indeed, is perhaps Racine's most exquisite creation, so subtly has he blended in her the ingredients of passion and refinement.

This is how she expresses herself:

> *Qu'il meure. Vengeons-nous. Courez. Qu'on le saisisse;*
> *Que la main des muets s'arme pour son supplice.*
> (Kill Bajazet! Avenge me. Run. Seize him;
> See the hands of the mutes prepare his doom.)

The staccato of Racine's first line clearly expresses Roxana's distraught state of mind, but it is only a prelude to the crescendo of the second line, where the alliterative wail of self-pity emphasised by the long-vowelled *main, muets, s'arme*, poised pathetically for a moment on *s'arme*, bursts into the alliterative and staccato hiss of revenge of *pour son supplice*, itself preluded by *saisisse*. In the translation, the wail and perhaps the pathos also are recaptured, but the splendid hiss, alas, is barely audible.

Or, again, the first two lines already cited from the dying speech of Phaedra may be examined; namely:

> The venom now has reached my very heart,
> Seizing this failing heart with a strange cold.

Phèdre says:

> *Déjà jusqu'à mon coeur le venin parvenu*
> *Dans ce coeur expirant jette un froid inconnu.*

Not only are the long drawn out vowels, evoking the ebbing life, and the repetition of *coeur* most effective, but so is the throb of the heart subtly suggested by the three *r*'s in *coeur, expirant, froid*, the last clotted with the *f*. While the English version has brought out the repetition of "heart" and the long vowels, in "reached," "seizing," "failing," "strange," the throb has had to be put into the first line, "reached my very heart," where it is far less effective, and by way of compensation, an irregular flutter introduced in the second line with the shift of the accent to "strange."

As a final example of Racine's alliterative and onomatopoeic challenge, the following masterly passage from the last act (Act V, Scene 3) of his last play (*Athalie*) may be cited: Jehoiada, the High Priest, commands a Levite to entrap the rapacious Athaliah, the moment she enters the Temple, and promptly thereupon to sound the trumpet of revolt against her:

> *Vous, dès que cette reine, ivre d'un fol orgueil,*
> *De la porte du temple aura passé le seuil,*
> *Qu'elle ne pourra plus retourner en arrière,*
> *Prenez soin qu'à l'instant la trompette guerrière*
> *Dans le camp ennemi jette un subit effroi.*
> *Appelez tout le peuple au secours de son roi;*
> *Et faites retentir jusques à son oreille*
> *De Joas conservé l'étonnante merveille.*

Rendered:

> Immediately this queen, in drunken pride,
> Has crossed the threshold of the Temple's gate,
> To make sure there is no return for her,
> Take care the trumpet's instant blare and war-drum
> Strike sudden terror into her Tyrian troops:
> Stir up the whole town to their king's defence;
> And detonate in their astonished ears
> The shattering miracle of Jehoash, saved.

The *Leitmotiv* (to use a later Wagnerian cliché) in Racine's verbal orchestra is to be found in the key phrase *porte du temple* in the second line, where the *p t* and *t p* knit by *r* and the nasal *em* serves as a prelude for the working up of these sounds, in crescendo, into the great climax of the last line; observe the cunning with which the climax is reached through the staccato brass shiver of *instant, jette un subit, faites retentir* (with the trumpeter's lips almost seen puffing at *dans le camp ennemi jette un subit . . .*, and *appelez tout le peuple*) to the repeated echoes of the *trompette guerrière*, through the moderate *secours de son roi* and the longer *oreille* to the tremendous reverberation of *étonnante merveille*, dooming, as with the walls of Jericho and the hosts of Midian, Athaliah's Godforsaken cause.

In the English, while much is recaptured with the *t n*'s and while the shiver of the brass ("detonate," "astonished," "shattering") is perhaps not inferior to the French, the long echoes of "care," "blare" and "Jehoash, saved" cannot quite achieve the miracle of the original. It was therefore necessary to strengthen the alliteration and onomatopoeia of the English passage by the insertion of the word "drum," which was naturally evoked by the roll of the *t*'s and *r*'s of the English line, "Strike sudden terror into her Tyrian troops" ("Tyrian troops" for *camp ennemi* is justified by the previous context, while "town" in the next line for *peuple* is also perhaps alliteratively acceptable).

Such are the shifts to which a conscientious translator is driven in order to recapture as far as possible the spirit of a great original.

It is therefore necessary to treat these translations as but a first step to the full enjoyment of an original, which, abounding in such, and even greater treasures, is as imperishable as the music of the French language and the beat of the human heart.

S.S.

PERFORMANCES OF RACINE'S PLAYS
AT LA COMÉDIE-FRANÇAISE, PARIS*
(*Founded 1680*)

In Alphabetical Order	*First Perfor-mance*	First Perfor-mance at the Comédie-Française	17th Century 1680-1700	18th Century 1701-1800	19th Century 1801-1900	20th Century 1901-1966	Total as of July 31, 1966
PLAYS	**DATES**		**NUMBER OF PERFORMANCES**				
ALEXANDRE LE GRAND	1665	1682	22	3	1	—	26
ANDROMAQUE	1667	1680	116	296	447	486	1,345
ATHALIE		1716	—	209	255	109	573
BAJAZET	1672	1680	67	184	162	95	508
BÉRÉNICE	1670	1680	54	78	24	263	419
BRITANNICUS	1669	1680	86	289	337	419	1,131
ESTHER		1721	—	8	151	72	231
IPHIGÉNIE EN AULIDE	1674–75	1680	95	348	333	48	824
MITHRIDATE	1673	1680	98	249	165	132	644
PHÈDRE	1677	1680	121	424	442	366	1,353
LES PLAIDEURS	1668	1680	143	507	574	138	1,362
LA THÉBAÏDE	1664	1680	7	8	2	3	20
TOTALS			809	2,603	2,893	2,131	8,436

In the same period (from 1680 to July 31, 1966) the most performed plays at the Comédie-Française of

1. Corneille were—*Le Cid* (1,471 performances), *Horace* (863), *Le Menteur* (825), *Cinna* (742), *Polyeucte* (708), *Rodogune* (455), *Nicomède* (371).

2. Molière were—*Tartuffe* (2,746), *L'Avare* (2,135), *Le Médecin Malgré Lui* (2,080), *Le Misanthrope* (1,815), *Les Femmes Savantes* (1,707), *Le Malade Imaginaire* (1,648), *L'École des Maris* (1,566), *L'École des Femmes* (1,417), *Les Précieuses Ridicules* (1,240).

* The information above has been taken from monographs prepared by Madame Sylvie Chevalley, *bibliothécaire-archiviste* (Archive Librarian) of the Comédie-Française, Paris, whose assistance is warmly acknowledged.

THE THEBAN BROTHERS

A Tragedy

To His Grace, the Duc de Saint-Aignan, Peer of France

Your Grace,

I offer you a work which is perhaps only notable for the honour of having pleased you. But this honour, indeed, is something so great for me, that had my play brought me but this benefit, I might say that its success had surpassed my hopes. And what hope could be fairer than the approval of one whose judgment is so sure, and who is himself the admiration of everyone? Therefore, your Grace, if The Theban Brothers *has been at all applauded, it is doubtless because none has dared to gainsay the judgment that you have passed in its favour; and it seems that you have transmitted to it that gift of pleasing which is the mark of all your actions. I hope, now that it is stripped of all the glamour of the stage, you will continue to look upon it with a favourable eye. If this is so, whatever enemies it may have, I fear nothing for it, since it will be sure of a Protector whom the enemy's ranks can never shake. It is well known, your Grace, that if you have a perfect knowledge of all that's beautiful, you do not undertake great deeds with a courage any the less noble, and that you have combined in yourself both these excellent qualities, either of which has made so many men great. But I must fear lest my praises become as tedious to you as yours have been advantageous to me: even though I might be only telling you what is known to everybody and what you alone wish not to know. It is sufficient that you allow me to say to you with deep respect that I am,*

> *Your Grace,*
>
> *Your very humble and*
> *very obedient servant*
> RACINE

*Preface**

The reader will allow me to beg a little more indulgence for this play than for the others which follow it. I was very young† when I composed it. Some verse which I had written at the time fell by chance into the hands of persons of taste. They pressed me to write a tragedy and suggested the subject of the Theban Brothers. This subject had previously been handled by Rotrou under the title of *Antigone*. But he made the two brothers die at the very beginning of his third act. The rest of his play was in some sort the beginning of another tragedy, dealing with altogether fresh subject matter. And he had combined in a single play two different plots, one of which forms the subject of Euripides' *Phoenician Women*, and the other of Sophocles' *Antigone*. I saw how this twofold plot might have harmed his play, which otherwise was full of fine passages. I based my theme more or less on Euripides' *Phoenician Women*. For, as regards *The Theban Brothers* in Seneca's works, I am inclined to the opinion of Heinsius, and hold with him that not only is it not a tragedy by Seneca, but that it is the work rather of a rhetorician, who had no idea of tragedy.

The catastrophe in my play is perhaps a little too bloody. Indeed, there is hardly an actor who does not die at the end. But this is *The Theban Brothers*. That is to say, the most tragic theme of antiquity.

Love, which as a rule‡ plays so great a part in tragedies, has a very minor role in this. And I doubt whether I would have given it a greater part had I to begin all over again. For it would be

---

* This Preface appeared for the first time in the edition of 1676 (without the letter of dedication to the Duc de Saint-Aignan).

† Twenty-four years of age.

‡ Precisely the contrary view had been advanced by Corneille in his *Premier Discours du Poème Dramatique*.

necessary to portray either one brother in love or both. And how would it look to give them other preoccupations than that famous hatred which possessed them entirely? Or else love must be relegated to one of the secondary characters as I have done. And then this passion, becoming as though foreign to the main theme, can only produce a moderate impact. In short, I am convinced that the tenderness or jealousies of love could find very little place among the incests, parricides, and all the other horrors which make up the story of Oedipus and of his unfortunate family.

THE THEBAN BROTHERS

The French alternative titles *La Thébaïde* (*The Sons of Thebes*) or *Les Frères Ennemis* (*The Hostile Brothers*), have been compounded into *The Theban Brothers*.
First performed by Molière's Company at the Palais-Royal on June 20, 1664, and printed the same year.

CHARACTERS

ETEOCLES	*King of Thebes*
POLYNICES	*Brother of Eteocles*
JOCASTA	*Mother of these two Princes and of Antigone*
ANTIGONE	*Sister of Eteocles and Polynices*
CREON	*Uncle of the Princes and of the Princess*
HAEMON	*Son of Creon, in love with Antigone*
OLYMPIAS	*Lady-in-waiting to Jocasta*
ATTALUS	*Lord-in-waiting to Creon*
SOLDIER *of* POLYNICES' *army*	
GUARDS	

The scene is at Thebes in a chamber of the royal palace.

ACT I

SCENE I

JOCASTA

Olympias, they have set out? Mortal pain!
What sobs my moment's sleep is going to cost me!
For six months, tears have kept my eyes awake,
Must slumber close them at this perilous hour?
Ah, would that death might close them evermore   5
And stop my witnessing the darkest crimes!
But are they yet at grips?

OLYMPIAS

         From the high walls
I saw them drawn up for the fight already;
I saw, already, swords flash all around;
And left the ramparts quick to come and warn you.   10
I saw Eteocles himself, with sword
In hand, walking ahead; with utmost zeal,
He shows the bravest how perils should be faced.

JOCASTA

Be sure, Olympias, they will slay each other.
Warn the princess and tell her to make haste;   15
I wait for her. O Heavens! support my weakness!
Olympias, we must run and stop these brutes,
Must part them both or at their hands must die.
Alas, we now behold the accursèd day
Whose dreadful thought alone was crushing me!   20
Neither my prayers nor tears at all availed;
And Fate insists her anger be appeased.

O thou, Sun, thou, who giv'st the world its light,
Why hast thou not left it in deepest night!
On such dark crimes wilt thou shine dazzlingly   25
And not shrink back when seeing what we see?
But why recoil from infamies so base?
The race of Laius[1] makes them commonplace;
Thou mayest see my sons' crimes without shame
After the deeds that brand their parents' name.   30
Thou'rt not amazed my sons are treacherous,
That both are wicked and both murderous:
Thou know'st from an incestuous blood they're raised,
And, were they virtuous, wouldst be amazed.

SCENE II

Enter ANTIGONE

JOCASTA

Have you, my child, heard our surpassing woes?   35

ANTIGONE

My lady, I have learnt my brothers' madness.

JOCASTA

Come, dear Antigone,[2] let's run at once
And stay their murderous arms as best we can.
Come, let us show them what's most dear to them;
Let's see if they can brush us both aside,   40
Or if they'll even dare, in their dark fury,
To shed our blood so as to spill each other's.

ANTIGONE

It is all over, Madam, here's the king.

[1] Laius, ruler of Thebes, was the husband of Jocasta and the father of Oedipus, who, fulfilling the oracle, was unwittingly to kill his father and marry his mother Jocasta. (See Sophocles' *Oedipus Tyrannos*.)

[2] Antigone and her two twin brothers, Eteocles and Polynices, were children of the incestuous union of their mother Jocasta with their half-brother Oedipus.

SCENE III

Enter ETEOCLES

JOCASTA

Olympias, hold me; I am crushed by grief.

ETEOCLES

My lady, what's the matter? . . .

JOCASTA

              Ah, my son!   45
What bloodstains do I see upon your clothes?
Is it your brother's? Is it not your own?

ETEOCLES

My lady, it is neither one nor the other.
Until now Polynices keeps his camp
And has not sought me out as yet to fight.   50
Only an impudent troop of Argives
Have tried to bar my sortie from our walls:
I made these rash intruders bite the dust
And it is their blood that offends your eyes.

JOCASTA

But what did you intend? What sudden zeal   55
Made you descend so promptly on the plain?

ETEOCLES

My lady, it was time to be abroad;
I lost my reputation lingering here.
The people, who already feared a famine,
Were on the point of censuring my sloth,   60
Reproaching me already for my crown

And for poor service in the rank they gave me.
I must content them; therefore, come what may,
No more shall Thebes be captive from today.
Leaving behind me not a single soldier,   65
I wish to make her merely judge our fighting.
I have sufficient force to take the field;
And if our arms are blessed by some good luck,
The prickly Polynices and his allies
Shall leave Thebes free or at my feet shall die.   70

JOCASTA

O Heavens! could you wish such blood stain your arms?
Ah, does the crown for you hold so much charm?
If it exacted fratricide to win it,
Would you, my son, wish at that cost to reign?
It rests alone on you, if moved by honour,   75
To give us peace without recourse to crime,
And triumphing today over your wrath,
Content your brother and together reign.

ETEOCLES

Do you call it reigning, carving up my crown,
And yielding abjectly what is my own?   80

JOCASTA

My son, you know both blood and justice give
To him, like you, his share in this high rank.
Sad Oedipus, when at his journey's end,
Commanded, each of you should reign his year;
And having but one realm to hand to you   85
Wished turn by turn that both of you be king.
You were so good as to accept these terms.
You were by fate first called upon to rule;
You mounted on the throne; he was not jealous:
And, you'll not let him mount it after you?   90

ETEOCLES

No, Madam, he must no more claim to rule.
Thebes has not wished to yield to this decree;

And when he wished to sit upon the throne,
She it was and not I who drove him hence.
And is Thebes then to dread his high hand less,   *95*
Having for six months suffered his assaults?
Would she obey this sanguinary prince,
Who has just waged against her ravenous war?
Would she accept as king, Mycenae's slave,
Who harbours only hate for every Theban,   *100*
Who is the king of Argos' sorry dupe,
Whom marriage binds to all our bitterest foes?
When Argos took him for his son-in-law,
He hoped through him to see our Thebes in ashes.
Love scarce had part in that most shameful match,   *105*
And burning hatred only lit its torch.
Thebes has crowned me to circumvent his chains;
She seeks through me an end to all her pains.
You must accuse her if I break my word,
I am her prisoner rather than her lord.   *110*

JOCASTA

Say, sooner, say, O thankless savage heart,
But for the crown, you have no feeling else.
But I mistake; the rank is not what pleases,
The crime alone is what entices you.
Well then, since you are lusting after it,   *115*
I offer you a double parricide:
Go, spill your brother's blood; if not enough,
I beg of you to shed your mother's too.
Then you will have no further foes to crush,
No further obstacles, nor further crimes,   *120*
And with no irksome rival for the throne,
Archcriminal, you'll sit and reign alone.

ETEOCLES

Well, Madam, have your way; be satisfied:
I must give up the throne and crown my brother;
I must, to further your unrighteous plan,   *125*
Descend from being his king to being his subject;
So as to raise you to the height of joy,

I must become the victim of his fury;
I must in dying . . .

JOCASTA

Heavens! what cruel words!
How ill you reach into my inmost heart!   *130*
I am not asking you to leave the throne:
Reign on, my son, that is what I too want.
But if so many miseries may move you,
If in your heart you harbour love for me,
If you are mindful of your very honour,   *135*
Associate your brother with the throne:
It is an empty splendour he'll receive;
Your reign through this will be securer, sweeter.
The nations, dazzled by this act sublime
Shall ever want as prince a king so fine;   *140*
And far from weakening you, this shining deed
Shall make of you the justest, greatest king:
Or, if my prayers must find you unrelenting,
If peace at such a price seems out of reach,
And if the diadem so charms your heart,   *145*
At least console me with a little peace,
And grant this favour to your mother's tears.
Meanwhile, my son, I shall approach your brother:
Perhaps compassion may impel his heart,
Or else, at least I'll bid my last farewell.   *150*
Allow me to set out this very moment:
I'll go without an escort to his tent;
I hope to move him with my rightful sighs.

ETEOCLES

You need not set out. You may see him here,
And if you find some magic in this meeting,   *155*
It rests with him alone to end our strife.
You may fulfil your wish this very hour
And let him see you here within this palace.
I'll go still further, and to make it plain
He is indeed wrong, calling me a traitor,   *160*
And that I am not an accursèd tyrant,

Let gods and people on the point pronounce.
If so the people wills, I'll give my place;
But if the people spurn him, let him yield.
I'm forcing nobody and pledge my word   *165*
To let the Thebans choose, themselves, their lord.

SCENE IV

Enter CREON

CREON

My lord, your sortie has spread gloom around:
Dreading your death, Thebes is in tears already;
On every side panic and horror reign,
The frightened people tremble on her ramparts.   *170*

ETEOCLES

This needless terror will be soon appeased.
My lady, I must go among my soldiers;
Meanwhile you may accomplish what you wish.
Call Polynices, speak to him of peace.
Creon, the queen commands here in my absence;   *175*
Make certain everyone obeys her voice;
Leave, to receive and to convey her will,
Your son Menoeceus whom I have selected.
As he is honourable as well as brave,
This leaves no room for umbrage to our foes;   *180*
His virtue is enough to reassure them.
Command him, Madam.

To CREON

And you, follow me.

CREON

What! my lord . . .

ETEOCLES

Creon, yes, the matter's settled.

CREON

And you are leaving thus your sovereign power?

ETEOCLES

You need not worry if I leave or no;   *185*
Do as I order, follow where I go.

Exit ETEOCLES

SCENE V

CREON

What have you done, my lady? How behaved,
To force a victor thus to take to flight?
This counsel ruins all.

JOCASTA

It will save all;
And through this very counsel Thebes be freed.   *190*

CREON

Indeed, my lady! In our present state
When, strengthened by more than six thousand men,
Thebes may rely on fortune's every chance,
Must the king dash sweet victory from his hands?

JOCASTA

Not always is your victory so sweet;   *195*
She's often followed by remorse and shame.
When brothers, armed to clash, would kill each other,
Not separating them is murdering both.
Can darker injury be dealt a victor
Than let him win so vain a victory?   *200*

CREON

Their anger is too great.

JOCASTA

It may be softened.

CREON

They both would reign.

JOCASTA

They both shall therefore reign.

CREON

High sovereignty may not be thus put off;
It's not a garment one may don and doff.

JOCASTA

The interest of the State shall be their law.   *205*

CREON

The interest of the State demands one king,
Who, with a constant order, rules his realms,
So that, home and abroad, his laws are known.
A reign that's chequered by two different kings,
Gives to the State not two kings, but two tyrants.   *210*
By orders often cancelling each other
One brother would destroy his brother's plans;
You'll see them ever conjuring some plot,
To change the State's complexion every year.
This measured span they are prescribed to follow   *215*
Swells their self-will in limiting their rule.
Both in their turn will make their peoples groan:
Like some mad torrent, lasting but a day,
That rushes more, the narrower it is,
And marks its passage with rampageous ruin.[3]   *220*

[3] One of the very few similes in Racine's secular plays; although this torrent image, repeated as a simile in Racine's next play *Alexander the Great* (lines 189–192) recurs often in attenuated metaphoric guise in later plays, Racine, in his maturity, rightly eschewed simile as inappropriate in dramatic dialogue, though in his last two plays simile appropriately reappears in the lyrical choruses.

JOCASTA

Rather, they will be seen, through noble plans,
Both vying for the love of their dear subjects.
Confess, however, Creon, your sole care
Is lest peace nullify your craven hope,
Securing to my sons the throne you seek,   225
And smash the trap by which you lie in wait.
As, after their demise, the right of birth
Puts in your hands supreme authority,
The blood that binds you to my royal sons
Makes you regard them as your greatest foes;   230
And your ambition, aiming at their fortune,
Gives you a common hatred for them both.
You fill the king with dangerous advice;
Serving one brother to destroy them both.

CREON

I do not feed at all on such delusions: 235
My reverence for the king is warm and true,
And my ambition is to see him stay
Upon the throne at which you think I aim.
My only care is how to keep him great;
I hate his foes and that is all my crime: 240
I do not hide it. But, from what I see,
Not everyone is criminal here like me.

JOCASTA

I am a mother; if I love his brother,
The king himself is no less dear to me.
He may be hated by some cowardly courtier;   245
But no true mother can betray herself.

ANTIGONE

Your interests, Creon, are the same as ours,
Not all the king's opponents are your foes;
You are a father. In the opponent's camp,
Perhaps you may recall you have a son.   250
For Polynices, Haemon's love is known.

CREON

I know it, lady, and I judge him rightly;
I must, indeed, pick him out from the rest,
Yet it is but to hate him all the more:
And in my righteous anger I should like   255
All men to hate him as his father hates.

ANTIGONE

After the feats his gallant arm achieved,
Not everyone resembles you in this.

CREON

I know it all too well—and to my sorrow:
Yet his revolt but underlines my duty;   260
And all his splendid exploits so admired,
Merely make him more odious to me.
Shame ever dogs the camp of a rebellion:
The more a rebel dares the worse his crime;
Aloft he holds his crime with arm aloft   265
And honour's absent where the king is not.

ANTIGONE

Listen more wisely to the voice of nature.

CREON

The dearer the culprit, the nearer the hit.

ANTIGONE

But can a father be so overborne?
You are too full of hate.

CREON

                    And you of love.   270
You sue too much, my lady, for a rebel.

ANTIGONE

For innocence it's always good to sue.

CREON

I know what makes him innocent to you.

ANTIGONE

And I know why your hate for him you fan.

CREON

Love looks with other eyes than everyman.   *275*

JOCASTA

You take advantage, Creon, of our plight
And run to licence; but beware my anger:
Your liberties will soon recoil on you.

ANTIGONE

The public interest scarcely troubles him;
His love of country hides another love.   *280*
I know it, Creon, but detest its course.
And if you're wise, you'll keep it ever hidden.

CREON

I shall, my lady, and wish in advance
To spare you also my abhorrent presence.
My deep respects only enhance your scorn.   *285*
I go to give way to my happy son.
The king calls me away. I must obey.
Farewell. Bring Polynices here and Haemon.

JOCASTA

Be certain, wicked man, they both will come;
And both shall hinder your nefarious plans.   *290*

Exit CREON

SCENE VI

ANTIGONE

The miscreant! How high his insolence!

JOCASTA

His proud words soon shall turn out to his shame:
And soon, if heaven will hearken to our hopes,
Peace will avenge us on this vaulting man.
But we must hurry, every hour is dear: 295
Let us call quickly Haemon and your brother;
To crown my plan I'm ready to accord
Every assurance they may like to ask.
And thou, just Heaven, if wearied by my woes,
My Polynices' heart to peace dispose,   300
Support my sighs and lend my tears fresh force
And grant me fitting tongue for my remorse!

Exit JOCASTA

ANTIGONE (*Lingering a moment after her mother*)

And if thou pitiest my innocent love,
O Heaven, in bringing Haemon to me, prove
Him faithful; and allow today to me   305
Once more my lover and his love to see!

ACT II

SCENE I

ANTIGONE, HAEMON

HAEMON

Must you refuse to stay behind with me,
After a whole year tortured by your absence!
Have you, my lady, called me near to you
Just promptly to remove so sweet a joy?   *310*

ANTIGONE

And will you have me promptly leave my brother?
Must I not to the temple take my mother?
Must I prefer, at your desire's caprice,
To foster first your love and then our peace?

HAEMON

You go too far to find bars to my bliss;   *315*
Without us they may quite well test the gods.
Permit my heart, at sight of your dear eyes,
To learn its own fate from its deities.[4]
May I ask them, without too much presumption
If they still have for me their wonted charm?   *320*
Will they accept my ardent love unangered?

[4] Such conceits disappear in Racine's plays after *Andromaque*. This, in his first play, is perhaps the worst, with a close second in line 72 of *Alexander the Great*, where Axiana's eyes are described as "tyrants." Subsequently Racine often made masterly use of "eyes" to illumine his psychological penetration.

And have they pity for the pain they caused?
Throughout the sad course of my cruel absence
Were you at all desirous I be true?
Did you at all think far from you death faced   *325*
A lover, doomed to die but at your feet?
Ah, when a soul is smitten with such love,
When a bold heart may dare to dream of you,
How sweet to worship such divine allure!
But how one suffers when it stays unseen!   *330*
One moment far from you seemed like a year.
I would have·ended all a hundred times,
Had I not reckoned, pending my return,
My very distance proved to you my love;
And that the memory of my loyalty   *335*
Might in my absence prosecute my suit;
And thinking of me you would also think
How much I loved you to obey you so.

ANTIGONE

Yes, I indeed believed your faithful heart
Would find a cruel punishment in absence;   *340*
And if I must confess my inmost feelings,
Haemon, I wanted it to make you suffer,
And that, away from me, some bitter-sweetness
Would make the days more slowly drag than usual.
But you need not complain: my heavy heart   *345*
Wished nothing for you it did not endure.
Above all, through the age this war has lasted,
The ground all covered with your armèd men,
O gods! how tortured has my heart not been
Seeing in both camps all it loves the most!   *350*
A thousand painful sights would sear my breast;
All those without our walls and those within;
With each assault, my heart felt a thousand blows
And a thousand times a day I suffered death.

HAEMON

But in our desperate plight what have I done   *355*
That my princess has not herself ordained?

I followed Polynices as you wished:
You made me do it by an outright order.
I pledged him ever since my warmest friendship;
I left my country, I forsook my father,   *360*
Drew down on me his anger in departing;
To cap it all, went far away from you.

ANTIGONE

I know it, Haemon, and give you your due;
In serving Polynices you served me;
Then he was dear to me, as he is now,   *365*
And deeds for his sake I deemed done for me.
We loved each other from our infancy;
I held a sovereign sway upon his heart,
I felt the sweetest joy in pleasing him,
And all my brother's sorrows were his sister's.   *370*
Ah! if I still held such sway over him,
He'd love the peace my heavy heart is seeking:
Our common misery would be assuaged:
I would see him and you would see me too!

HAEMON

He hates the sight of this accursèd war,   *375*
I saw him sighing both with grief and rage,
When, to ascend the throne of his forefathers,
He was compelled to take this cruel course.
Let us hope Heaven, moved by our miseries,
Will soon succeed in reconciling them: *380*
May it restore affection to their hearts,
And may it guard the love that is in yours!

ANTIGONE

Alas! you may be sure your last desire
Will easier prove than to assuage their rage.
I know my brothers both and I can tell you,   *385*
Haemon, their hearts are harder far than mine.
But Heaven has sometimes wrought even greater wonders.

SCENE II

Enter OLYMPIAS

ANTIGONE

Well! Shall we hear the oracles' decree?
What must we do?

OLYMPIAS

        Alas!

ANTIGONE

            What do you know?
Olympias, is it war?

OLYMPIAS

          Ah, worse, far worse!   390

HAEMON

What great disaster does their wrath proclaim?

OLYMPIAS

Prince, hear their answer and then judge yourself;
Thebans, to end these wars
The last of royal birth
Must, as decree the stars,   395
Die bleeding on your earth.

ANTIGONE

What has our wretched blood then done to you,
O gods! that you should damn it utterly?
Has not my father's death[5] left you appeased?
Must all our blood be stifled by your anger?   400

HAEMON

My lady, this decree is not for you;

---

[5] Beautifully recounted in Sophocles' *Oedipus at Colonus*.

Your virtue is your refuge against death:
The gods know to distinguish innocence.

ANTIGONE

I do not dread their vengeance for my sake.
My innocence would be a weak support;[6]   *405*
Oedipus' child, on his account I die:
And uncomplaining I await my death;
And if I must confess what I am dreading,
It is for you I dread, dear Haemon, you.
You stem, like us, from this unhappy blood;   *410*
And I see only too well angry Heaven
Will make you, like us, direly buy this honour,
And make the Theban princes all regret
They were not offspring of the least of men.

HAEMON

Can one repudiate so great a boon?   *415*
My heart is flattered by a death so fair;
And it is sweet to spring from royal blood
Had one to yield such blood as soon as born.

ANTIGONE

What! if our family has angered Heaven,
Must it take vengeance even upon you?   *420*
Are father and his children not enough,
Without its seeking innocent victims further?
It is for us to purge our parents' crimes:
Then punish us, great gods; but spare the rest.
My father, Haemon, murders you today;   *425*
And more perhaps than he, I am your slayer;
Heaven punishes you and your family,
Both for my father's crimes and for my love;
And this our love is far more fatal to you
Than Oedipus's crimes and Laius's blood.   *430*

---

[6] An early rejection by Racine of the aesthetically too tidy doctrine of poetic justice advocated by a number of writers of tragedy (rarely of the first rank). Racine has the powerful support of Shakespeare, most tragic in the sacrifice of Cordelia, and, of course, of the great Greeks.

HAEMON

My love, my lady? What is fatal in it?
Is it a crime to love celestial beauty?
And since accepting it does not displease you,
In what way does it merit Heaven's ire?
You are alone a party to my sighs: 435
It is for you to judge if they offend:
According as your sovereignty decree,
Will they prove criminal or blameless be.
Let Heaven pronounce my death as it may will,
I'll cherish both the reasons for it still;   440
Dying with honour for my kings' blood true,
And happier far to die for love of you.
What then should I do in our doom so sore?
Could I have any heart to live on more?
In vain the gods would wish my life to spare;   445
For what they'd not do, I'd do in despair.
But after all perhaps our fears are vain:
Wait . . . Here comes Polynices and the queen.

SCENE III

Enter JOCASTA *and* POLYNICES

POLYNICES

In heaven's name, Madam, do not hamper me!
I see full well that peace will not be made.   450
I hoped the infinite justice of the gods
Would make their voice heard against usurpation,
And, weary at the sight of so much blood,
That they would give to each his rightful rank;
But since they plainly stand for what's unjust,   455
In conjuration with such criminals,
Must I still hope a contumacious people
Will follow justice when the gods do not?
Must I elect as judge an insolent rabble,

A proud usurper's tame, tempestuous tools,   460
Whose craven calculation serves my foe,
Who keeps inciting them behind the scenes?
Reason may never move a multitude.
I've brooked, before, the black looks of this mob,
Who drove me off and, far from greeting me   465
As King, look on their injured prince as tyrant.
As honour never had a hold on them,
They fancy everyone must dream of vengeance;
No hand can stem their hostile feelings' spate:
When once they hate, they must forever hate.   470

JOCASTA

My son, if it is true the people fear you,
And that the Thebans dread to see you reign,
Why do you seek at cost of so much blood
To rule a people proved implacable?

POLYNICES

Is it the people, who must choose their master?[7]   475
A king, once hated, is he no more king?
Is their hate or their love the first requirement
Deciding if a king should reign or go?
The people may at will fear, cherish us;
Our blood gives us the throne and not their whims.[8]   480
And what blood royal gives, they must accept;
A prince they cannot love they must respect.

JOCASTA

You'll be a despot whom your realms will hate.

POLYNICES

That name is not fit for legitimate kings.
My rights preserve me from that loathsome title.   485

---

[7] Rousseau's *Contrat Social* was still in the womb of Time!
[8] It was in obstinate defence of this doctrine of the Divine Right of Kings that
Charles I, father of Henrietta, who was to grace with her presence the première
of Racine's next play, *Alexandre*, had lost his throne and head in London in 1649,
only a few years before the play was written.

Their subjects' hate is not what makes a despot;
By that name call Eteocles himself.

JOCASTA

He's loved by all.

POLYNICES

A most belovèd despot!
Who tries, by a hundred dastard deeds, to keep
The rank that he has violently seized;   490
His arrogance makes him, contrarily,
His people's slave and his own brother's despot.
To reign alone, he stoops low to obey,
And makes himself despised to make me hated.
It is with reason they prefer the traitor: 495
The people love a slave and dread a master.
I would betray the majesty of kings,
Letting the people arbitrate my claims.

JOCASTA

Must strife forever cast a spell on you?
Are you already irked by this brief truce?   500
Must there be no end, after all our woes,
You, to shedding blood, I, to shedding tears?
Will you yield nothing to a mother's moan?
My daughter, if you can, hold back your brother:
The cruel boy had love for you alone.   505

ANTIGONE

Ah! if for your sake he is deaf to pity,
What could I hope for from our former love,
Erased too well by such long separation?
I scarce have place still in his memory;
He only loves, delights to shed our blood.   510
Seek no more in him that high-minded prince,
Who once evinced such horror for all crime,
Whose noble soul was full of gentle kindness,
Who esteemed his mother and adored his sister:

Nature for him is now but a bad dream;   515
He spurns his sister and he scorns his mother;
The ruffian, in his overweening pride,
Takes us for strangers or his enemies.

POLYNICES

Do not lay that crime on my bleeding heart;
Say rather, sister, it is you who've changed;   520
Say the unjust usurper of my rank
Has also snatched from me my sister's love.
I know you still and I am still the same.

ANTIGONE

Do you love me as much as I love you,
O harsh boy, deaf to my despairing sighs,   525
Exposing me to all this further pain?

POLYNICES

But you, my sister, do you love your brother,
Presenting me here with unjust demands,
With aim to tear the sceptre from my grasp?
Gods! Could Eteocles be more inhuman?   530
You back too much a tyrant torturing me.

ANTIGONE

No, no, I am more mindful of your interests.
Do not believe my tears would harm you so;
Nor that they are in league with your opponents.
This peace I long for would become a prison,   535
Were it to cost his crown to Polynices;
And, brother, the one favour which I ask,
Is that I be allowed to see you more.
For just a few days let us see you here,
And give us time to search out some solution   540
That may restore you to your father's rank,
Without your spilling our so precious blood.
Can you refuse this small consideration
To a sister's tears and to your mother's sighs?

JOCASTA

But what fresh fears can be upsetting you?　　　　545
Why do you want so suddenly to leave us?
Was not the truce to last the whole day long?
Is it to end as soon as it's begun?
You saw Eteocles lay down his arms;
He wishes me to see you and you do not.　　　　550

ANTIGONE

Yes, brother, he is not like you, unbending;
His mother's tears appeared to influence him;
Our grief today appeased his indignation.
You call him cruel but are crueller far.

HAEMON

My lord, there is no hurry; you may calmly　　　　555
Permit the princess and the queen proceed:
Grant to their pressing prayers this entire day;
And let us see if their plan may succeed.
Do not allow your brother the glad chance
Of saying, but for you, peace could be made.　　　　560
You will have satisfied your mother, sister,
And, above all, have satisfied your honour.
But what does this excited soldier want?

SCENE IV

Enter a SOLDIER

THE SOLDIER

Sir, fighting has begun, the truce is broken:
As ordered by their king, Creon and the Thebans　　　　565
Attack your army and abjure their word.
Brave Hippomedon, in your absence, tries
To hold up the assault with all his might.
At his command, I come to warn you, Sir.

POLYNICES

The traitors! Come on, Haemon, we must go. 570
(*To the* QUEEN)
You see, my lady, how he keeps his word:
He wants to fight, attacks; I rush to meet him.

JOCASTA

Polynices! My son! . . . He hears no more.
My cries, like my distress, are all in vain.
Antigone, run after this barbarian: 575
At least, beg Haemon make sure they are parted.
My strength is failing; I can no more fly;
Alas! all I can now do is to die.

ACT III

SCENE I

JOCASTA, OLYMPIAS

JOCASTA

Olympias, go and see the shattering sight;
See if their savagery has not been stayed,   580
If nothing could deflect either of them.
They say Menoeceus went forth with this plan.

OLYMPIAS

I do not know what plan inspired his heart;
A hero's daring shone upon his face;
But you must hope, my lady, to the end.   585

JOCASTA

Olympias, go, see all and tell me all.
Throw light upon my dark anxieties.

OLYMPIAS

But should I leave you here thus all alone?

JOCASTA

Go. In my state, I welcome solitude,
If with my crushing cares I could but find it!   590

Exit OLYMPIAS

SCENE II

JOCASTA (*Alone*)

Must these, my fatal cares, for ever last?
Will the gods' vengeance never be appeased?
Must I then suffer all these cruel deaths,
Before they let me sink into my grave?
How much less dire, Heaven, were thy victims' plight   595
If thy bolt crushed the guilty ones outright!
How infinite thy chastisements appear
When thou let'st live those writhing in thy fear!
Full well thou knowest, since I cringed undone,
When I found myself wife of my own son,   600
How the mildest torments, that in my heart swell,
Equal all evils that are borne in hell.
And must, O gods, an unintended crime
Draw down on us your anger for all time?
Did I know him, alas! the son I wed?   605
Yourselves, you led him to my very bed.
Your spite, it was, that brought me to the abyss:
The vaunted justice of the gods is this!
They lead our footsteps to the edge of crimes
They make us perpetrate, unpardoned paradigms!   610
To fashion miscreants first their malice stretches,
In order to create illustrious wretches!
Ah, why cannot they, when their furies flare,
Strike down such criminals as find crime fair!

SCENE III

Enter ANTIGONE

JOCASTA

Well, is it done? Has one or other traitor   615
Just perpetrated his brave fratricide?
Speak, speak, my daughter.

ANTIGONE

Ah! indeed, my lady,
The oracle's fulfilled and heaven content.

JOCASTA

What! Both my sons are dead!

ANTIGONE

Another's blood
Gives the State peace and quiet to your heart;   620
A royal blood that's worthy of its source,
A hero gives his life to save the State.
I rushed to curb Haemon and Polynices;
They were already far, before I left;
They heard me no more and my piteous cries   625
In vain called out to both of them by name.
They have both flown towards the field of battle;
And as for me, I went upon the walls,
From where the spellbound people gaped like me
Upon the impending fight that froze their marrow.   630
At this hour, big with fate, our youngest prince,
The honour of our blood, our kingdom's hope,
In short, Menoeceus, Haemon's happy brother,
And most unhappy to be son of Creon,
Resplendent with devotion to his country,   635
Set fearless foot between the hostile camps;
And forcing Greeks and Thebans both to hear him,
"Stop," he cried, "stop, you hard, unnatural brutes!"
His fine, imperious voice was heard unchallenged:
The soldiers, spellbound by this novel sight,   640
Immediate stayed the dark course of their fury;
The prince continued promptly with these words:
"Hearken all ye to what decree the fates
Who wish to set a limit to your hates.
I am the last, of royal blood descended,   645
That, as the gods ordain, must now be ended.
Receive this blood, then, that my hand shall shed,
And receive peace with it in place of dread."
This much he says and then he stabs himself.

The Thebans, seeing their great hero die,   650
Gaze on his noble sacrifice with terror,
As though salvation spelt for them their doom.
I saw Haemon, in tears, leave his position
To come down and embrace his bleeding brother:
And, following his example, Creon too,   655
Threw down his arms to mourn his dying son,
And both the camps, beholding their retreat,
Have left off fighting and have separated;
While I, with trembling heart and troubled soul,
Turned from this piteous sight with tearful eyes,   660
In marvel at his noble frenzy lost.

JOCASTA

Like you I marvel and I shake with horror.
O gods, can there remain some obstacle
To Theban peace after this miracle?
May not this shining end appease your ire,   665
Since even my sons have been disarmed by it?
Will you refuse his sacrifice sublime?
If virtue touches you as much as crime,
If like your punishment your prize is great,
What crime will such blood not obliterate?   670

ANTIGONE

Yes, yes, his virtue shall be recompensed;
Menoeceus' blood has fully paid the gods;
And the Olympians deem one hero's blood
Alone worth more than that of a thousand knaves.

JOCASTA

Learn to know better Heaven's dire revenge.   675
It always puts a pause between my pains;
But when its hand appears to succour me,
It then prepares alas! its deadliest blow.
It set a term upon my tears, last night,
To waken me to see all set to fight.   680
If with some hope of peace it flatters me,
A cruel oracle then shatters me.

It brings my son to me—a boon to treasure—
But ah! how dearly does it sell this pleasure!
This son is heartless with his ears closed tight;   685
Then all at once heaven tears him off to fight.
Thus cruel still, its anger still will burn,
It feigns to be appeased, to grow more stern;
It halts its shower of blows to make them pour,
And draws its arm back, but to crush me more!   690

ANTIGONE

In this last miracle let's place our hopes.

JOCASTA

The hatred of my sons will hinder all.
Harsh Polynices only heeds his rights;
The other heeds the people's voice and Creon's,
Yes, craven Creon's, whose ungenerous spirit   695
Will wrest from us the fruit of Menoeceus' blood.
In vain to save us has this great prince died;
The father harms us more than son can serve.
This faithless father of two youthful heroes . . .

ANTIGONE

My lady, here he comes with the king, my brother.   700

SCENE IV

Enter ETEOCLES *and* CREON

JOCASTA

My son, is this the way you keep your word?

ETEOCLES

This clash, my lady, was not due to me,
But to some soldiers, both of mine and Argos,
Who by degrees embroiled with one another
Have imperceptibly engaged the army   705

And turned a petty clash into great combat.
The battle would have doubtless been most fierce
And its result have settled all our quarrel,
Had not the heroic death of Creon's son
Restrained the hands of all the combatants.   *710*
This prince, the last of royal blood descended,
Thought Heaven's dread finger pointed straight at him,
And he himself plunged forth to seek out death,
Borne nobly on by love of fatherland.

JOCASTA

Ah! if his patriot love alone could make him   *715*
Impregnable to life's sweet flatteries,
Cannot, my son, this same love curb a little
The impetuous flow of your ambition?
His fine example beckons you to follow.
You will not have to cease to reign nor live: *720*
You may, by yielding something of your rank,
Do more than he did, shedding all his blood;
You only have to cease to hate your brother;
You will achieve more than his death achieved.
Gods! is it harder then to love a brother   *725*
Than to hate life and rush to seek out death?
And must another find it easier far
To shed his blood than you to love your own?

ETEOCLES

Like you I'm spellbound by his shining courage,
And even jealous of his splendid death.   *730*
But none the less, my lady, I must tell you
A throne is harder to renounce than life.
Honour may often render life accursed;
But rare are kings who glory in obeying.
The gods desired his blood; so without guilt   *735*
This prince could not deny the State its victim;
But the same country, clamouring for his blood,
Clamours I reign and keeps me in my rank.
Till she remove me I must stay, her king.
She has but to pronounce, I'll heed at once,   *740*

And Thebes will see me promptly abdicate
And run to meet my death to appease her fate.

CREON

Menoeceus, ah, is dead. Heaven wants none else.
Let his blood flow without now adding yours;
And since he shed his blood to give us peace,   *745*
Grant it, my lord, to our legitimate wish.

ETEOCLES

What! Creon too would now pronounce for peace?

CREON

For having loved this savage war too much,
You see the pain in which heaven plunges me:
My son is dead, my lord.

ETEOCLES

                    We must avenge him.   *750*

CREON

In my dire grief on whom to be avenged?

ETEOCLES

Creon, your foes are those of Thebes herself;
Avenge her, and avenge yourself.

CREON

                         Among her foes
I find your brother and I find my son!
Must I spill my own blood or else shed yours?   *755*
Must I, avenging one son, lose another?
My blood is dear to me and yours is sacred,
Shall I be sacrilegious or unnatural?
Shall I then stain my hand with blood revered,
Redeem my fatherhood by slaying my son?   *760*
Such cruel remedies cannot console,
And they would spell disaster not revenge.
My only consolation, in my pain,

Is that at least my sorrows serve your reign.
I shall find solace if the son, I pity,   765
Gains by his death the calm of Thebes' fair city.
Heaven promises this to my bleeding son;
Complete the peace, my lord, he has begun;
Grant him this heavenly prize claimed by his pain,
So that his dear blood be not shed in vain.   770

JOCASTA

Since you are now alive to all our woes,
Menoeceus' blood at last may peace impose.
Let Thebes take courage from his feat so great;
Since he has changed your heart, he'll change her fate.
From now on peace is not an empty lure: 775
Since Creon wishes it, I deem it sure.
These iron hearts will soon begin to melt:
Who Creon tames may tame my sons as well.

(*To* ETEOCLES)

Let this great change disarm and soften you;
Renounce, my son, renounce a hate we'll rue;   780
Comfort your mother and console Creon,
Give Polynices me and him Haemon.

ETEOCLES

But this means thrusting over me a lord.
This, Polynices wants, you have his word;
Above all he demands to mount the throne,   785
And will return, sceptre in hand alone.

SCENE V

Enter ATTALUS

ATTALUS

Sire, Polynices seeks an interview;
This is what we have just learnt from a herald.

He offers you, my lord, to come himself
Or to await you in his camp.

CREON

     Softened   *790*
Perhaps, he dreams to end a sluggish war,
And his ambition takes no more to force.
Through this last combat he has learnt today
That you are no less powerful than he.
To serve his anger wearies even the Greeks; *795*
I learnt but now his royal father-in-law,
Preferring a sure peace to war's alarms,
Retains Mycenae, making him king of Argos.
With all his courage, doubtless he desires
Merely to win an honourable withdrawal.   *800*
Since he would see you, know, he chooses peace.
Today must crown or shatter it for ever.
In this plan try yourself to fortify him,
And promise everything except the throne.

ETEOCLES

The throne is what he's after, nothing else.   *805*

JOCASTA

But see him first at least.

CREON

     Yes, since he seeks it:
Alone you will fare better than we could;
Your brother-blood will loving flow once more.

ETEOCLES

Then let me find him.

JOCASTA

     In Heaven's name, stay, son,
Wait for him rather, and receive him here.   *810*

ETEOCLES

Just as you wish, my lady! Let him come,
With promise of safe conduct for his person.
Let's go.

ANTIGONE

     Ah! if this day brings peace to Thebes,
It will be, Creon, your great handiwork.

Exeunt ETEOCLES, JOCASTA *and* ANTIGONE

SCENE VI

CREON

The love of Thebes is not what's moving you,   *815*
Haughty princess; and your elusive soul
That seems to woo me after all your scorn,
Dreams less of peace than of my son's return.
But we'll soon see if proud Antigone
Will look down on the throne as on my heart;   *820*
And when the gods have made me king, we'll see
Whether my happy son will rival me.

ATTALUS

And whom would not a change so rare astonish?
Creon himself, Creon pronounces peace!

CREON

So you think peace is what is moving me?   *825*

ATTALUS

Yes, Sire, I do, though least expecting it;
And seeing in fact this noble purpose move you
I'm struck with wonder at your high resolve
Impelling you, at last, to drown your hate.
This is the dead Menoeceus' finest feat.   *830*

He, who for country sacrifices hate,
Might well for her his life too immolate.

CREON

Ah, doubtless, he who by his lofty will
Can love his enemy may well love death.
What! would you have me stultify my vengeance,   *835*
Embracing my own enemy's defence?
The cause of my son's death is Polynices,
Should I then rush to be his base protector?
Were I somehow my utter hate to drown
Could I renounce my craving for the crown?   *840*
No, no; you'll see me with a constant keenness,
Hate all my foes and cherish my own greatness.
The throne was always my most ardent aim:
I blush to serve where once my fathers reigned;
I burn to join the rank of my forefathers,   *845*
I dreamt of it the moment I was born.
For two years now this noble care consumes me;
I take no step that leads not to the throne:
I fan the fury of my princely nephews,
And my ambition is the spur of theirs.   *850*
At first I joined the unjust Eteocles,
Making him bar the throne to Polynices.
You know since then I aimed myself to mount it;
And put him on it but to drive him thence.

ATTALUS

But, Sire, if you find war such recompense,   *855*
How comes it you now snatch their swords from them?
And since their discord is your whole desire,
Why, on your counsel, should this talk transpire?

CREON

War is more dread to me than to my foes,
As heaven's most cruel anger now has shown: *860*
It sets against me my own stratagem;
And uses my arm to transfix my breast.

War hardly broke out when to punish me
Haemon abandoned me for Polynices;
Through me the brothers became mortal foes   865
And I became the foe of my own son.
Today, through me, the truce at last was broken,
I spurred the soldiers, all the camp arose.
Fighting began, and then my desperate son
Came forth to die, ending my well-planned scrap.   870
But I still have one son, whom yet I love,
Rebellious though he be, my rival even.
Without his death, I wish my foes to die,
Too much 'twould cost me if it cost two sons.
Besides, the brothers' hatred is too great.   875
Do not think it would ever suffer peace.
I can myself incite their hate so well
That they would rather both succumb than love;
The hates of other foes may not endure;
But when the bonds of nature once are broken,   880
Dear Attalus, nothing can bind again
Those whom such ties were powerless to restrain:
One hates a brother with a hate that's dire:
But absence may abate their mutual ire:
However much we hate a foe we dread,   885
When he is far from us, one half is shed.
Then do not wonder if I wish them speak:
I wish, in speaking, their resentments break;
That full of hatred they could not efface,
Each smothers other, seeking to embrace.[9]   890

ATTALUS

You need, my lord, but fear yourself from now;
For with the crown remorse shall gird your brow.

CREON

Upon the throne, of cares there is a feast:
Remorse is one that troubles me the least.

---

[9] Precursor of Nero's famous line (1314) in *Britannicus* (Act IV, Scene 3):
"I'll hug my rival, but to smother him."

A soul, possessed of royal pomp and sway,   *895*
From all that's past will turn its thought away;
A mind, from every other aim estranged,
Deems it has not lived if it has not reigned.
But come. About remorse I have no care,
No more have I a heart that crime can scare: *900*
All first offences take a little force;
But one commits the next without remorse.

ACT IV

SCENE I

ETEOCLES, CREON

ETEOCLES

Yes, Creon, it is here he soon must come;
And we may both await him in this place.
Let's hear his wishes; but we may be sure   905
That nothing will be furthered by our talk.
I know my brother and his haughty moods;
I know his hatred is still absolute;
No one, I think, can ever stem its tide;
And as for me, my hate will still abide.   910

CREON

But if at last he leaves you sovereign power,
You must, it seems to me, appease your hate.

ETEOCLES

I doubt my heart will ever be appeased:
It's not his pride, it's he himself I hate.
Our hatred for each other is fanatic;   915
And has not just been fashioned in a year;
Such hate was born with us; and its dark fury
With life itself flowed deep into our hearts.
From tenderest infancy we stood forth foes,
Indeed, we were so even before our birth:[10]   920

[10] This idea of prenatal taint was emphasised by Racine by an amendment including the insertion of four lines in the 1697 edition—the last in his lifetime—when he was preoccupied by his Jansenist doctrines of predestined doom.

Fatal and tragic brood of incestuous blood!
While one same womb was still enclosing both,
In our mother's flesh, intestinal war
Engraved on her the source of our contentions.
You know how they burst forth within the cradle,   *925*
And in the grave perhaps will follow us.
Heaven, one might say, with a predestined doom
Wished thus to scourge the incest of our parents;
And wished, through our blood's paradigm, to prove
All that is darkest in man's hate and love.   *930*
And Creon, now that I await his coming,
Do not believe my hate for him will wane,
The nearer he, the more I find him odious;
And this must doubtless strike him in the face.
I would regret his leaving me my seat: *935*
Flee he must, flee, not merely beat retreat.
Creon, I will not hate him half and half;
I fear his anger far less than his love.
To give free rein to all my burning hate
I wish his fury to give me good cause;   *940*
And since my heart no truck can contemplate,
I wish him to detest that I may hate.
His rage, as you shall see, is still the same,
His heart, as ever, at the crown will aim;
He'll ever loathe me, ever wish to reign;   *945*
And I may conquer him but never gain.

CREON

Defeat him then, my lord, prove he defiant.
However proud, he's not invincible;
And since mere reason will not move his heart,
See what an arm that ever wins can do.   *950*
Yes, though I found some sweet allure in peace,
I shall be first to take up arms once more;
And if I asked, you both should end the strife,
I ask still more, you sole reign all your life.
Let wars spread far and wide and never cease,   *955*
If Polynices we must have with peace.
Let no one come and praise its boons again;

War and its horrors please us, if you reign.
The whole of Thebes is speaking through my lips;
Do not subject us to this prince's grip: 960
If peace is possible, "peace," we shall sing;
But if you love your people, save their king.
Meanwhile, hear what your brother has in plan,
And hide, my lord, your anger, if you can;
Pretend . . . But some one comes.

SCENE II

Enter ATTALUS

ETEOCLES

                   Are they at hand?   965
Attalus, are they coming?

ATTALUS

                   Here they are,
My lord. They saw the princess and the queen,
And will soon be in the adjoining chamber.

ETEOCLES

I feel my temper rise. Let them appear.
How much one hates a foe when he is near![11]   970

CREON

Ah, here he is!
              Sweet fortune, my war wage,
Delivering both to their unbridled rage!

Exit ATTALUS

[11] Compare Hermione's similar but finer recoil at the first approach of the
unloved Orestes at the end of Act II Scene 1 of *Andromache*: "Ah me! I did not
think he was so near."

SCENE III

Enter JOCASTA, POLYNICES, ANTIGONE *and* HAEMON

JOCASTA

At last I soon shall reach my heart's desire,
Since heaven has now brought both of you together.
After two years, once more you see your brother,   975
In the same palace where you both were born;
And I in my undreamt of happiness,
May now embrace the two of you together.
Begin, my sons, this precious unity;
Let each of you his brother recognise;   980
Both, view your features in your brother's face;
To judge them better, pray observe more closely;
Above all let blood speak and play its part.
Come, Eteocles; Polynices, come . . .
What! far from coming nearer, you draw back!   985
What means this dismal welcome, these dark looks?
Is it not, each, in hesitating mood,
To greet his brother waits that he be greeted,
Clinging to the honour of yielding last,
Neither of you would be first to embrace?   990
A strange ambition, aiming but at crime,
Where the most stubborn passes as most noble!
The victor in this shameful fight should blush;
And those, subdued the first, most generous shine.
Let's see which of you two will have more heart,   995
Who will be first to triumph over his temper . . .
What! you do nothing! You should move, the first;
And coming from so far you should begin:
Come, Polynices, embrace your brother,
And show . . .

ETEOCLES

My lady, why this sorry game?   *1000*
All these embraces hardly meet the case:
Let him speak and, having said, leave us in peace.

POLYNICES

What, must I once more speak what's in my mind?
All that has happened leaves it clear to read:
The war, the fighting, so much blood that's shed,   *1005*
All that says straight the throne is now my due.

ETEOCLES

This very fighting and this very war,
This blood that reddens earth so many times,
All that says straight the throne is still my due,
And as long as I breathe is not for you.   *1010*

POLYNICES

Unjustly, as you know, you sit upon it.

ETEOCLES

Unjust or no, so long as you're not on it.

POLYNICES

If you will not step down, you'll fall from high.

ETEOCLES

If I fall, with me you shall surely die.

JOCASTA

O gods! how cruelly I am deceived!   *1015*
Had I so strongly urged this fatal meeting,
But to embroil them deeper still than ever?
My sons, is this the way to speak of peace?
In Heaven's name, leave aside such tragic thoughts;
Do not rekindle now your past dissensions: *1020*
You are not here upon some monstrous field.
Am I the one to put arms in your hands?
Look round upon these walls where you were born;

Does not their sight stir pity in your hearts?
Here it is that you both first saw the light; *1025*
Here everything breathes only peace and love:
These friends, your sister, all condemn your hates;
And lastly I, who ever strove for you,
Who would, to bind you, sacrifice . . . Alas!
They turn their heads away and do not hear! *1030*
Their adamantine hearts will never melt;
The voice of nature fails to move them more!

(*To* POLYNICES)

And you, whom I believed more sweet and gentle . . .

POLYNICES

I want from him only what he has promised:
He cannot reign and not become forsworn. *1035*

JOCASTA

Excessive justice often turns to wrong.
The throne to you is due, I cannot doubt it;
But you are toppling it, wishing to mount it.
Do you not weary of this dreadful war?
Would you, relentless, desolate this land, *1040*
Destroy this empire which you wish to gain?
On corpses only would you dream to reign?
Thebes, fearful, rightly deems a prince no good
Who inundates her land with streams of blood:
Could she accept your rule, unquestioning? *1045*
You are her tyrant ere you be her king.
If growing great means often vice has grown,
If virtue withers, when one mounts the throne,
When you will reign, how you will be their bane,
If you are cruel when you do not reign? *1050*

POLYNICES

If I am cruel, I am forced to be;
I am not master of my cruelty;
I hate the horrors that I must commit;
Unjustly do the people fear my writ.

But I indeed must soothe my motherland,   *1055*
My soul is stricken by her moaning, and
Her guiltless blood, each day, too lightly spills;
I must arrest the course of all her ills;
And letting neither Thebes nor Greece still burn,
To the author of my troubles I must turn: *1060*
Today either his blood or mine suffices.

JOCASTA

Your brother's blood?

POLYNICES

                    Indeed, my lady, his,
We must thus finish with this evil war.
Yes, cruel man, such is the plan I bring.
I wished myself to summon you to duel;   *1065*
I feared to tell it anyone but you;
Anyone else would have condemned my thought,
And no one would announce it here to you.
I now announce it. It is for you to prove
If you can keep what you have snatched from me.   *1070*
Show yourself worthy of so fine a prey.

ETEOCLES

I accept your plan and I accept with joy.
Creon knows what I wished in this regard:
I would have kept the throne with less delight.
I think you worthy now to bear the crown   *1075*
That I will thrust on you with the tip of my sword.

JOCASTA

Then hurry, savages, to tear my breast;
Begin your monstrous plan by murdering me.
Do not consider me to be your mother,
Consider I am mother of your brother.   *1080*
If you are questing for your brother's blood,
Quest for its source in my unhappy womb:
I am the common enemy of both,
Since the enemy of each took life from me.

This enemy without me would not breathe!   *1085*
If he die, must I not in my turn die?
Make no mistake, in his death I must share;
You must slay both or else must not slay one;
To shun your being half-mild or half-cruel,
You must destroy me or else save your brother.   *1090*
If courage pleases you, if honour spurs,
Barbarians, blush to contemplate such crimes;
Or if this crime pleases you each so much,
Barbarians, blush to contemplate but one.
And yet, it is not love that holds you back,   *1095*
If you save my life in pursuing his:
You would take good care, monsters, not to spare me,
If I prevented you at all from reigning.
Ah Polynices, thus to treat your mother?

POLYNICES

I spare my country.

JOCASTA

       And you slay your brother!   *1100*

POLYNICES

I scourge the wicked.

JOCASTA

       And his death will see
You guiltier, more wicked far than he!

POLYNICES

Must I then crown this traitor with my hands,
And go from court to court, seeking a master?
A vagabond and tramp, leave here my realms,   *1105*
Obeying laws that he does not respect?
Shall I be victim of his very crimes?
Is then the crown the portion of transgression?
What rights, what duties has he not defiled?
And none the less he reigns and I'm exiled!   *110*

JOCASTA

But if the king of Argos gives you a crown?

POLYNICES

Must I seek elsewhere what my blood endows?
Shall I bring nothing, marrying his daughter?
And must my rank depend on his mere favour?
Must I be driven from my rightful throne   1115
To beg position from an alien prince?
No, no, I wish to owe the crown to whom
I owe my birth and not pay humble court.

JOCASTA

Whether you hold from father, father-in-law,
The hand of both of them is ever dear.   1120

POLYNICES

No, no, there's all the difference in the world;
The one would make me slave, the other king.
What, shall my greatness be a woman's work!
My soul would blush at such a shameful splendour,
Shall then the throne be barred me, but for love?   1125
I would not reign if I had not been loved?
I wish to rule by right or never rule;
And if I sit on thrones, to sit as master;
That all the people must obey but me
And I'm at liberty to make them hate me.   1130
In brief, I must be sovereign in my sight,
Be not a king, or else a king by right;
Let my blood crown me; if justice be not done,
I wish to call in aid my arm alone.

JOCASTA

Do more, owe everything to your great heart;   1135
Let your right arm alone carve you an empire;
Scorning to follow other monarchs' steps,
Be, my son, be the work of your own hands.
By glittering feats win for yourself a crown;
Let noble laurels glisten on your brow;   1140
In triumph reign and with one stroke unite
A hero's glory and the royal purple.

Indeed! would your ambition be confined
To reigning turn by turn for one brief year?
Seek for your great, unconquerable heart   *1145*
Some throne where you alone may rightly mount.
A thousand shining sceptres bide your sword,
Unstained with dear blood dripping in our sight.
I'll view your triumphs in the happiest hue
And even your brother'll conquering go with you.   *1150*

POLYNICES

You want me, flattered by such grand illusions,
To leave a usurper on my father's throne?

JOCASTA

If so much ill you wish, indeed, for him,
Raise him yourself to this disastrous throne.
This throne has ever proved a perilous chasm;   *1155*
Girt both with thunderbolts as well as crime:
Your father and the kings preceding you,
Scarce seated on it, have been overthrown.

POLYNICES

Were I to meet the thunderclaps of heaven,
I'd mount it rather than go cap in hand.   *1160*
Jealous of the fate of these hapless heroes,
Madam, I wish to rise and fall with them.

ETEOCLES

I'm sure to spare you such a futile fall.

POLYNICES

Believe me, I shall not be first to crawl!

JOCASTA

My son, his rule is loved.

POLYNICES

That makes no odds.   *1165*

JOCASTA

The people are for him.

POLYNICES

For me, the gods!

ETEOCLES

The gods' will barred you from this lofty rank,
Since they have put me first upon the throne.
They knew full well when they decreed this choice,
One reigns on still whenever one once reigns.   *1170*
No throne did ever more than one lord see;
Two do not fit, however broad it be!
One, late or soon, must needs come tumbling down,
His other self would press from him the crown.
Judge by the spleen with which I view this fool   *1175*
If I with him can ever share my rule.

POLYNICES

So loathsome are you now, I cannot bear
Heaven's light with you a moment more to share.

JOCASTA

Go then, I give consent, blot out your light;
To this fell fight I both of you incite;   *1180*
Since all my struggles move you not at all,
Why wait? Avenge me, hurry, fight and fall.
Go, run, surpass your fathers' crimes by far;
Show, as you kill, how brotherly you are:
The greatest guilt has given you your breath,   *1185*
An equal crime must in its turn bring death.
No more do I condemn your furious passion;
No more for my blood have I sweet compassion;
Your conduct teaches me no more to sigh;
And I go, knaves, to teach you how to die.   *1190*

Exit JOCASTA

SCENE IV

ANTIGONE

My lady . . . Heavens! Alas! will nothing move them?

HAEMON

Nothing can shake their savage constancy.

ANTIGONE

Princes . . .

ETEOCLES

Come, let us choose our duelling place.

POLYNICES

Let us run. Sister, farewell.

ETEOCLES

Farewell, princess.

ANTIGONE

Stop! Stop! dear brothers. Guards, you hold them back;   *1195*
Add and unite your sorrows all with mine.
It would be cruel to respect them now.

HAEMON

My lady, nothing more can now restrain them.

ANTIGONE

Ah, noble Haemon, you alone I beg:
If virtue pleases you, if you still love me,   *1200*
And, if their murderous hands may yet be tied,
Alas, to save me, save these fratricides.

ACT V

SCENE I

ANTIGONE (*Alone*)[12]

Unhappy princess, ah! what must I do?
Your mother has just died in your arms;
    Why not end all your alarms   *1205*
As she has done, and kill yourself, you too?
Have you the heart fresh miseries to brave?
Your brothers are at grips, nothing can save
    Them in their cruel mood.
Their conduct spurs you to cut short your years;   *1210*
    And you alone shed tears
    While others shed their blood.

In what dread chasms my misfortune falls!
    Where should my sorrows fly?
    Shall I live? Shall I die?   *1215*
A lover holds me back, a mother calls;
In the dark grave I see her wait for me;
What reason wishes, love forbids it be,
    And my intent removes.
How many grounds have I to end the strife!   *1220*
    But ah! how one values life
    When one values him one loves!

Yes, love, my fainting spirit you revive;
    My victor's voice I recognise.
    Dead in my heart hope lies,   *1225*

[12] This soliloquy of Antigone in stanza form was doubtless suggested to Racine by Rotrou's Antigone, who similarly soliloquizes in stanza form in Act III Scene 1 of Rotrou's *Antigone*.

And yet you live and order I should live;
Haemon, you say, would follow me in death,
That I am forced still to preserve my breath
    To save him I adore.
Ah, Haemon, see how strong my love and true: *1230*
    For myself I would live no more,
    But I will live on for you.

If ever you doubted my passion's might . . .
But here's some fatal news about the fight.

SCENE II

Enter OLYMPIAS

ANTIGONE

Well, dear Olympias, have you seen the crime?   *1235*

OLYMPIAS

I ran in vain. Already it was over.
I saw the tearful people leave our ramparts
All running down and crying out, "To arms";
To tell in brief the reason for their panic,
Madam, the king is dead; his brother conquers.   *1240*
They talk of Haemon, telling how, courageous,
He tried a long while to abate their rage,
But all his brave attempts have been in vain.
I gathered this from many mixed reports.

ANTIGONE

Ah, I am certain Haemon is most noble;   *1245*
His great heart ever shrank from every crime.
I had besought him stop their dastard deeds;

Could he at all have done it, he'd have done it.
Alas! their madness could not be contained;
It wished to be engulfed in streams of blood.   *1250*
Unnatural princes, now you rest content:
Death only could restore the peace between you.
The throne for both of you was much too cramped;
There had to be a greater space between you;
So heaven had to end your clash by placing   *1255*
One with the living, the other with the dead.
Unhappy, both of you, deserving pity!
And yet much less unfortunate than I,
Since of the many ills that on you fall
You feel not one, while I, alas, feel all!   *1260*

OLYMPIAS

But this misfortune brings to you less pain
Than had death taken Polynices from you.
You showered all your care upon this prince:
The interests of the king moved you much less.

ANTIGONE

I loved him truly with an open love;   *1265*
I loved him much more than I loved his brother;
The fact that he was virtuous and unhappy
Gave him this greater share in my regard.
But ah! he is no more so generous-hearted.
He is a criminal whose crime has crowned him: *1270*
His brother moves my heart now more than he:
His misery has made him dear to me.

OLYMPIAS

Creon comes.

ANTIGONE

He looks sad; I know the cause.
The king's death leaves him to the victor's anger.
He is the noxious source of all our woes.   *1275*

SCENE III

Enter CREON *and* ATTALUS *with* GUARDS

CREON

Lady, what do I learn on entering here?
Is it true, the Queen . . .

ANTIGONE

Yes, she is dead.

CREON

O gods! May I not know in what strange manner
The light of her unhappy days was dimmed?

OLYMPIAS

Herself she sought, my lord, the way to death;   *1280*
And sudden laying hands upon a dagger,
She ended her misfortunes and her life.

ANTIGONE

She went before the downfall of her son.

CREON

My lady, it is true the unfriendly gods . . .

ANTIGONE

Impute to you alone my brother's death,   *1285*
And never blame the anger of the gods.
You have alone led him to this dire combat:
He heeded your advice which caused his death.
Thus kings prove victims to their flatterers;[13]

---

[13] A constant theme in Racine, from this his first, to *Athaliah*, his last play.
(See in particular Act IV, Scene 6 of *Phaedra*, and Act IV, Scene 3 of both *Britannicus* and *Athaliah*.)

Their end you hasten, fawning on their crimes;   *1290*
You are the authors of the fall of kings,
But kings, in toppling, tear their flatterers down.
Creon, as you see, his deadly defeat
To you is fatal, as to us it's fell;
Heaven, slaying him, is now avenged on you,   *1295*
And you perhaps have cause to weep like us.

CREON

Madam, indeed; and spiteful destiny
Makes me mourn two sons if you mourn two brothers.

ANTIGONE

My brothers and your sons! gods! What means this?
Who else than Eteocles then is dead?   *1300*

CREON

But do you not yet know the bloody tale?

ANTIGONE

I know that Polynices proved victorious,
And Haemon vainly tried to separate them.

CREON

My lady, much more mortal was the fight;
You do not yet know all my loss and yours;   *1305*
But now alas! let me relate them all.

ANTIGONE

Pitiless fortune, come, thy fury show!
Ah, doubtless now I'll face thy heaviest blow!

CREON

You saw, my lady, in what raging temper
The princes both, stormed out to rend each other;   *1310*
How with an equal zest they rushed from here,
How never had their hearts been more at one.
The thirst for bathing in his brother's blood
Achieved what twin blood never had achieved:
They seemed united in their passing hate;   *1315*

And firmest friends to cut each other's throat.
They first selected, as their field of battle,
A spot near both the camps beneath the walls;
And there assuming all their former fury
Begin at last their dread and dastard duel.   *1320*
With threatening gestures and with blazing eyes,
They seek a passage in each other's breast,
And, rage alone inciting their strong arms,
Both seem to hurl themselves, provoking death.
My son, whose spirit was weighed down with sorrow,   *1325*
And who was mindful, Lady, of your orders,
Throws himself between them, scorning for you
Their absolute commands, that stayed us all;
He holds their arms, repulses them, beseeching,
And risks their fury, seeking still to part them.   *1330*
But all in vain he strains to stem their temper;
The raging twins for ever come to grips.
He still holds firm, and never loses heart;
Deflects the rain of a thousand deadly blows,
Until the king's too sharp and savage sword,   *1335*
Whether it sought his brother or my son,
Levels him at his feet, about to die.

ANTIGONE

And sorrow still is leaving me alive!

CREON

I run and raise him, take him in my arms;
He whispers, recognising me, "I'm dying,   *1340*
For my fair princess I would die again.
You run, dear father, to my help in vain;
It is to these mad monsters you should fly:
Father, part them, and let me happy die."
With these words he expires. This savage sight   *1345*
Stays not at all their dark and desperate rage;
And Polynices only seemed afflicted:
"Wait, Haemon," cried he, "you shall be avenged."
His grief, indeed, gives fresh force to his fury,

And soon the duel turns to his advantage.   *1350*
The king, struck by a blow that pierced his side,
Yields victory to him, sunken in his blood.
At once the two camps give vent to their shock,
To lamentation ours, the Greeks to joy;
The people, frightened by their king's demise,   *1355*
Attest their terror from their towers' tops.
Exulting in his crime, proud Polynices
Gazes with pleasure on his dying victim;
He seems to wallow in his brother's blood.
"You'll die," he says to him, "and I shall reign.   *1360*
See in my hands the empire and the victory;
Go, blush in hell at my surpassing glory;
And, still more painfully to reach the grave,
Remember, knave, you die now as my slave."
Thus saying, he approaches, with proud gesture,   *1365*
The dying king stretched out upon the dust,
And to disarm him far extends his arm.
The king, who seems dead, watches all his steps;
He sees him, waits for him; his burning soul
Seems yet to linger for some mighty purpose.   *1370*
He harbours still the passion for revenge,
With all his strength delaying his last sighs.
About to yield his ghost, he clings to life,
And his death becomes the victor's trap of doom:
In the fateful moment, when his monstrous brother   *1375*
Is poised to pluck the sword to which he clings,
He stabs him in the heart; his gloating soul,
Having achieved this stroke, gives up his life.
The stricken Polynices wails aloud,
His gibbering ghost in fury flees to Hades.   *1380*
Lady, dead though he be, he keeps his anger,
And one would say threatens his brother still.
His face, on which foul death has spread its grip,
Remains more proud and terrible than ever.

ANTIGONE

O dark ambition, fraught with destined doom!   *1385*
Clear consequence of cruel oracles!

Of all the royal blood but we remain;
And Creon, would to Heaven but you remained,
And that in desperation I had followed
My mother's death before their angry end!   *1390*

CREON

Yes, it is true the gods' consuming wrath
To make us perish, all, seems now exhausted;
For, lady, as you see, their stern decree
Crushes me no less than it sears your soul.
In snatching my sons . . .

ANTIGONE

                    Ah! Creon, you reign,   *1395*
And the throne's your sweet indemnity for Haemon.
Leave me, I pray, a little solitude,
And on my anxious grief do not intrude.
My troubles, also, would then burden you.
Elsewhere you'll find more pleasing company;   *1400*
The throne awaits you and the people call;
Taste all the pleasure of your novel greatness.
Farewell—we give each other only pain:
Creon, I wish to weep; you wish to reign.

CREON (*Halting* ANTIGONE)

Ah, Lady! reign and mount upon the throne: *1405*
This high rank fits Antigone alone.

ANTIGONE

I am impatient that you take your seat.
The crown is yours.

CREON

                    I place it at your feet.

ANTIGONE

I would refuse it at the gods' decree;
And Creon, you dare offer it to me!   *1410*

CREON

I know this high rank has no greater glory
Than offering you the splendour of the Crown.
I know myself unworthy of such fortune:
But if one may achieve this signal glory,
If by some shining feat one may deserve it;   *1415*
What must I do, my lady?

ANTIGONE

Follow me.

CREON

What would I not do to win such a grace!
Only command what I shall have to do:
I'm ready . . .

ANTIGONE (*Going away*)

We shall see.

CREON (*Following her*)

I await your orders.

ANTIGONE (*Going away*)

Await them.

Exeunt ANTIGONE *and* OLYMPIAS

SCENE IV

ATTALUS

Would her anger be appeased?   *1420*
Do you think you'll win her?

CREON

Yes, dear Attalus;
No happiness is equal now to mine;

And you shall see in me, this happy day,
The ambitious on the throne, the lover crowned.
I asked of Heaven the princess and the throne; 1425
It grants to me the sceptre and Antigone.
To crown my head and heart this very day,
It arms, on my behalf, both hate and love;
It kindles for me two opposing passions;
It melts the sister, and it steels the brothers; 1430
It spurs their anger, and it curbs her pride,
Clearing my way to their throne and her heart.

ATTALUS

It is indeed true all your hopes have prospered,
And happy you would be, were you not father.
Love and ambition leave you wanting nothing; 1435
But nature gives to you great cause for tears:
Losing your two sons . . .

CREON

Yes, their loss afflicts me.
I know what fatherhood requires of me:
True I was father, but, first, born to reign;
I lose much less than I believe I've gained. 1440
The name of father is a common title;
It is a blessing Heaven refuses scarce:
I find no charm in such a general bliss;
It is no bliss if no one is made jealous.[14]
But the sceptre is a sparing gift of Heaven: 1445
This high rank parts us from the rest of men;
A very few are blessed with such a boon:
The earth has fewer kings than gods in Heaven.
Besides, you know Haemon loved the princess
And that in her turn she too worshipped him: 1450
Were he alive, his love would ruin mine.
Depriving me of son, Heaven takes my rival.
Then speak to me of happy themes alone,
Allow me to give vent to all my joy;

---

[14] Racine's genius in illuminating the dark malice of human *Schadenfreude* is apparent from his first play.

Conjure no more pale shadows from the shades,   *1455*
But tell me what I gain, not what I lose:
Speak of my throne, speak of Antigone;
Soon I shall have her heart, the throne I have.
All that has taken place is but a dream:
Father I was and subject, lover I am and king,   *1460*
The princess and the crown so charm my mind,
That . . . But Olympias comes.

ATTALUS

Gods! all in tears.

SCENE V

Enter OLYMPIAS

OLYMPIAS

Why are you dallying? The princess is dead.

CREON

Olympias, dead!

OLYMPIAS

Superfluous regrets!
She merely entered the adjoining chamber   *1465*
And with the very dagger that the queen
Had used, promptly pierced her beautiful heart
Before I could perceive her deadly purpose:
The wound she gave herself, my lord, proved mortal,
And sudden she fell dying in her blood.   *1470*
Imagine what I felt at sight of this.
But with her spirit ready to break free,
"Haemon," she said, "I kill myself for thee";
And at that moment ended her fine life.
I felt her fair form frozen in my arms: *1475*

And I believed my shade would follow hers;
Happy a thousand times, if my bleak plight
Had plunged me with her in the tomb's black night!

Exit OLYMPIAS

LAST SCENE

CREON

Thus from a hated lover swift she flies!
Ah, lovely girl, yourself, you shut your eyes,   *1480*
For ever close those fair eyes I adore,
Close them, indeed, never to see me more!
Though you loved Haemon, to your death you run
Far less to follow him than me to shun!
But were you still to be as harsh to me,   *1485*
If in the shades my presence loathed would be,
Were after death your anger still to swell,
Ah, heartless girl, I'll follow you to hell!
You'll ever see the object of your hate,
My sighs will ever pour my pain in spate   *1490*
Whether to soften you or to defy;
And there to shun me you can no more die.
Then let me die . . .

ATTALUS *and* GUARDS

My lord, what dire intent![15]

CREON

You murder me in saving thus my life!
Love, rage, delirium, come, lend me your aid;   *1495*
Come now and cut short my accursèd days!
Defeat the barrier of these cruel friends!
And see, O Heaven, thy oracle faithful ends!

[15] Some editions here indicate "snatching his sword" beneath "Attalus and Guards" making it clear, what Creon's next line implies, that Creon is prevented from commiting suicide.

I am the last of Laius' sad blood born;
Kill me, grim gods, or you will be forsworn.   *1500*
Take back, take back this sceptre, I detest;
You've snatched Antigone, then snatch the rest:
The throne and all your presents plague my view,
A thunderbolt is all I ask of you.
Do not refuse it to my crimes, my prayer,   *1505*
In all your victims' doom give me my share.
But I beg you in vain; my guilt alone
Makes me already feel the wrongs I've done.
Polynices, Eteocles, Jocasta, Antigone,
My dear sons, I have lost to mount the throne,   *1510*
So many others I have wronged in life,[16]
Jab in my heart the executioner's knife.
Stop . . . My death will redeem your own death spasm;
The bolt is falling, earth's a yawning chasm;
I feel my thousand torments still increase   *1515*
And now sink down to hell in search of peace.

(*He falls into the hands of the* GUARDS)[17]

THE END

✿✿✿

[16] (The tension in this speech as a whole foreshadows Orestes' last speech at the end of *Andromaque*.) With these lines in particular, compare Athalida's similar movement of remorse at the end of *Bajazet*. Thus, in his very first play, occurs, however improbably in the mouth of the villainous Creon, the scene of "moral recognition," typical of Racinian tragedy, which was to reach an almost cosmic climax in Act IV Scene 6 of *Phèdre*.

[17] It is a moot point whether this stage direction implies that Creon falls dead to fulfill the oracle (more or less), or, what would be far more probable, falls unconscious, like Orestes, as a result of the emotional stress to which he has been exposed.

ALEXANDER THE GREAT

A Tragedy

To The King

Sire,

*Here is my second undertaking, no less presumptuous than the
first. Not content with having put Alexander's name at the head
of my work, I add to it further, Your Majesty's; in other
words, I bring together all that is greatest in the present
century and the centuries that are past. But Sire, I hope Your
Majesty will not condemn my second, when you have not
disapproved of my first.*

*Whatever attempts may have been made to distort my hero, he
had but to appear before Your Majesty for him to be recognised
as Alexander. And what better judge than a king whose fame is as
widespread as this conqueror's, and before whom one may say
that all peoples of the earth fall silent as Scripture records of
Alexander?* I am well aware this silence is a silence of wonder
and amazement, that up to now it is not so much the force of
your arms that has impressed them as that of your qualities.*

*But, Sire, your reputation is no less splendid for not being
based on conflagrations and ruins, and already Your Majesty
has reached the pinnacle of fame by a path more novel and more
difficult than that by which Alexander ascended. It is not
extraordinary to see a young man winning battles, to see him set
the whole world ablaze. It is not impossible for youth and
fortune to bear him victorious into the heart of India. History is
full of young conquerors. And it is well known with what zeal
Your Majesty yourself sought out opportunities to distinguish
yourself at an age when Alexander could but impatiently envy
the victories of his father. But Your Majesty will permit me to
say that no king has ever been seen like you, who at
Alexander's age has displayed the qualities of Augustus, who,
almost without stirring from the heart of his kingdom has
spread his light to the ends of the earth and who has begun his
career where the greatest princes have sought to end theirs.
The ancients have argued whether fortune had not a greater*

* Maccabees, I, 1:3.

*hand in Alexander's conquests than merit. But what part can
fortune claim in the deeds of a king who owes to his own counsels
alone the prosperity of his kingdom, and who needs only himself,
to become the dread of Europe?*

*But, Sire, I am forgetting that in wishing to praise Your
Majesty, I am embarking on too vast and difficult an enterprise.
I must first experiment further with other heroes of antiquity;
and I anticipate that while I gain more strength, Your
Majesty will have covered yourself with even fresher fame;
that we perhaps shall see you once more, at the head of an
army, complete the comparison one may make between Your
Majesty and Alexander, and add the title of Conqueror to that
of the wisest king in the world. Then shall your subjects have to
devote all their vigils to the recital of so many glorious deeds,
and not let Your Majesty have cause to complain with Alexander,*
that there was no one in your time who could leave to posterity
a memorial of your virtues. I do not hope to be fortunate enough
to distinguish myself by the worth of my works; but I am sure
that I shall stand out at least by the zeal and deep veneration
with which I am, Sire,*

> *Your Majesty's most humble,*
> *most obedient and most loyal*
> *servant and subject,*
> RACINE

---

* Plutarch, in his *Life of Alexander*, Chap. XV, recounts how Alexander envied
Achilles, who after his death had found (in Homer) a great herald of his exploits:
The Iliad was Alexander's favourite work.

First Preface*

I shall not relate here what history tells of Porus, I should have to copy the entire eighth book of Quintus Curtius; and I shall undertake still less to make a precise apology for all the places criticised in my play. I have not claimed to give the public a perfect play; I know myself too well to have dared to flatter myself with such a hope. However successful the production of my *Alexander* and however loudly the first personages of the world and the Alexanders of our age have come down on its side, I do not allow myself to be dazzled by their high applause. I prefer to believe that they have wished to encourage a young man, and to spur me on to greater achievements. But I confess that whatever mistrust I had of my powers, I could not help harbouring some regard for my tragedy when I have observed the trouble certain persons have taken to denigrate it. One does not make so much commotion over a work of which one has no opinion; one is content not to see it again after the first time and to let it fail of itself, without even deigning to contribute to its failure. However, I have had the pleasure of seeing the faces of my critics grace my play on more than six consecutive occasions. They have not been afraid to expose themselves so often to hearing something which offended them. They have abundantly lavished their time and their trouble to come to criticise it; to say nothing of the pain caused to them perhaps by the applause which their presence did not prevent the public from giving me. It is not, as I have already said, that I believe my play to be faultless. It is well known with what deference I have listened to the candid advice of my true friends, and it will be even noticed that I have profited in certain passages from the criticisms they have made to me. But

* Printed in the first edition of 1666 and then, with omissions, in the edition of 1672.

I should have achieved nothing had I paid heed to the subtleties of certain critics who would subject public taste to the distempers of a sick mind, who go to the theatre with the set object of not enjoying themselves, and who fancy they can prove to the whole audience, by shaking their heads and by affected leers, that they are deeply versed in the *Poetics* of Aristotle. Indeed, what am I to say to those critics who condemn the very title of my tragedy, and who do not wish me to call it *Alexander* although Alexander is the mainspring of the plot, and the theme of the play is none other than that conqueror's generosity. They say that I have made Porus nobler than Alexander. And how is he nobler? Is not Alexander ever the victor? Not content with vanquishing Porus by the force of his arms, he triumphs even over Porus's pride by the generosity he shows in restoring to him his realms. They find it strange that Alexander, having won the battle, does not return at the head of his army, and that he should converse with his beloved, instead of dashing off to fight a bunch of desperadoes bent on dying. Yet, if we are to believe one of the greatest captains of our time, even Ephestion should not have gone off for this purpose. They cannot stomach Ephestion recounting the death of Taxiles in Porus's presence, because his account is too much to Porus's advantage. But they do not ponder that one only censures praise given in the presence of a person praised, when it smacks of flattery, and that it has quite the opposite effect when it is uttered by a hostile mouth, and when he who is praised, is plunged in misfortune. This is called doing justice to virtue and respecting it even in chains. It seems to me that this behaviour accords well with the idea which historians have given us of Alexander's favourite. But at least, they say, he should spare his master's patience and not laud so highly before him his enemy's valour. Those who are of this view doubtless have forgotten that Porus has just been defeated by Alexander, and that praises heaped on the vanquished redound to the glory of the victor.

I make no reply to those who blame Alexander for restoring Porus to his throne in Cleophilia's presence. It is enough for me that what passes for a defect among these critics, who have read history only in novels, and who imagine that a hero must never take a step without his beloved's permission, has been praised by those, ,who themselves great heroes, have the right to judge the temper of their equals. Finally, the most important objection they make is that my plot is too simple and too barren. I do not represent to those critics the taste of antiquity. I see well that they have scant knowledge of it. But why complain, so long as all my scenes are well filled, so long as they are logically linked to one another, so long as all my actors never come on the stage without one's knowing the reason which makes them come; and so long as, with little incident and little plot, I have been fortunate enough to write a play which has perhaps held their attention in spite of themselves from the beginning to the end? But what consoles me is to see my critics agree so ill; some say that Taxiles is not gentleman enough; others that he does not deserve his tragic end. Some maintain that Alexander is not loving enough; others that he only comes on the stage to talk of love. Thus I do not need my friends to take the trouble to defend me, I have but to refer my enemies to my enemies; I leave to them to defend a play which they attack so ill-concertedly and with such opposite views.

Second Preface*

There is hardly a tragedy in which history has been so faithfully followed as in this one. Its plot is derived from several authors, but chiefly from the eighth book of Quintus Curtius. There one finds all that Alexander did when he entered India, the embassies he sent to the kings of that land, the various receptions they gave to his envoys, the alliance which Taxiles made with him, the hauteur with which Porus rejected the conditions offered him, the enmity between Porus and Taxiles, and finally the victory that Alexander won over Porus, the noble reply which this brave Indian gave to the victor who asked him how he wished to be treated, and the nobility with which Alexander restored to him all his realms and added many others.

This action of Alexander has passed for one of the finest which that prince performed in his life, and the peril to which he was exposed by Porus in the battle appeared to him the greatest he had ever faced. He admitted it himself, stating that he had found at last a danger worthy of his valour. And it was on this very occasion that he cried: "O Athenians, how many travails I endure to win your praise!" I have tried to portray in Porus an enemy worthy of Alexander, and I may say that his character has given extreme pleasure on our stage, to the extent that I have been reproached for making this prince greater than Alexander. But these critics do not reflect that in battle as in the hour of victory Alexander is in fact greater than Porus; that there is not a line in the tragedy but in praise of Alexander; that the very curses of Porus and Axiana are so many eulogies of the Conqueror's worth. Porus has perhaps a more engaging quality because he is unfortunate. "For," as Seneca says, "our natures are such that we admire

* First published in the 1676 collective edition.

75

nothing more than a man who knows how to bear misfortune with dignity." "*Ita affecti sumus, ut nihil aeque magnam apud nos admirationem occupet, quam homo fortiter miser.*"

The love of Alexander and Cleophilia is not my invention: Justinus speaks of it, as well as Quintus Curtius. These two historians relate that a queen in India named Cleophilia surrendered to that monarch with the town in which he held her besieged, and that he restored to her her kingdom in consideration of her beauty. She had a son by him, whom she named Alexander. Here are Justinus' words: "*Regna Cleofidis reginae petit, quae, cum se dedisset ei, regnum ab Alexandro recepit, illecebris consecuta quod virtute non potuerat; filiumque ab eo genitum, Alexandrum nominavit, qui postea regnum Indorum potitus est.*"* It appears, following this passage, that the Indians looked upon this Cleophilia as the Romans after them looked upon Cleopatra. Moreover there is some similarity between the adventures of these two queens; and Cleophilia behaved towards Alexander more or less as Cleopatra behaved towards Caesar. One had a son she called Alexander, the other had a son she called Caesarion. One could add this resemblance to the parallel drawn between these two conquerors, all the more because they resembled each other in the manner they made love. This passion never plagued them beyond the realms of reason. And even if Cleophilia had been the sister of Taxiles, as she is in my tragedy, I am convinced that Alexander's love for her would not have prevented him from restoring Porus to his throne in her presence.

---

* "He demands the realms of Queen Cleophilia, who, when she had surrendered herself to him, received back her kingdom from Alexander, gaining by her charms what she could not retain by her strength; and the son, born of him, she named Alexander, who thereafter ruled over the kingdom of the Indians."

ALEXANDER THE GREAT

First performed on December 4, 1665, by Molière's Company at the Palais-Royal; first edition, 1666.

CHARACTERS

ALEXANDER
PORUS ⎫
TAXILES ⎬   *Kings in India*
AXIANA   *Queen of another part of India*
CLEOPHILIA   *Sister of Taxiles*
EPHESTION
ALEXANDER'*s Suite*

The scene is on the banks of the Hydaspes[1] in Taxiles' camp.

---

[1] The modern Jhelum, one of the five tributaries of the Indus which, with its four sister streams, the Chenab, the Ravi, the Beas and the Sutlej, gives its name Punjab ("Five Waters") to the State through which they flow.

ACT I

SCENE I

TAXILES, CLEOPHILIA

CLEOPHILIA

What! do you mean to fight a king whose power
Seems to force heaven to champion his defence?
Before him Asia's kings have fallen fast,
And he holds fortune his obedient prisoner!
Open your eyes, brother.[2] Know Alexander: 5
See thrones reduced to ashes all around,
Peoples enslaved and sovereigns in chains;
And draw back from the doom that dragged them down.

TAXILES

Do you wish me, struck by a craven fear,
To place my head beneath his threatening yoke,   10
And hear the Indian peoples murmuring
I have, myself, forged both their chains and mine?
Shall I leave Porus? and betray these princes
Assembled to set free our provinces,
And who, with brave, unhesitating choice,   15
Know equally to live or die as kings?
Can you find one, who, lifting not a finger,
Faints at the mere mention of Alexander,
And, thinking him already lord of the world,
Runs slavishly to him entreating chains?   20
Far from being frightened by his conquering fame,

---

[2] Cleophilia and Taxiles were not related in history. Racine makes them brother and sister for the purposes of his plot.

They'll storm him in the heart of victory;
And you, my sister, wish Taxiles now,
Ready to fight him, to beseech his aid!

CLEOPHILIA

Hence it is only you whom he approaches;   25
Only your friendship Alexander craves:
Just when the threatening bolt is poised to crash,
He strives in secret to protect you from it.

TAXILES

And why am I the one his anger spares?
Of all those whom Hydaspes sends against him,   30
Have I alone deserved his base compassion?
Can he not tender friendship too to Porus?
He doubtless deems him far too noble-hearted
Ever to listen to such shameful pleas:
He seeks a courage that will less resist him;   35
And deems perhaps I'm worthier of his pains.

CLEOPHILIA

Do not charge him with seeking out some slave;
Say rather he deems you his worthiest foe;
And that, in plucking from your grasp your arms,
He reaps his triumph over all the rest.   40
His choice will mark no stain upon your name,
His friendship's not the portion of poltroons;
Although he burns to conquer all the world,
You never see a slave among his friends.
Ah! if his friendship can besmirch your fame,   45
Why did you not spare me so dark a stain?
You know the attentions daily showered on me:
It but remained with you to stay their flow.
You see me now the mistress of his heart;
A hundred secret notes pledge me his love;   50
To reach my heart, the furnace of his passion
Illuminates the two opposing camps.
Instead of hating him, or forcing me to hate,

You've scolded me for being too reserved;
You have encouraged me to bear his love   55
And in my turn perhaps to love him, brother.

CENTER TAXILES

Without a blush at the power of your spell,
You may compel this hero to surrender;
And without striking fear into your heart,
Euphrates' conqueror could down your weapons: 60
But the State today depends upon my fate.
I hold her destiny chained to my chance;
And though your words are seeking to persuade me,
I must stay free to see that she be free.
I know the anxiety my purpose gives you;   65
But like you, sister, must obey my love.
Axiana's lovely eyes, hostile to peace,
Arm all their charms against your Alexander;
Queen of all hearts, she spurs all to the fight
For that same freedom toppled by her spell;   70
The fetters foes would fix fill her with shame,
Her eyes are the sole tyrants without blame.
My sister, I must serve her shining anger;
I must go . . .

CENTER CLEOPHILIA

                Well, go to your doom to please her;
Obey the bidding of your precious tyrants,   75
Serve them or rather run and serve your rival.
Suffer they crown him with your very laurels;
For Porus fight, as Axiana bids;
And by fine feats, supporting her harsh part,
Ensure to Porus sway upon her heart.   80

CENTER TAXILES

Ah, sister, do you think Porus . . .

CENTER CLEOPHILIA

                Yourself,
Can you a moment doubt Axiana loves him?

Do you not see with what perfidious zeal
She flaunts his worth before your very eyes?
However brave another, if one heed her,   *85*
It is around him only Victory wings:
Without him all your projects would be vain:
India's freedom, his hands alone sustain;
Without him all our walls would now be ash:
Only he can dam Alexander's dash.   *90*
She makes a god of this seductive suitor,
And yet you doubt she may make him her lover?

TAXILES

I tried my best to doubt it, cruel sister.
Alas! support Taxiles in his error.
Why do you paint for him this hateful sketch?   *95*
Ah, help him rather to belie his eyes:
Tell him Axiana is a haughty beauty,
As cold to all men as she's to your brother;
Beguile me with some hope . . .[3]

CLEOPHILIA

By all means, hope;
But hope no further from your useless wooing.   *100*
Why by such powerless struggles seek a conquest
That Alexander hands to you himself?
It's not against him you must fight for her:
The foe who aims to wrest her from you is Porus.
Injurious Fame, in praising him alone,   *105*
Seems to forget our other warriors' names:
Whatever others do, he reaps the glory,
And leads you like his subjects to the fight.
Ah, if subjection's sweet, if subject you would be,
The Greeks and Persians show to you a master;   *110*
You'll find a hundred kings your chained companions;
Porus and all the world will be among them.
But Alexander does not want you fettered;
He leaves upon your brow these sovereign symbols,

[3] In this and other speeches of Taxiles may be discerned the embryo that was to give birth to the master creation of Hermione in *Andromaque*, Racine's next play.

Your haughty rival dares now to disdain.   *115*
Porus subjects you, he will make you reign;
Instead of being the poor dupe of Porus,
You will be . . . But here comes your noble rival.

CENTER TAXILES

Ah, sister, I'm confused—my troubled heart,
At sight of Porus, tells me he is loved.   *120*

CENTER CLEOPHILIA

You must become, with little time to squander,
Porus's slave, or friend of Alexander.

Exit CLEOPHILIA

SCENE II

Enter PORUS

PORUS

My lord, unless I err, our boastful foes
Will make less progress than they fondly fancied.
Our chiefs and soldiers, burning with fine zest,   *125*
Blaze forth their male assurance on their brows;
They spur each other on; and our least warriors
Are promising themselves abundant laurels.
From rank to rank I saw their spreading zeal
Burst out at sight of me in generous shouts;   *130*
And they complain that, idling in the camp,
They spend their strength instead of testing it.
Shall we allow such splendid hearts to fret?
Our foe, my lord, is seeking his advantage;
He still feels weak and to procrastinate,   *135*
Ephestion demands an interview,
And hopes by idle talk . . .

TAXILES

But we must hear him.
We do not yet know Alexander's will:
Perhaps he wishes to make peace with us.

PORUS

Peace! Ah! could you accept it at his hands?   140
What! we have seen him, by such wanton warfare,
Disturb the happy calm our lands enjoyed,
And, sword in hand, invade our prosperous realms,
Attacking kings who wronged him not at all;
We've seen him pillaging whole provinces,   145
Swelling our rivers with our subjects' blood;
And when heaven is about to abandon him,
Shall I await a haughty tyrant's pardon?

TAXILES

Do not, my lord, say heaven abandons him;
He is forever fanned by all its grace;   150
A king, at whose word all these kingdoms quake,
Is not an enemy that kings disdain.

PORUS

Far from disdaining, I admire his courage:
I pay the homage due to his high worth;
But, in my turn, I wish to earn the tributes   155
I feel compelled to pay his qualities.
Let Alexander to the skies be raised,
But if I can I'll see he is abased,
And on the very altars I'll attack him
That other trembling men erect to him.   160
Thus Alexander looked on every king
Whose realms still with his roll of victories ring:
In Asia, had some fear held back his sword,
Would Darius[4], dying, hail in him his lord?

---

[4] Darius, the Persian King, was defeated by Alexander at the Battles of Issus and of Gaugamela (Arbela), and fled before him to his doom, in the satrapy of Bessus. (See footnote to line 802.)

TAXILES

Sir, had Darius better known himself,   *165*
He would still reign, where reigns another master.
And yet this pride that caused his tragic end
Had some foundation which your scorn has not:
The might of Alexander was scarce known;
This thunderbolt was still veiled in the clouds.   *170*
Darius, lulled asleep in deep repose,
Had never even heard of his new foe.
He did hear soon enough: his soul, dumbfounded,
Saw all his mighty forces fall apart;
And was laid low by an all-conquering arm;   *175*
The crashing thunder shook his eyes awake.

PORUS

But tell me, at what price will Alexander
Sell the base peace he wants to bait you with?
Question, my lord, a hundred different peoples
Thrown into chains by his deceptive peace.   *180*
Make no mistake; his mildness is an insult:
And in his friendship's wake weeps slavery:
Useless to dream of only half-obeying;
If you are not his slave, you are his foe!

TAXILES

My lord, with neither bold nor cowardly show,   *185*
You may content him with some empty homage.
Let's flatter with esteem this quenchless prince,
Whose bubbling pride must ever bear him on.
He is a leaping torrent which must tear
All obstacles away that hem its path;   *190*
And, swollen with a hundred nations' ruins,
Must stun the whole world with its noisy dash.[5]
Why irritate him with a savage pride?
Let's greet him smiling as he passes by;
And yielding rights to him we'll soon take back,   *195*
Render him duties that will cost us nothing.

[5] See the footnote to Act I, Scene 5, line 220, in *The Theban Brothers.*

PORUS

Will cost us nothing! Dare you, Sir, believe it?
Shall I then count my honour lost as nothing?
Your realm and mine would be too dearly bought
If they cost Porus the least craven act.[6]   200
But do you think this contumacious prince
Would leave no trace of his adventure here?
How many kings, wrecked by this deadly reef,
Reign only so much as his pride may please!
Our crowns, becoming now his conquest's spoils,   205
Would float above our heads while we would reign,
And both our sceptres, prey to his least whim,
Will tumble from our hands at his mere word.
Do not say he hurtles from realm to realm:
He never leaves a prince free from his bonds;   210
And better to bend peoples to his will,
He often finds them monarchs in the dust.
But these base troubles do not move my heart:
Your interest alone inspires my words.
Porus will have no part in all this say;   215
When honour speaks, her only he'll obey.

TAXILES

Like you, what honour bids me, I'll obey,
But she enjoins me salvage all I may.

PORUS

If you would salvage anything at all,
Let's march and Alexander's stroke forestall.   220

TAXILES

Contempt and rashness are but shifty guides.

PORUS

Shame overtakes faint hearts with rapid strides.

[6] Compare with *Bajazet*, Act II, Scene 3, lines 595–6: "This sad last blood
would be too dearly bought,/If I must save it by a craven act."

TAXILES

The people love the kings who save them pain.

PORUS

They value still more those who nobly reign.

TAXILES

Such views will please but haughty hearts that swell.　　225

PORUS

They will please kings, and maybe queens as well.

TAXILES

As though the queen had only eyes for you.

PORUS

A slave is ever odious in her view.

TAXILES

But, do you think, my lord, love orders you
To hazard with you both her realm and person?　　230
Do not delude yourself, confess, I pray,
You heed your hate and not your love today.

PORUS

I will confess, indeed, my righteous rage
Loves war as much as peace is dear to you;
I will confess, inflamed by noble fury,
I go to test my pluck on Alexander.　　235
My spirit, restless at his exploits' fame,
Has long awaited this most happy day:
Before he sought me out, my fretting pride
Already made of me his secret foe.　　240
In the fine frenzy of my jealousy,
I blamed his tardiness in crossing Asia;
I longed so deeply he should hurry here,
That I was coveting the Persian's chance;
And even now, were he to shun my sword,　　245

Were he to seek mere passage to depart,
You'd find me, armed to stop him, even alone,
Reject the peace he wishes to accord.

TAXILES

Yes, doubtless, such a high and mighty zeal
Will promise you a splendid place in history;   250
And were you to succumb, with all your dash,
At least you'll fall with a resounding crash.
Farewell. The Queen comes. Vaunt to her your prowess;
Unfurl your pride: it surely will impress.
I would but irk you while you nobly speak;   255
Your hearts would blush to think my heart so weak.

Exit TAXILES

SCENE III

Enter AXIANA[7]

AXIANA

Taxiles shuns me! For what unknown cause . . .

PORUS

He does well to conceal his shame from you;
And since he dare not stomach danger more,
With what face could he stay and meet your eye?   260
Let's leave him, Lady, since he must surrender,
To worship Alexander, with his sister.
Let's quit this camp, where, incense in his hand,
Taxiles faithfully awaits his lord.

AXIANA

What did he say, my lord?

---

[7] Axiana is a fictitious character, invented by Racine to heighten the love interest.

PORUS

He went too far: 265
The slave already dares to boost his master;
He wants me to submit ...

AXIANA

Pray, calm yourself
And let me try and stay him from his course:
In spite of me, his sighs assure his love.
However that may be, I'll tax him further.   270
We must not force him, by your harsh disdain,
To execute a plan not yet made plain.

PORUS

You doubt it still? And you would still rely
Upon a faithless lover's perjured faith,
Who'd hand you to his overlord today,   275
Hoping to get you back from him tomorrow!
Well, help him, you yourself, to outwit you.
He may tear you away from my deep love;
But cannot filch, with all his jealousy,
My fame for having fought and died for you.   280

AXIANA

And you believe, after such insolence,
My lord, my love would be his recompense.
You fancy I should give my heart to him,
And ratify the gift they made of me?
Can you, unblushing, charge me with such crime?   285
Have I been flashing such regard for him?
Had I to choose between you and Taxiles,
Do you imagine I would hesitate?
Do I not know Taxiles always wavers,
Love holds him back when fear would draw him off?   290
Do I not know, his pale heart, but for me,
Would soon succumb to all his sister's wiles?
You know how Alexander held her prisoner,
And how at last she came back to her brother;

But I soon fathomed she had undertaken   295
To trap him in the snare that caught her heart.

PORUS

And you can still remain where she resides!
Why do you not abandon this false sister?
Why do you wish punctiliously to spare
A prince . . .

AXIANA

       It is for you I wish to win him.   300
Shall I see you, crushed by our realms' defence,
Attack alone a prince who conquers kings?
I wish to bring you succour from Taxiles,
Who will, despite his sister, fight Alexander.
Why have you not this burning zeal for me?   305
But by such common cares your soul's untouched:
Provided your great heart might nobly perish,
What may succeed your death scarce troubles you.
You wish to hand me helpless, havenless,
To Alexander's wrath, Taxiles' love,   310
Who, treating me as a proud conqueror,
Would claim my heart as your death's recompense.
Then go, my lord, and satisfy your soul;
Go, fight and quite forget to save your life;
Forget how heaven, propitious to your prayers,   315
Prepared perhaps a happy lot for you.
Perhaps in her turn Axiana charmed
Was going . . . But, my lord, run to your army;
Such long discourse must now be wearying you;
And I am keeping you here much too long.   320

PORUS

Ah, stop, dear lady, know my passionate love.
You, mistress of my days and of my heart:
Fame in my heart holds sway, I will not hide it,
But then what sovereign sway your charms divine!
I'll say no more to conquer Alexander,   325
Your men and mine would have attempted all;

That it would be unequalled bliss for me,
Alone to triumph in my rival's sight:
I tell you nothing more. Speak, no, dictate:
My heart puts at your feet my fame and hate.   *330*

AXIANA

Fear nothing, for your great, obedient heart
Is not in hands that may perhaps betray it:
No, jealous of his fame, I do not aim
To stop a hero bent on victory.
Run, hurl yourself against your haughty foe;   *335*
But do not cut yourself off from your friends:
Deal gently with them and with tranquil mind
Let me exert my influence on Taxiles;
Please feel more kindly towards him than you do:
I'm going now to make him fight for you.   *340*

PORUS

Well, Lady, go. I gladly give consent:
Let's see Ephestion, since he's been sent.
But hoping soon to put an end to prattle,
I await Ephestion and then the battle.

ACT II

SCENE I

EPHESTION

Yes, while your kings deliberate together,   345
And preparations for our talks are made,
Permit me, Madam, also to convey
The secret reasons that have brought me here.
Loyally privy to my master's ardour,
Before the eyes that sparked it, pray permit   350
I speak of it and dare ask for this hero
The peace he wishes to accord your kings.
After his many sighs, what may he hope?
Are you still waiting for your brother's word?
Do you insist his heart, shy and unsure,   355
Should never sue without fear of refusal?
Must he display the whole world at your feet?
Must he pronounce for peace? Must he wage war?
Command and Alexander will obey
Whether to merit you, or win your love.   360

CLEOPHILIA

Can I believe a prince at the height of glory
Can still remember my indifferent charms;
That dragging victory after him and dread,
He may still stoop to woo me with his sighs?
Prisoners like him soon shatter all love's chains,   365
Fame spurs them on to ever higher aims;
And love in their hearts, interrupted, hushed,
Is soon beneath the weight of laurels crushed.

While I was captive in this hero's camp,
I placed upon his heart a gentle stamp;   *370*
But I believe, Sir, when he set me free,
In his turn, Alexander free would be.

EPHESTION

Ah! had you seen him burning with impatience,
Count the dull days of your protracted absence,
You would be sure, that, spurred on by his love,   *375*
He sought you only when he rushed to battle.
It is for you, this conqueror of kings
Has hurtled headlong through your wide domains,
Shattering, in passing, with his lightning blows,
All that obstructed him in nearing you.   *380*
Your flags and our flags are in the same field.
From his retrenchments he can see your own:
But despite all his exploits, this shy victor
Fears he may still be distant from your heart.
What good for him to run from land to land   *385*
If from your heart he is forever banned?
If, to evade his fervent protestations,
You daily seek to doubt his declarations;
And if your mind, a thousand times mistrusting . . .

CLEOPHILIA

Alas! such fears are but effete defences;   *390*
Our hearts, forming a thousand foolish cares,
Forever doubt the joy they most desire.
Yes, since this hero wants me to be frank,
I listen gladly to his love's recital.
I feared time may have limited its flow;   *395*
I wish him still to love me, love me always.
Indeed, when first his strong arm forced our frontiers,
And held me prisoner in the walls of Omphis,
My heart, that saw him master of the world,
Already languished loving in his chains;   *400*
And, far from murmuring at so harsh a fate,
Made of it, I confess, a happy state;
And, losing all remembrance of its freedom,

Even while asking it, feared to obtain it:
Judge, if his coming plunges me in joy.   *405*
But must I see him covered all in blood?
Is he to enter as an enemy?
And does he seek me but to torture me?

EPHESTION

No, Madam: conquered by your powerful spell,
He halts today the terror of his arms;   *410*
He offers peace to these misguided kings,
And stays the hand that would have crushed them all.
He fears lest victory, pliant to his prayers,
Drive home his blows even in Taxiles' breast.
His heart, susceptible to your just fears,   *415*
Will have no laurels watered by your tears.
The solicitude his love is showing, bless;
Please, spare his valour such a sad success;
And move your kings, before he strike anew,
To accept a boon they owe alone to you.   *420*

CLEOPHILIA

You may be sure, my lord; my anxious heart
Is ever troubled by such rightful fears;
I tremble lest my brother's bloody death
Redden the arm of my dear enemy.
But I oppose his flaming zeal in vain,   *425*
Axiana, Porus, tyrannize his heart;
A queen's fair spell and a great king's example,
Rise up against me, dare I wish to speak.
What must I not fear in this dire confusion!
I fear for him, I fear for Alexander.   *430*
I know a hundred kings were crushed by him,
And all his feats; but Porus too I know.
Our peoples have been seen triumphant following
Him, throwing back the Persians and the Scythians,
And proud of all the laurels, won for them,   *435*
They'll conquer when he leads or die avenged;
And I fear he . . .

EPHESTION

Ah, leave such empty fears.
Let Porus run to meet his destined doom;
Let India arm her peoples all behind him;
And let Taxiles only turn his steps!   440
But here they come.

CLEOPHILIA

My lord, achieve your task;
And by your sage advice scatter this storm;
Or, if it must burst, mind it so befall
That it on other heads than our heads fall.

Exit CLEOPHILIA

SCENE II

Enter PORUS *and* TAXILES

EPHESTION

Before the battle lowering over your heads   445
Places your every realm among our conquests,
Alexander wishes to postpone his feats
And for the last time offers to you peace.
Your peoples, blinded by delusive hope,
Dreamt to withstand Euphrates' conqueror: 450
But Hydaspes, despite all these scattered squadrons,
Now sees our standards flapping on her banks:
And you would see them on your very trenches,
Your fields all covered deep with bleeding corpses,
Had not our hero, laden with his laurels,   455
Himself allayed our warriors' reckless zeal.
He does not come here, stained with royal blood,
To daze your kingdoms with a barbarous triumph,
Nor seeks to dazzle with a sorry splendour,
Raising his greatness on the graves of kings.   460
But do not, in your turn, beguiled by glory,

Rush, teasing victory, right into his arms;
And when his anger still is in abeyance,
Be satisfied with having called for it;
Do not wait longer to pay him the homage,   465
Your hearts, in spite of you, accord his courage;
And, taking the aid his arm is offering you,
Honour your realms with such a great defender.
And this is what my great king bids me tell you,
Ready to drop his sword or take it up.   470
You know all his intentions: choose today
If you would lose all or, from him, hold sway.

TAXILES

Sir, do not think a barbarous arrogance
Blinds us to qualities of heart so rare;
And that our peoples, stubborn in their pride,   475
Clamour, in spite of you, to be your foes.
We give their due to glittering examples:
You worship gods who owe their shrines to us;[8]
Heroes, who passed as mortals in your land,
On coming here have been adored as gods.[9]   480
But uselessly you seek to turn our brave
Peoples to slaves instead of worshippers:
However great the splendour dazzling them
They will not offer incense by compulsion.
Kingdoms enough, now fallen to your blows,   485
Have seen their kings' heads bow beneath your yoke.
With all these kingdoms, crushed by Alexander,
Is it not time, my lord, he looked for friends?
This captive crowd, cringing at their master's name,
Props flimsily his power but newly born.   490
Their eyes are ever watching to be free;
Your empire's simply full of hidden foes.
They mourn in secret all their crownless kings;
Your chains, too long extended, have grown loose;

[8] It is interesting that the young Racine, barely twenty-six, should have shown such breadth of view, rare in his day, in ascribing to the Hindu pantheon some precedence over the Greek.

[9] Reference to Hercules and Bacchus, mentioned in Quintus Curtius (Book VIII, Chap. X).

Already Scythia, with rebellious heart,   *495*
Would snap the fetters you intend for us.
Then why not try, taking as pledge our friendship,
How far a faith not bound by oath can go?
And leave at least one land that sometimes may
Applaud the fame of all your feats in freedom.   *500*
At this price I accept Alexander's friendship,
Awaiting him already as a king
May await a hero still in step with fame,
Who can subdue my heart but not my realm.

PORUS

When the Hydaspes, summoning its lands,
Saw all its kings rush to defend its banks,   *505*
I thought, in this great enterprise it had
Engaged with me but tyrant-hating chiefs;
But since a king kissing the hand that threatens,
Begs a mean place among the tryant's friends,   *510*
It falls to me to answer for my State
And speak for those Taxiles has betrayed.
What is the King, your master, wanting here?
What is this great support his arm would grant?
How does he dare to take beneath his wing   *515*
Peoples who have no enemy but him?
Before his fury ravaged all the earth,
Indus enjoyed a universal peace;
If any neighbours dared disturb her calm,
She nurtured bold defenders on her banks.   *520*
Then why attack us? By what savage deeds
Have we provoked your master's indignation?
Have we been ever seen inside his country
Laying angry waste to lands unknown to us?
Must all these realms, these deserts, these great rivers,   *525*
Be brittle barriers between him and us?
And may none live at the end of the world
Without knowing his name or the weight of his chains?
What strange devouring courage, that, injurious,
Burns all as soon as it begins to shine;   *530*
That has its pride alone as rule and reason;

That wants to change the whole world to a prison,
And that, in overlordship of us all,
Would number all mankind among its slaves!
No kings, nor kingdoms else! His impious hands   535
Would place all men beneath the self-same yoke.
In greedy pride I know he gulps us down:
We only, of these many kings, still reign.
Did I say, we? No, none remains but me
In whom the trace of kingship is still found.   540
But this has filled my heart with shining pride;
In calm content I see the whole world tremble,
In order that mankind, saved but by me,
Should it be free, by Porus' hand be freed;
And everywhere, in deep peace, men should say: 545
"Alexander would have vanquished all one day;
But at earth's corner on a king did stumble,
Through whom the whole world saw its fetters crumble."

EPHESTION

Your purpose shows at least a noble heart;
But it is late, my lord, to brave the storm;   550
If the declining world has but this prop,
I pity it and pity you yourself.
I will not keep you; march against my master:
I only wish you knew what he was like;
And that report would have, in pity, tried   555
To tell you half at least of his great deeds.
You would see . . .

PORUS

What should I see and what learn
To place me so beneath your Alexander?
Would it not be the Persians lightly crushed,
Your arms grown weary murdering cowardly crowds?   560
What glory, tell me, beating down a king,
Already conquered by his own effeteness;
A nerveless people, only half alive,
Groaning beneath the gold they bore as arms,
And who, in heaps collapsing without fight,   565

Opposed but corpses to bold Alexander?
The others, dazzled by his least exploits,
Crawled on their knees to beg of him his laws;
And heeding, in their fear, some oracle,
Could not believe a god might be withstood.   *570*
But we, who look on conquerors otherwise,
We know the gods we worship are not tyrants;
And that, whatever titles slaves may give him,
Jove's son here passes only as a man.
We do not mean to scent his path with flowers;   *575*
He'll find us everywhere armed to the teeth;
He'll see his conquests blocked at every step;
A single rock will cost him more lives here,
More trouble, more assaults, almost more time,
Than the empire of all the Persians cost his arm.   *580*
Foes of the sloth which ruined that base people,
The gold we bear does not corrupt our souls.
Fame is the only boon that may entice,
And the only one for which my heart would fight;
It . . .

EPHESTION (*Rising*)

That also is what Alexander seeks.   *585*
His heart may not stoop to unworthier aims.
Fame only, thrusting him forth from his realms,
Turned his young footsteps to the throne of Cyrus,
And, shaking the pillars of the strongest empire,
Spurred him to winning wars and making kings.   *590*
And since you dare deny him, in your pride,
The honour of the pardon he would give,
Your eyes, today, in witness of his victory,
Will see how zealously he fights for glory:
Soon sword in hand you'll see him march and rout . . . *595*

PORUS

Go then: I'll wait for him, or seek him out.

Exit EPHESTION

SCENE III

TAXILES

Carried away by your impatience, you . . .

PORUS

No, I'll not claim to trouble your alliance:
Ephestion, irate only against me,
Will take his king the tale of your submission.   *600*
Axiana's soldiers, pledged to follow me,
Await the battle, ranged beneath my banners;
I'll bear the splendour of her throne and mine,
And you, my lord, will be judge of the fight;
Unless your heart, burning to make amends,   *605*
Embrace the quarrel of your latest friends.

SCENE IV

Enter AXIANA

AXIANA (*To* TAXILES)

My lord, what are they saying? Our enemies
Are making boast Taxiles is half-won;
That he'll not fight a king whom he esteems.

TAXILES

An enemy's report should be distrusted,   *610*
Madam; in time they will know me better.

AXIANA

My lord, deny then this insulting tale:
Confound the impudence of those who spread it;
Like Porus go, compel them to be silent,
And make them feel, in righteous indignation,   *615*
They have no deadlier enemy than you.

TAXILES

My lady, I go now to place my army;
Give less heed to this rumour that disturbs you;
As Porus does his duty, I'll do mine.

Exit TAXILES

SCENE V

AXIANA

Your dark reserve, you coward, tells me nothing;   620
And, to convince me, that is not at all
The bearing of a king who speeds to victory.
We cannot longer doubt, we are betrayed:
For his sister's sake he saps his realm and fame;
And seeking in his hate, my lord, to crush you,   625
He waits for you to fight, to burst on you.

PORUS

In losing him, I lose a weak support;
I know him too well to rely on him.
I looked with unconcern upon his shuffling;
I feared far more his rickety resistance.   630
A traitor, leaving us to please his sister,
Weakens us much less than a cowardly ally.

AXIANA

And yet, my lord, what are you undertaking?
You fight oblivious of Alexander's strength;
Almost alone, running to face their blows,   635
You oppose only yourself to all these foes.

PORUS

Would you want me, in terror, like the traitor,
To conjure ways to hand you to a master;
That Porus, caught defenceless in his camp,

Decline the battle he has just sought out?   *640*
No, no, I'll not believe it. I know better
The fine flame honour kindles in your breast:
You were the one—remember—whose great spell
Spurred all our kings, nay dragged them off to war;
Who, in your pride, refusing to surrender,   *645*
Reserved your hand for Alexander's conqueror.
Conquer I must and fly to it, far less to shun
The name of captive, than that name to earn.
Lady, I run and in my heart I burn,
Dead or victorious, still your chains to earn;   *650*
And since I have been sighing all in vain
To win your heart that dreams alone of glory,
I go now, in the blaze that victory brings,
Glory to bind so tightly to my person,
That I perhaps may yet induce your heart   *655*
From love of glory to love of the victor.

AXIANA

Then go, my lord. Taxiles will, perhaps,
Have braver subjects in his camp than he;
In a last effort I shall go and stir them.
Thereafter, in your camp, I'll bide your fate.   *660*
You need not learn the beating of my heart:
Triumph and live.

PORUS

                What are you waiting for?
Why can I not know, from this very hour,
If my sad sighs have agitated you?
Would you, fair Axiana—for harsh fate   *665*
Perhaps condemns me not to see you more—
Would you, a hapless prince, as he lies dying,
Be unaware to what bliss he was due?
Speak.

AXIANA

    What shall I tell you?

PORUS

Divine Princess,
If you should feel for me some happy weakness,   670
Your heart, which pledges me such praise today,
Might pledge to me a little love as well.
Can it be deaf to all my ardent sighs?
Can it . . .

AXIANA

My lord, go, challenge Alexander.
You win, if that ace of the warrior's art   675
Defends himself no better than my heart.

ACT III

SCENE I

AXIANA, CLEOPHILIA

AXIANA

What, Madam! I am held here in duress!
I may not see my army march to war!
Beginning his black treason now with me,
Taxiles keeps me prisoner in his camp!   680
This is the passion for me he paraded!
My abject worshipper stands forth as master!
His love already, weary of my coldness,
Enslaves my limbs in absence of my heart!

CLEOPHILIA

Ah! look more kindly on the valid fears   685
Of one who has been conquered by your spell;
And be more gracious, Madam, towards the zeal
That makes him so concerned about your weal.
While all around us two gigantic armies,
Contending feverishly in equal zest,   690
Let fly their lightning shafts on every side,
Wherever else would you direct your steps?
Where else could you escape the hurricane?
Your life is safe in the calm shelter here:
Here all is peace . . .

AXIANA

            It is this very peace,   695
Whose base security I cannot bear.
What! when my subjects, fighting in the plain

And led by Porus, perish for their Queen,
Flaunting their faith at price of all their blood;
When the dying's cries are almost in my ears, 700
You talk of peace; and your Taxiles' camp
Preserves a bland composure in the storm?
By an insulting calm my grief's beguiled!
By gay frivolities my eyes defiled!

CLEOPHILIA

My lady, would you my adoring brother 705
Hazard your life that is so dear to him?
He knows the dangers . . .

AXIANA

Safe that I might be,
This gallant lover safe imprisons me!
And while his rival risks for me his life,
He guards me bravely here, far from the strife! 710

CLEOPHILIA

Ah, happy Porus! The least separation,
In your impatience, turns to desolation;
To hear you speak, the cares to which you yield
Would make you seek him in the battlefield!

AXIANA

Much more, my lady; with my dying breath, 715
I'd seek him in the very jaws of death,
Lose all my realms and see without a smart,
Through them, your Alexander buy your heart.

CLEOPHILIA

If you seek Porus, why desert me, dear?
Soon Alexander will conduct him here; 720
Allow us, watching over you to hover,
To guard his conquest for your lucky lover.

AXIANA

My lady, you exult; your heart already
To Alexander flies and hails him victor;

But, crediting your flattering love alone,   725
Perhaps your great pride bursts a little soon:
Your dashing wishes somewhat high aspire,
Too soon believing all that you desire.
Yes, yes . . .

CLEOPHILIA

Here comes my brother; we shall hear
Which of us two has been mistaken, dear.   730

AXIANA

Ah! I can hope no more; his proud conceit
Flaunts in my face my Porus's defeat.[10]

SCENE II

Enter TAXILES

TAXILES

If, Porus, Madam, had, with less contempt,
Followed the candid counsels of his friend,
He would indeed have saved me from the pain   735
Of telling you myself of his disgrace.

AXIANA

What! Porus . . .

TAXILES

All is over; his courage, foiled,
Is plunged now in the evils I foresaw.
It is quite true (in reverence for his valour,
I shall not further crush my fallen rival),   740
It is quite true his arm, disputing victory,

---

[10] This scene between the two ladies, spiced as it is with irony, recalls the famous verbal duel between Célimène and Arsinoë that was to delight Paris six months later in Molière's *Le Misanthrope* (Act III, Scene 4). In the last couplet Axiana resumes the tragic tone.

Has dyed in gore the glory of his foes;
That victory, prize of all these splendid feats,
Balanced awhile between him and Alexander:
But vexed with me, he nonetheless, had rushed   745
Too ardently ahead, in feverish haste.
I've seen his ranks severely shaken, shattered,
Your soldiers in disorder; and his, scattered;
Him in the end, swept backwards by their flight,
Despite himself, flee from the victor's might;   750
And, too late, of his vain ire disabused,
Desire the very help he had refused.

AXIANA

He had refused! Indeed! Does your mean heart
Require to be besought to play your part?
Must one, despite you, drag you off to fight   755
And force you, recreant, to do what's right?
The lead of Porus, since I have no choice,
Tell me, was that not strong enough a voice?
This hero's perils, and I, pale of hue,
The whole State toppling, could not influence you!   760
Serve well the lord who holds your sister's hand;
Go, do with me what his harsh lips command.
Mete out to all the vanquished equal pains,
Fetter your mistress, put your rival in chains.
It is indeed all over: your base part   765
Has lodged this princely hero in my heart.
I worship him! and, by the end of day,
At once my hatred and my love will say;
Will vow to him my firm love in your view,
And near him swear undying hate for you.   770
Farewell, you know me: love me if you will.

TAXILES

Ah! only look to me for deep esteem,
My lady; and expect no threats nor fetters:
Alexander better knows what's due to queens.
Allow his gentleness bid you retain   775
A throne that Porus should have less imperilled;

And I myself would be seen blindly hacking
The sacrilegious hand that would dare sap it.

AXIANA

My crown restored by either one of you,
Would then become the bounty of my foe;   *780*
And I'd be placed upon my very throne
By the same tryant hand that drove me from it?

TAXILES

Fair queens and kings whom his great courage conquered,
Have let their mishaps be assuaged by him.
Look at the wife and mother of Darius: *785*
They treat him like a brother and a son.

AXIANA

No, no, I will not traffic with my heart,
Coddling a tyrant, reigning by compassion.
Do you believe I'll ape a feeble Persian?
That I will fawn at Alexander's court?   *790*
That with my victor hurtling through the world
I'll flaunt his darling fetters everywhere?
If he gives kingdoms, let him give you ours;
And let him deck you with the spoils of others.
Reign; neither Porus nor I shall envious be;   *795*
And you will be a meaner slave than we.
I hope Alexander, jealous of his name,
And galled, your guilt has soiled his victory's fame,
Will soon, by your own death, wash off the stain.
Traitors like you often thankless remain: *800*
And so whatever favours he may shower,
Remember treacherous Bessus's dying hour.[11]
Good-bye.

Exit AXIANA

---

[11] Bessus, the fugitive Darius' satrap in Bactria, attempted to seize the Persian throne for himself by murdering his defeated master. Alexander caught up with them as Darius lay dying, ordered the execution of the regicide Bessius, and himself married Darius' daughter, as a token of his own legitimate succession.

SCENE III

CLEOPHILIA

      Yield, brother, to this bubbling fury:
With time and Alexander you shall win;
Whatever she may say, her acid temper   *805*
Will not persist in turning down a realm:
Lord of her fate, you are lord of her heart.
But tell me, have you seen the conqueror?
What treatment should we now expect of him?
What did he say?

TAXILES

        I saw your Alexander.   *810*
At first his splendid youth, that all attest,
Seemed to belie the number of his feats.
Full of his fame, I dared not, I confess,
Concede such glory to such patent youth;
But yet the lofty courage of his brow,   *815*
The fire in his eyes, his majesty,
Proclaim him Alexander, and his features
Bear the unfailing portent of his greatness;
And his proud presence furthering his plans,
He conquers with his eyes as with his arm.   *820*
As he came from the field, my dazzled gaze
Saw in his eyes the star of victory shine,
And yet, on seeing me, he shed his greatness
And made his goodness sparkle in its turn.
All his high spirits could not hide his love.   *825*
"Return," he told me, "to my fair princess;
Dispose her eyes once more to see a victor,
Who places at her feet his heart and victory."
He follows me. I have no more to say;
Over your destiny you have full sway;   *830*
I also leave you conduct over mine.

CLEOPHILIA

You shall have full power, or else I have none.
All will obey you, if the victor hears me.

TAXILES

I go . . . But they are coming. He, himself!

SCENE IV

Enter ALEXANDER, EPHESTION *and* ALEXANDER's *Suite*

ALEXANDER

Ephestion, go and bring me Porus here;   835
See his life is spared and the vanquished's blood.

Exit EPHESTION *and Suite*

SCENE V

ALEXANDER (*To* TAXILES)

Is it then true, my lord, a queen in blindness
Prefers to you a crass, courageous king?
But do not fear him: for his empire's yours;
With this prize, curb the anger of the shrew.   840
Lord of two realms, and arbiter of hers,
Go, with your vows, and offer her three crowns.

TAXILES

My lord, this is too much. Pray, be less lavish . . .

ALEXANDER

You may repay my bounty at your leisure.
Do not delay, go where your love finds balm   845
And crown your ardour with so fine a palm.

Exit TAXILES

SCENE VI

ALEXANDER

Lady, I pledge his love my full support:
Can I do nothing for me, all for him?
In lavishing on him my victory's fruits,
Am I to have a sterile fame alone?   850
The sceptres I have given or restored,
My friends' brows crowned with Alexander's laurels,
The riches I have conquered, showered on them,
Make it quite clear I yearn for other conquests.
Did I not promise you my strong right arm   855
Would set me soon before your charms divine?
But at the same time, do you not remember
You promised me a place within your heart?
Now I have come: yes, love has fought for me;
And victory has itself redeemed my faith;   860
Before you, all yields; you too must surrender;
Your heart has promised, would it now deny?
Ah, could your heart alone elude today
An ardent conqueror, seeking it alone?

CLEOPHILIA

No, no, I do not claim my heart, unmoved,   865
Alone denies your title of all-conquering:
I render what I owe your shining virtues,
That hold a hundred peoples at your feet.
The Indians, beaten, are your least achievements;
The proudest hearts before you pale with fear;   870
And, when you wish, your kindness in its turn
Can make the dourest with devotion burn.
And yet, my lord, these triumphs, all that charm,
Often disturb my mind with real alarm:
I fear lest, glad at having won my heart,   875
You leave it then to languish, sigh and smart;

Lest proof against my passion and my pain,
Your heart an easy conquest may disdain.
Heroes like you love lightly, it would seem:
Your fame has ever been your sweetest dream;   *880*
And even now, perhaps, while still you plead,
The fame of conquering me is all you need.

ALEXANDER

Alas! how ill you know the surging need
Of a passion breaking out with every sigh.
I will admit at one time, while at war,   *885*
My heart could dream of nothing else than fame;
Peoples and kings, subjected to my rule,
Alone were worthy objects of desire.
All Persia's beauties filed before my eyes,
Together with her kings, and failed to conquer: *890*
My heart was hardened with a proud contempt,
And could not pay their charms the least respect:
In love with fame, invincible throughout,
It gloried in appearing quite unmoved:
How differently do your despotic eyes,   *895*
My heart, alas! with sweetness hypnotise!
It wants no more the conqueror's name of Great;
It comes with pleasure to admit defeat:
Happy, if your heart, in its turn, alight,
Would let your fair eyes but admit their might!   *900*
Must you then ever doubt their victory?
Ever reproach me with my exploits' glory,
As though the cunning knots that hold me fast
Should only tangle men of lesser cast?
By novel feats I'm going to show you   *905*
What love in Alexander's heart can do:
Now that my arm, obedient to your laws,
Must vindicate at once my name and yours.
I shall make famous, through war's shining din,
Peoples unknown yet to the rest of men,   *910*
With altars to your name in such abodes
Where their wild hands deny them to the Gods.

CLEOPHILIA

You will, indeed drag victory captive there;
But I must doubt, my lord, if love would follow.
So many realms and seas, dividing us,   *915*
Would soon, alas! efface me from your heart.
When furious Ocean sees your flag unfurled
Achieve some day the conquest of the world;
When at your feet you see the kings fall dumb,
And trembling earth grow silent as you come,[12]   *920*
Will you, my lord, remember, a young queen
Deep in her realms bewails you, far, unseen,
And calls to mind the rapturous moments past,
When this great hero swore his love would last?

ALEXANDER

Do you imagine, savage to myself,   *925*
I would abandon here so rare a beauty?
But you yourself perhaps would rather spurn
The splendid throne of Asia where I'd place you?

CLEOPHILIA

My lord, you know that I must heed my brother.

ALEXANDER

If he alone could clinch my happiness,   *930*
The whole of India, subject to his laws,
Would soon solicit him on my behalf.

CLEOPHILIA

My love for him seeks no material gain.
Only appease an irritated queen;
And do not let his rival, who has braved you,   *935*
Become today far happier than he.

ALEXANDER

Without doubt Porus was a noble rival:
Never has such rare courage won my praise.
I saw him, reached him in the heat of battle;

[12] An echo from Maccabees I, 1:3.

And I say once more he did not shun me: 940
We sought each other out. So fine a pride
Was on the point of ending our great quarrel,
When a band of soldiers rushed between us,
Making us bury our blows in the crowd.

SCENE VII

Enter EPHESTION

ALEXANDER

Well, are they bringing this bold prince to me?   945

EPHESTION

They seek him everywhere, but until now
In spite of all their efforts, death or flight
Hides, Sire, this captive from their scrutiny.
But a knot of his men, cut off in flight,
Stopping the chase of your victorious soldiers,   950
Seem to prepare dearly to sell their deaths.

ALEXANDER

Disarm the vanquished, see there's no excess.
My lady, let us bend a proud princess,
So that Taxiles may promote my love;
And since my peace must now depend on his,   955
We'll seal his happiness to crown my bliss.

ACT IV

SCENE I

AXIANA (*Alone*)

Am I to hear but these victorious cries
Of my triumphant, taunting enemies?
And may I not at least remain alone,
In dire misfortune, brooding on my pain?   960
Pressed by a lover I may not forgive,
In spite of me, they dream to make me live:
They watch, pursue me. But do not imagine,
Dear Porus, they can stop me following you.
Of course, you never could survive our shame: 965
So many men are hunting you in vain;
Your whereabouts would by your feats be spread,
And they can find you only mid the dead.
Alas! on leaving me, your passionate plea
Seemed to foresee the ills now crushing me,   970
When your fine eyes, deep gazing into mine,
Asked me how far my heart could pine for you;
When reckless of the outcome of the war,
Requital of your love was all your care.
And why with all that cunning did I hide   975
A secret fatal to your peace of mind?
How many times your eyes, compelling me,
Had placed my silent heart in jeopardy!
How many times, responsive to your fire,
Have I not, in your presence, breathed desire!   980
But I still wished to doubt your victory;
I read my sighs as yearning but for glory;
I thought this, all I loved. Great King, forgive!
Without you, now I know I cannot live.

I shall confess our honour held some sway,   *985*
As I so often said. But I should say
You, only, showed me where true honour leads.
I learnt to know it, seeing your great deeds;
However fine the fervour it would kindle,
In anyone but you its charm would dwindle.   *990*
But what good now my useless sighs to pour,
Lost in thin air, these sighs you hear no more?
It's time my soul, descended to the grave,
Vow you that love you did for so long crave;
It's time my heart, in tested pledge and true,   *995*
Show all, it cannot live on after you.
You think, after your death, I could still live
Beneath the laws a victor deigns to give?
I know he is about to come to me
And give me back my throne in clemency.   *1000*
He hopes perhaps, he hopes to choke my hate,
As trophy to his pity counterfeit!
Then let him come. He'll see me, dignified,
Die as your queen, just as my king you died.

SCENE II

Enter ALEXANDER

AXIANA

Indeed, my lord, indeed, do you delight   *1005*
In seeing flow the tears your arms occasion?
Or do you envy me, in my sad state,
The sorry freedom to bewail my woes.

ALEXANDER

Your grief is free as much as it is proper:
My lady, you lament a noble prince.   *1010*
I was his foe; but not to the extent

Of blaming tears, in tribute of his death.
Before I crossed the frontiers of your India,
His splendid courage made him known to me;
He stood out from among the greatest kings,   *1015*
I knew . . .

AXIANA

Then why come here and fall on him?
By what law must you ferret courage out
And wage war on it to earth's farthest ends?
Can merit never dazzle your vain eyes
And not impel your pride to blot it out?   *1020*

ALEXANDER

I sought out Porus, true: say what you will,
I did not seek him out for his destruction.
I will confess, a glutton for renown,
I was led on by rumours of his battles;
The mere name of a king, till then unconquered,   *1025*
Drove my heart on to tackle fresh exploits.
While I was hoping, through my various battles,
To fix on me alone the whole world's eyes,
I saw the widespread fame of this brave warrior
Balance with me the palm of sweet Renown;   *1030*
And, seeing his arm strike terror all around,
I found in India a fit field for me.
Weary of kings who fell without a fight,
I heard with pleasure his reputed valour.
So fine a foe gave me fresh buoyancy;   *1035*
I came in search of glory and of danger.
His courage, Madam, passed my expectations:
Victory, that once so firmly followed me,
Almost abandoned me to follow him.
He wrestled with me for the smallest laurels;   *1040*
And I dare say, in losing victory,
My foe himself has seen his glory grow;
So fine a fall has raised his reputation,
And he would not wish never to have fought.

AXIANA

Alas! this noble wish indeed had made him   1045
Abandon every care to guard his life;
Since, on all sides, betrayed and persecuted,
He hurled himself against so many foes.
But you, if it were true, his warrior's ardour
Had given shining scope to your ambition,   1050
Why did you not, my lord, fight worthily?
Had you to trap his courage with your tricks,
And, far from bearing off a perfect palm,
To owe his fall to others' acts than yours?
Triumph; but know Taxiles in his heart   1055
Already fights you for the fame of victor;
The traitor fancies, with some show of right,
You've been victorious merely through his ruse:
And it's a pleasing sight in all my pain
To see him dip his finger in your fame.   1060

ALEXANDER

Your pain would denigrate my fame in vain:
Never have I been seen to steal a victory,[13]
And by such craven guile, I deem beneath me,
Deceive my foes instead of daunting them.
Although, it seems, outnumbered everywhere,   1065
I could not stoop to ambush in the dark;
They blamed their downfall on my arm alone;
And everywhere the sun shone on my battles.
I pity, it is true, your ravaged fields;
I wanted to prevent your princes' fall;   1070
But had they followed my advice and wish
I would have saved them both or fought them both.
Believe. . .

AXIANA

        I believe all, believe you resistless:
Yet is there nothing sacred but your courage?

---

[13] "I do not steal victory," the famous retort of Alexander when counselled at Arbela to attack the Persians in the night. (Plutarch, *Life of Alexander*, Chap. XXXI.)

Is all that matters, throwing kings in chains,   *1075*
Making the whole world groan with scarce a thought?
How had these myriad captive cities harmed you,
These myriad corpses heaped on Hydaspes' banks?
What have I done, that you should come and crush
A hero who alone could win my love?   *1080*
Did he burst through the borders of your Greece?
Did we raise up whole nations against you,
Inciting them to undermine your fame?
Alas! we could admire and not be envious.
Blessed in our realms, enchanted with each other,   *1085*
Our destined lot was happier than yours:
His whole ambition was to win a heart
That would perhaps today have called him lord.
Ah! had you shed this noble blood alone,
Could one accuse you of this single crime,   *1090*
Do you, my lord, not feel yourself accursed
Coming so far to break such tender bonds?
No, howsoever kind you deem yourself,
You're but a tyrant.

ALEXANDER

      Madam, I see clear,
You want me, in the throes of a base anger,   *1095*
To break out into rank recrimination.
Perhaps you hope to tire my clemency
And make me compromise its reputation.
But even had your courage not entranced me,
You but attack a victor, who's disarmed.   *1100*
My heart, despite you, bent on pitying you,
Respects the dire misfortune that engulfs you.
It is this fatal blindness that afflicts you,
That finds in me merely a hateful tyrant.
Else you would surely grant, my glorious wars   *1105*
Not always have been stained by blood and tears.
You'd see . . .

AXIANA

      Alas! my lord, can I not see
Your blazing deeds, that sharpen my despair?

Have I not seen your victories everywhere
Through moderation kill opposing pride?   *1110*
Do I not see defeated Scythia, Persia,
Relish their yoke and loud proclaim your worth,
Vying, indeed, with your own countrymen,
In blind concurrence to secure your life?
But what poor comfort to my wounded heart   *1115*
To see elsewhere your goodness hymned by all?
Do you believe my hate would be less deep,
To see all kiss the hand that tortures me?
Can all these kings avenged or helped by you,
Can all these happy peoples bring back Porus?   *1120*
The more they love, the more I hate you, Sire,
And all the more because I must admire,
Because the world compels me to condone,
Because I'm left to hate you all alone.

ALEXANDER

I shall excuse your tender love's excesses;   *1125*
But after all, they should surprise me, Madam:
If I've correctly gauged the general view,
You had not singled Porus out for favour;
Balancing between Taxiles and him,
Your heart was silent while he was alive;   *1130*
And when he can no longer hear you now,
My lady, you begin to fix on him.
You think, susceptible to your new care,
His ashes still require your flame to flare?
Pray do not be engulfed by sterile grief;   *1135*
More weighty matters elsewhere call to you,
Your tears have graced his memory enough:
Reign, and hold high the glory of your rank;
And, giving back your desolate heart its poise,
Rally your kingdoms shaken by his fall,   *1140*
From this great crowd of kings find them a lord,
More loving than ever, Taxiles . . .

AXIANA

What! the traitor!

ALEXANDER

I beg you, please, to moderate your feelings;
He is not stained by treachery to you.
As master of his realms he could decide   *1145*
To seek with them a shelter from the storm.
He was obliged by neither oath nor duty
To rush into the abyss where Porus plunged.
Indeed, remember, Alexander too
Supports this loving prince's happiness.   *1150*
Reflect, united by so wise a choice,
All Indus and Hydaspes will be yours;
That I will gladly further all your interests,
Once they are coupled with Taxiles's.
He's here. I do not wish to gag his wooing;   *1155*
I leave him to explain his love himself:
My presence is already harsh to you:
Sweet lovers' talk must search out solitude;
I shall not trouble you.

Exit ALEXANDER

SCENE III

Enter TAXILES

AXIANA

Come, powerful king,
Great emperor of India; yes, you, knave.   *1160*
He wants to quell my anger for your sake;
He says your only wishes are to please me,
That my reserve has but inflamed your love:
And more; that I must love you in my turn.
But do you know where love would have to take you?   *1165*
Know by what secret you may move my heart?
Are you prepared . . .

TAXILES

Ah, Lady, let me show you
How far so warm a hope can lead my will!
What must I do?

AXIANA

You must, if you love truly,
Love glory as intensely as I love,   *1170*
Woo me by a thousand noble deeds alone,
And hate this Alexander as I hate;
Must boldly march into the midst of danger;
And draw your sword to fight, to win or die.
Turn, turn your eyes on Porus and yourself,   *1175*
And judge which of you more deserved my love.
Taxiles, yes, my heart did seem to balance,
But it distinguished clearly slave from king.
I loved him, worship him; and since harsh fate
Forbids him in such bliss participate,   *1180*
By you I choose his glory to be seen:
My tears will keep his memory ever green;
You'll ever find me, in my deepest grief,
Speaking to you of him—my sole relief!

TAXILES

So I must burn in vain for a heart of ice,   *1185*
On which the face of Porus is engraved.
If I did go, to please you, and brave death,
Madam, I should be doomed, but still not please.
I cannot then . . .

AXIANA

You can regain my trust;
And wash away your crime in hostile blood.   *1190*
Chance smiles on you: and Porus from the grave
Rallies his soldiers all around his flag;
His spirit only seems to stay their flight.

Your men too, your men, shamed by your disgrace,
Show on their brows, blazing with righteous rage,   *1195*
Repentance of the crime to which you forced them.
Go, stir the fire that is consuming them;
Avenge our freedom that is still alive;
Become defender of my throne and yours;
Run, make sure Porus finds a fit successor . . .   *1200*
You hold your tongue! I see upon your face
So fine a plan intimidates your heart.
I cite a hero's instance all in vain;
You wish to serve. Go, serve, and let me be.

TAXILES

This is too much. You are perhaps forgetting,   *1205*
If you compel me, I may speak as master;
That I may tire of suffering your scorn;
That you and your States, all are in my hands;
That after such respect, which makes you prouder,
I can . . .

AXIANA

    I understand, I am your prisoner: *1210*
You wish perhaps to fetter even my heart;
To make it, trembling, gratify your sighs?
Well, strip yourself at last of your false mildness;
Call fear and terror to your dastard aid;
Speak as a tyrant ready to pursue me;   *1215*
My hate cannot increase, come then, subdue me.
Above all, do not threaten me anew.
Your sister comes to urge you what to do;
If her advice is, as my wishes, plain,
You'll help me soon my Porus to regain.   *1220*
Good-bye.

TAXILES

    Ah! rather . . .

Exit AXIANA

SCENE IV

Enter CLEOPHILIA

CLEOPHILIA

　　　Leave this thankless queen,
Who, in her hate, has sworn to harass us:
Whose sole joy is to drive you to despair.
Forget . . .

TAXILES

　　　No, no, I wish to worship her.
I love her; even if my deep desire   *1225*
Is answered only by immortal hate,
In spite of all her scorn, of all your pleas,
In spite of me, I simply have to love.
Her anger, after all, was not surprising;
I must blame you, blame me alone for this.   *1230*
But for your counsels, sister, that betrayed me,
If I were not loved I'd be hated less;
But for you, I should see her, saved by me,
Still wavering between Porus's heart and mine;
And ah! how sweet a bliss would that not be   *1235*
To place her choice in some uncertainty!
I can no longer live, crushed by her hate;
I have to throw myself at her proud feet.
I'll hurry there; and to her hate to pander
I'll fight you, sister, fight your Alexander.   *1240*
I know how both of you with passion pine;
But it's too much for your peace to kill mine;
And quite indifferent how your love may end,
I'll see all die or see my heart content.[14]

[14] Another of Taxiles' speeches containing the seed of some of Hermione's
great tirades in *Andromache*.

CLEOPHILIA

Then go, and hurry to the battlefield,   *1245*
And let the zeal inflaming you not droop.
Why does your drifting heart still dally here?
Run. They're at grips, and Porus waits for you.

TAXILES

What! Porus is not dead! Porus appears!

CLEOPHILIA

Yes, he. Such heavy blows ring with his stamp.   *1250*
As he foresaw, the rumour of his death
Has stayed the arm of a credulous conqueror.
He comes now to surprise their sleeping valour,
To disarrange a victory yet unsure;
He comes, you need not doubt, as a raging lover   *1255*
To bear his mistress off or die before her.
Further, your camp, seduced by her intrigues,
Are clamouring stridently to follow Porus.
Then go yourself, go, as a generous lover,
To aid a rival, loved so tenderly.   *1260*
Farewell.

Exit CLEOPHILIA

SCENE V

TAXILES (*Alone*)

Must fate, resolved to play me false,
Resuscitate a rival to destroy me?
Those eyes, that wept for him, once more he'll see,
Those eyes, preferring him, though dead, to me!
It is too much. Let's see what fate decrees,   *1265*
Whom with her noble conquest it will please.
Come. No more time in craven anger spend,
Lest, without us, so great a quarrel end.

ACT V

SCENE I

ALEXANDER, CLEOPHILIA

ALEXANDER

Did you fear Porus even in defeat?
In your eyes was my victory incomplete?   *1270*
No, no, he is a prisoner in my power,
Surrounded on all sides by those I order.
Ah! far from fearing him, pray, pity him.

CLEOPHILIA

It is this very state that makes me fear him.
His reputation for surpassing valour   *1275*
Distressed me less than his misfortune does.
As long as he was followed by great armies,
His forces and his feats did not dismay me;
But he is now, my lord, a fallen king;
And so I reckon him among your friends.   *1280*

ALEXANDER

He has forfeited all claims to such a name;
And has too well earned Alexander's hate.
He knows with what regret I reached that pass;
But now my hate's as great as he had willed.
I even owe the world a harsh example: *1285*
I must avenge the horrors of the war;
Must punish him for ills he could prevent,
And for compelling me to punish him.[15]

---

[15] Racine's penetrating psychology is apparent even in this early play.

Twice vanquished, hated by my fair princess . . .

CLEOPHILIA

My lord, I do not hate him, I confess;   1290
And if today I were allowed to hear
What his misfortunes' voice is telling me,
I'd say to you he was our greatest prince;
His arm was long the bastion of our realms;
He wished, perhaps, in marching against you,   1295
To be thought worthy of your blows at least,
And that the same fight where you both would shine,
Would speed his name forever in your wake.
But, if I fight for him, my generous zeal
Would harm my brother and destroy his hopes.   1300
As long as Porus lives—ah! poor Taxiles!
His ruin is assured and maybe mine.
Yes, if his love remains ungratified,
He'll hold me guilty and will punish me.
And even now that you are making ready   1305
To fly afresh, from conquest on to conquest,
When Ganges' waves will part you from my brother,
Who will, my lord, restrain his wilful anger?
My soul, forlorn, will languish far from you.
Alas! were he to bid my sighs be silent,   1310
What would become of my distracted heart?
Where will the victor be to whom I gave it?

ALEXANDER

Lady, this is too much. Give me your heart,
And I will keep it, do what Taxiles may,
Far better than so many realms I've conquered   1315
And which I only kept to tender you.
My lady, one last victory and I'll come—
My glorious goal—to hold sway in your heart,
Myself to be your slave and hand to you
The fate of Alexander and of men.   1320
The Malli await me, about to pay me homage.
So near the Ocean, what can I do more

Than go and show myself to this proud element[16]
As conqueror of the world and as your lover.
Then . . .

CLEOPHILIA

> What, my lord, forever wars on wars;   *1325*
> Do you seek subjects even in the stars?
> Do you want as witness of your splendid show
> Regions their very peoples hardly know?
> What do you hope to fight in climes so rude?
> They will oppose to you vast solitude,   *1330*
> Dim deserts never brightened by the sky,
> Where nature seems herself to droop and die.
> Who knows if jealous fate, in secret strife,
> Failing to eclipse the glory of your life,
> Does not await you in this desert waste,   *1335*
> To see your grave at least remain untraced.
> Do you dream to drag your army there, war-sated,
> Ten times renewed and ten times decimated?
> Your soldiers, drawing pity, with worn faces,
> Shed half their number in a hundred places,   *1340*
> And through their groans impart to you quite clear . . .

ALEXANDER

Madam, they'll march as soon as I appear:
These brave hearts, who in camp, in idle leisure,
Count groaning every blow in gloomy pleasure,
Will follow me revived. Cursing their groans,   *1345*
They'll vie before my eyes for further wounds.
Meanwhile we will support Taxiles' suit:
His rival must no longer pluck the fruit.
I told you, Lady, and I say once more . . .

CLEOPHILIA

Here comes the queen.

[16] Alexander, from the Punjab, went down the Indus Valley to the Arabian Sea, returning to Babylon by water with his troops marching back along the coast. He was to die not long after.

SCENE II

Enter AXIANA

ALEXANDER

       Well, Madam, Porus lives,   *1350*
Heaven seems to have been gracious to your prayers;
And gives him back . . .

AXIANA

       Alas! it cuts him off!
No hope avails me to beguile my grief;
His death was doubtful, now it will be sure:
He runs to it; perhaps the only reason   *1355*
To see me once more and to succour me.
But what could he do, one, against a host,
That his great fight did all in vain affright?
A band of men, his lionheart inspired,
Have all in vain struck terror in your camp.   *1360*
He must die in the end, and bravely fall,
Engulfed by heaps of dead who block his path.
Ah, could I only, rushing out from here,
Show him Axiana dying first before him!
Taxiles holds me back while he, the traitor,   *1365*
Has gone to feast upon my hero's blood;
He goes to gloat on him in death's embrace,
If he at all dare to confront him still.

ALEXANDER

My lady, no, I've taken care to spare him:
He will soon come to put your mind at rest.   *1370*
You will see him.

AXIANA

       You'd stretch to him your grace!
The arm that crushed him would become his stay!

I'd see him saved by Alexander's hands!
What further miracle may I not see?
I do remember, Sire, as you did promise,   1375
Victorious Alexander had no foes:
Or rather never was this warrior one:
Glory alone set you to fight each other.
He wished to test himself on one so brave;
And you attacked him but that you might save.   1380

ALEXANDER

His mounting scorn, defying all my ire,
Doubtless deserved a conqueror more severe;
His pride seems to be strengthened by his fall;
But I will cease to be his enemy:
I throw off, Madam, both the hate and name,   1385
I make Taxiles judge of my displeasure;
He, only, as he wills, may doom or spare him;
And it is only he whom you must win.

AXIANA

A beggar at his feet! Is this my place?
And you refer me to Taxiles' grace?   1390
On one so craven must we spend our breath?
Alas! your hate has sworn brave Porus' death.
No, to destroy him was your only goal.
How easy to seduce a generous soul!
My credulous heart, forgetting all its hate,   1395
Was struck with virtues you repudiate.
Then girt yourself, my lord, with might severe:
Make bloody end of such a fine career:
After so many foes by you reprieved,
Sentence the only one you should have saved.   1400

ALEXANDER

Porus, you love; but save his life, ah no!
Refuse the benefits I would bestow;
Tarnish my pity with base jealousy;

But blame yourself, if, in the end, he die.
He's here. His own opinion I'll await: *1405*
Let Porus be supreme judge of his fate.

LAST SCENE

Enter PORUS, EPHESTION *and* ALEXANDER's *Guards*

ALEXANDER

This, Porus, is the fruit of all your pride!
Where are your dazzling but delusive dreams?
Your lofty arrogance is turned to shame.
I owe a victim to my outraged fame: *1410*
Nothing can save you. Nonetheless I would
Offer once more a pardon, thrice withstood.
This queen alone, meeting my grace with strife,
Wishes most faithfully to end your life,
Without a moment's pause would choke your breath,   *1415*
Merely to see you love her till your death.
Why buy this hollow fame so dearly? Give
Taxiles what his heart demands—and live.

PORUS

Taxiles!

ALEXANDER

Yes.

PORUS

Well done, I applaud your pains;
All he has done for you this service gains.   *1420*
He, tyrant, made me taste defeat, dishonour,
Gave you his sister, sold to you his honour;
Delivered me to you. Could you, in dream,
One even of his benefits redeem?

But I've forestalled the precious pains you ply: *1425*
Go to the battlefield and see him die.

ALEXANDER

Taxiles!

CLEOPHILIA

What do I hear?

EPHESTION

Yes, he is dead.
He himself rushed to meet his dismal fate.
Porus was vanquished; far from surrendering,
He seemed to be attacking, not defending.   *1430*
His prostrate soldiers, dying at his feet,
Were sheltering him with their expiring bodies.
Enclosed as in a fortress, he, intrepid,
Held out still more against an entire host,
Forbidding access to the boldest warriors,   *1435*
With shattering blows of terror and of death.
I spared him still; and his exhausted strength
Would soon have put his life into my power,
When on this field of death, Taxiles running:
"Stop," shouted he, "this prisoner is my due.   *1440*
Porus, the game is up, you now must die;
You'll either yield the queen, or say good-bye."
Porus, his wrath revived on hearing him,
Raised once again his mighty, weary arm;
And proudly, calmly, seeking out his rival: *1445*
"Do I not hear," he cried, "the false Taxiles,
This traitor to his land, his mistress, me?
Come, knave, Axiana's yours," continued he,
"I will indeed yield you this splendid prize,
But first you must make certain Porus dies: *1450*
Draw near." With these sharp words, these bristling
    rivals
Each hurled himself at once upon the other.

We massed ourselves in wedge against their fury;
But Porus runs through us and clears a way,
Reaches Taxiles, strikes him through the heart,   *1455*
And flushed with victory to our men surrenders.

CLEOPHILIA

My lord, now it must fall to me to weep;
The whole weight of your arms has crashed on me.
My brother vainly looked to you for help,
And ah! your glory's fatal but to him.   *1460*
What use to him your friendship in the grave?
Will you, my lord, see him die, unavenged?
Will you then suffer, after murdering him,
Porus come gloating before you and me?

AXIANA

Yes, heed, my lord, the tears of Cleophilia.   *1465*
I pity her. She justly mourns Taxiles:
Her whole attempt to spare him has been vain;
She made of him a coward but could not save him.
It is not Porus who attacked her brother;
He himself rushed to meet his condign wrath.   *1470*
What did he come to seek in the thick of the fight?
Did he come to shield his friend from the victor's might?
He came to crush, in his extreme distress,
A king, Victory herself would surely bless.
But why remove from you your fine excuse?   *1475*
Is Taxiles not dead? Then end our truce.
Sire, sacrifice to him Porus the Great;
Avenge yourselves. But know I share his fate.
Yes, Porus, yes, as Alexander knows,
My heart does not love feebly. Taxiles groaned   *1480*
At it. You only did not know. My bliss
Is full, now, as I die, to tell you this.

PORUS

Yes, Alexander, take your satisfaction:
Defeated though I was, you see my deed.
Fear Porus, fear his hand though weaponless,   *1485*

That can avenge his fall amid a host.
My name may lend your enemies fresh wings,
And rouse a hundred fettered, sleeping kings.
Choke in my blood these seeds of future wars,
And conquering march securely towards the stars.   *1490*
Moreover do not dream a heart like mine
Salute a conqueror or plead and whine.
Speak; while I keep my glory free from shame,
Let's see how you will act in victory's name.

ALEXANDER

Porus, I see your pride must still defy: *1495*
You dare to threaten me with your last sigh.
My triumph should indeed blench at your boast,
Your name may do more mischief than a host:
I should safeguard myself. Tell me one thing,
How would you have me treat you now?

PORUS

As king.[17]   *1500*

ALEXANDER

Well then, it is as king I now will treat
You. I'll not leave my victory incomplete;
You wished it so, you cannot then complain.
I give you back your kingdom, Porus: reign.
And with my friendship, take your Axiana: *1505*
I sentence both to bonds that shall not break.
Live, both, and reign; alone, of all your friends,
Your sovereignity to Ganges' banks extends.

(*To* CLEOPHILIA)

This treatment, Lady, justly may amaze.
But such is Alexander's vengeful way.   *1510*
I love you; and my heart, moved by your sigh,
Would make a thousand for your anguish die.

[17] This was the historic reply Porus gave to Alexander. (Plutarch, *Life of Alexander*, Chap. LX.)

But you yourself might deem your honour harmed
By the death of a foe who is disarmed:
He would triumphantly defy his doom,   *1515*
And he would go as conqueror to his tomb.
Allow me, crowning my last enterprise,
To place my virtue whole before your eyes.
Let Porus reign through my command; and then
You may yourself command the rest of men.   *1520*
Assume the sentiments this rank ordains,
Make everyone admire your dawning reign;
And, viewing the splendour all around you spread,
Tell me Taxiles' sister's wrath is dead.

AXIANA

Yes, Madam, reign; allow me to express   *1525*
My admiration of your hero's heart.
Love him and still possess the sweet advantage
Of seeing all the earth adore your lover.

PORUS

My lord, until today the world in fear
Forced me to marvel at your great career: *1530*
But nothing forced me, in the general terror,
To grant in you more virtue than in me.
Now I avow your total victory:
Your virtues, I confess, equal your glory.
Go, Sire, bring all the world beneath your laws;   *1535*
Your feats will have my aid and my applause:
I'll follow you, convinced I must dare all
To hold the world in Alexander's thrall.

CLEOPHILIA

What may my sad and downcast heart say, Sire?
I do not speak a word against your virtue: *1540*
To Porus you restore his life and crown;
I will believe your fame demands it thus;
But do not press me: in my present state,
I can but hold my tongue and weep my fate.

ALEXANDER

Yes, Lady, let us weep so true a friend;   *1545*
And by our sighs display our shining zeal;
And let a proud tomb tell the ages dim
How you have mourned and I remembered him.

THE END

❊❊❊

ANDROMACHE

A Tragedy

To Madam*

Madam,

It is not without reason that I place your illustrious name at the head of this work. And with what other name could I dazzle my readers' eyes than hers by whom my audiences have been so fortunately dazzled? It was known that Your Royal Highness had deigned to interest yourself in my tragedy. It was known that you had helped me with your enlightened judgment to add fresh beauties to it. And lastly, it was known that you had honoured it with tears at the very first reading I gave you of it.
Forgive me, Madam, if I take the liberty of vaunting this happy beginning of its career. It gives me glorious consolation for the hardness of those who insist on remaining unmoved by it. I let them condemn my Andromache *as much as they wish, provided I am allowed to appeal from all the subtleties of their minds to the heart of Your Royal Highness.*
But, Madam, it is not only with your heart that you judge the worth of a work, it is with an intelligence that no false brilliance may deceive. Can we put upon the stage a story in which you are not as well steeped as we? Can we set to work a plot without your comprehension of its inmost springs? And can we conceive of sentiments which, however noble or delicate, are not infinitely below the nobility and delicacy of your thoughts? It is well known, Madam, and Your Royal Highness hides it in vain, that in the high and glorious rank to which nature and fortune have delighted to raise you, you do not despise this obscure glory which men of letters have marked out for themselves. And it seems that you have wished to have as much the advantage over our sex with your knowledge and the solidity of your mind, as you shine in yours with all the graces that hover over you. The Court turns to you as the arbiter of all that is pleasing. And we who strive to please the public, have no longer to go asking the learned if we work within the rules. The sovereign rule is to please Your Royal Highness.

* Henrietta of England, sister of Charles II and wife of Monsieur, Louis XIV's brother.

This no doubt is the least of your excellent qualities. But, Madam, it is the only one about which I can speak with some knowledge: the others are beyond my reach. I cannot speak of them without demeaning them by the inadequacy of my thoughts, and without stepping out of the deep veneration with which I am,

Madam,

Your Royal Highness's
very humble, very obedient
and very loyal servant,

RACINE

First Preface*

V̲irgil, in the third book of the *Aeneid*.

It is Aeneas who speaks:

The sight of high Phaeacia soon we lost,†
And skimm'd along Epirus' rocky coast.
Then to Chaonia's port our course we bend,
And, landed, to Buthrotus' heights ascend.
By chance, the mournful queen, before the gate,
Then solemniz'd her former husband's fate.
Green altars, rais'd of turf, with gifts she crown'd:
And sacred priests in order stand around,
And thrice the name of hapless Hector sound.
With eyes dejected, in a lowly tone,
After a modest pause, she thus begun:
"Oh, only happy maid of Priam's race,
Whom death deliver'd from the foe's embrace!
Commanded on Achilles' tomb to die,‡
Not forc'd like us, to hard captivity,
Or in a haughty master's arms to lie.
In Grecian ships, unhappy we were borne,
Endur'd the victor's lust, sustain'd the scorn!
Thus I submitted to the lawless pride
Of Pyrrhus, more a handmaid than a bride.
Cloy'd with possession, he forsook my bed,
And Helen's lovely daughter sought to wed;
Till young Orestes, pierc'd with deep despair,
And longing to redeem the promis'd fair,
Before Apollo's altar slew the ravisher."

* In the editions of 1668 and 1673.
† Dryden's translation of the original Latin, quoted by Racine.
‡ The reference is to Polyxena (daughter of Priam and Hecuba), sacrificed to Achilles' shade by his son Pyrrhus (see Euripides' *Hecuba*). Racine's Hermione (Act IV, Scene 5, line 1338) upbraids Pyrrhus with this savagery.

Here, in a few verses, lies the whole subject of this tragedy. Here is its scene, the plot which unfolds there, the four chief characters, and even their characteristics. Excepting those of Hermione, whose jealousy and temper are sufficiently indicated in the *Andromache* of Euripides.

But, in truth, my characters are so famous in antiquity, that even those who have but a nodding acquaintance of it will clearly notice that I have depicted them just as the ancient poets have represented them to us. I therefore did not deem it proper to change their moral attitude in any way. The only liberty I have taken is to soften a little the brutality of Pyrrhus, which Seneca in his *Troades* and Virgil in the Second Book of the *Aeneid*, have pushed much further than I thought I ought.

Nonetheless, people have been found to complain that he rages against Andromache, and that he wishes to marry his captive at any price. I admit that he is not sufficiently resigned to his mistress' will, and that Celadon* knew perfect love better than he. But what could I do? Pyrrhus had not read our novels. He was violent by nature. And every hero cannot be a Celadon.

However that may be, the public have been too kind to me for me to trouble about the individual annoyance of two or three people who would insist on our reforming all the heroes of antiquity to make perfect heroes of them. I sympathise with their desire to see on the stage only spotless characters. But I beg them remember that it is not for me to change the rules of drama. Horace urges us to depict Achilles fierce, inexorable, violent, just as he was and just as his son is depicted. And Aristotle, very far from asking perfect heroes of us, insists on the contrary that tragic characters, namely those whose misfortune causes the catastrophe of the tragedy, should be neither entirely good, nor entirely evil. He does not want them to be utterly good, because the punishment of a good man would excite in the spectator indignation rather than pity; nor that they be utterly evil because one cannot at all pity a scoundrel. So they must be moderately good, that is to say, good with some defect and should fall into misfortune through some fault which arouses pity and not detestation.

* The hero of *Astrée*, a romantic novel of the time by Honoré d'Urfé.

Second Preface*

[The opening paragraphs, up to "... the *Andromache* of Euripides," are the same in both Prefaces. The Second Preface then continues:]

It is almost the only thing I have borrowed in this play from that author. For, although my tragedy bears the same title as his, its plot is nevertheless very different. Andromache, in Euripides, fears for the life of Molossus, who is her son by Pyrrhus, and whom Hermione wants to see slain along with his mother. But in my play there is no question of Molossus. Andromache knows no other husband than Hector, nor other son than Astyanax. I believed thus to be conforming to the idea we have now of that princess. Most of those who have heard of Andromache, know her but as the widow of Hector and as the mother of Astyanax. One cannot imagine her loving another husband nor another son. And I doubt whether Andromache's tears would have made on the mind of my audiences the impression they have made, if they had flowed for another son than him whom she bore to Hector.

It is true that I was compelled to make Astyanax live a little longer than he has lived; but I write in a country where such a liberty cannot be ill-received. For, not to mention Ronsard, who has chosen this very Astyanax as the hero of his *Franciade*, who does not know that the lineage of our ancient kings is traced to this son of Hector, and that our old chronicles have saved this young prince's life, after the destruction of his country, to make of him the founder of our monarchy?

How much bolder Euripides has been in his tragedy of *Helen*! In it he openly shocks the common belief of entire Greece. He supposes that Helen has never set foot in Troy; and that after the sack of that town, Menelaus finds his wife in Egypt, which she

* This replaced the First Preface in all editions during Racine's lifetime, beginning with the edition of 1676.

had never left. All that based on a view entertained only by the Egyptians, as one may find in Herodotus.

I do not believe that I needed this example of Euripides to justify the small liberty that I have taken. For there is a great difference between destroying the very foundation of a legend and altering a few of its incidents, which change their aspect in every hand which treats of them. Thus Achilles, according to most poets, can only be wounded in the heel, although Homer makes him wounded in the arm and does not portray him as invulnerable in any part of his body. Thus Sophocles makes Jocasta die immediately after the recognition of Oedipus,* quite unlike Euripides who makes her live until the fight and death of her two sons.† And it is with respect to some contradictions of this nature that a former commentator of Sophocles‡ remarks very appositely "that one must not delight in cavilling at poets for the few changes they may have made in the legend; but rather strive to consider the excellent use they made of these changes, and the ingenious way in which they have modified the legend to suit their theme."

---

* Sophocles' *Oedipus Tyrannos*.
† Euripides' *Phoenician Women*.
‡ Sophocles' *Electra* [Racine's note].

ANDROMACHE

First performed in November 1667 by the players of the Hôtel de Bourgogne, and printed in 1668.

CHARACTERS

ANDROMACHE   *Widow of Hector, captive of Pyrrhus*
PYRRHUS   *Son of Achilles, King of Epirus*
ORESTES   *Son of Agamemnon*
HERMIONE   *Daughter of Helen, betrothed to Pyrrhus*
PYLADES   *Friend of Orestes*
CLEONE   *Lady-in-Waiting to Hermione*
CEPHISE   *Lady-in-Waiting to Andromache*
PHOENIX   *Tutor of Achilles and then of Pyrrhus*

Suite of ORESTES

The scene is at Buthrotus, a town in Epirus,
in a chamber in the palace of Pyrrhus.

ACT I

SCENE I

ORESTES

Yes, since I find my faithful friend once more,
My luck henceforth is certain to be better;
Why, fortune's frown already seems to fade,
Now she has taken pains to reunite us.
Who would have thought upon this mournful shore   5
I'd find Pylades straight upon my landing?
That after losing you for more than six months,
You'd run to greet me at the court of Pyrrhus?

PYLADES

For this I thank Heaven, that, through countless checks,
Seemed to have barred to me the road to Greece,   10
Since that most fateful day when stormy seas
Scattered our vessels by Epirus' shores.
How many terrors troubled me in exile!
How many times your misery made me weep,
Forever fearing for you some fresh peril   15
That my poor friendship could not share with you!
And most of all I feared that deep affliction[1]
In which your spirits have so long been steeped.
I dreaded lest the gods might offer you,
In cruel aid, the death you always sought.   20
But here you are, Orestes, and it seems

---

[1] The first of many hints in the play of the effect on Orestes' psyche of his having, at Apollo's order, murdered his mother, Clytemnestra, to avenge his father's murder at her instigation. (See Aeschylus' *Agamemnon* and *Choephori*.)

A happier fate has brought you to Epirus.
The splendid trappings of your retinue
Are not those of a wretch who seeks to die.

ORESTES

Alas! who knows the fate that leads me here?   25
Love for a heartless girl has drawn me hither.
But who can tell the lot it has in mind,
And whether it is life or death I'll find?

PYLADES

Would you indeed, enslaved as you are now,
Entrust the issue of your life to love?   30
What spell makes you forget your passion's pains
And to submit once more to bear love's chains?
Do you think Hermione, in Sparta deaf,
Will show you greater favour in Epirus?
Ashamed of all your fruitless prayers and moans,   35
You hated her, and mentioned her no more.
Friend, you deceived me.

ORESTES

                    I deceived myself.
Please do not overwhelm a wretch who loves you.
To you my heart is an ever open book.
You saw my love take birth, my earliest sighs.   40
Indeed, when Menelaus[2] bestowed his daughter
On Pyrrhus, the avenger of his house,
You saw my anguish; you have seen me since
Dragging from sea to sea my chains and my despair.
Yes, in my abject state, against my will,   45
You followed me in misery everywhere
And, ever intervening in my frenzy,
From my own self you saved me every day.
But when I thought, indifferent to my fears,
Hermione showered all her charms on Pyrrhus,   50
You know how then my heart, provoked to rage,
Wished by forgetting her to punish her.

    [2] Brother of Orestes' father, Agamemnon, leader of the Greek expedition to
Troy.

To all, to me, my victory seemed complete;
I fancied all my ferment sprang from hate;
Cursing her pride and whittling down her beauty,   55
I challenged her to trouble me again.
And thus I thought to smother all my love.
In this deceptive calm I came to Greece;
I found her kings already deep in conclave,
Apparently perturbed about some peril.   60
I hastened thither, thinking war and fame
Would fill my mind with cares of greater weight;
That, with my spirit back to former health,
My heart at long last would be free of love.
But marvel at the Fates whose dire pursuit   65
Holds out for me the very trap I shun.
On every side I hear Pyrrhus abused;
All Greece is ringing with the clash of rumour:
False to his blood and promise he's accused
Of rearing at his court the foe of Greece,   70
The young Astyanax, Hector's sad son,
Last scion of Troy's buried line of kings.
I am informed to snatch her son from death
Andromache deceived the shrewd Ulysses,[3]
Who tore some other infant from her arms   75
And had him killed believing him her son.
They say, indifferent to Hermione,
My rival elsewhere bears his heart and crown;
Without believing, Menelaus is hurt,
Complaining of a marriage still postponed.   80
The very gloom in which his soul is steeped
Gives birth in mine to secret joy and hope;
I feel exultant, yet at first pretend
Revenge alone rekindles my excitement.
But soon the heartless girl resumed her sway.   85
I recognised my ill-extinguished flame;
I felt my hatred dwindle with my wrong,
Or rather felt I loved her all along:
And so I canvassed all the Greeks' support.

[3] One of the Greek leaders in the Trojan expedition, renowned for his cunning.
He is the hero of Homer's *Odysseus*, and appears also in Racine's *Iphigénie*.

They sent me here to Pyrrhus; hence my coming.   *90*
My mission is to try and tear from him
This child whose life endangers all our states:
Happy if I might, in my pressing passion,
Prise my princess from him and not Astyanax!
For do not fancy the most potent perils   *95*
Can hold at all in check my flaming love.
Since all my strivings to resist are vain,
My destiny now sweeps me blindly on.
I love: and come to seek Hermione,
To win her, snatch her, or else die before her.   *100*
You who know Pyrrhus, what does he intend?
What goes on in his Court and in his heart?
Is he still slave to my Hermione?
Pylades, will he give her back to me?

PYLADES

I would mislead you if I dared to promise   *105*
He would desire to place her in your power;
Not that he seems delighted at his conquest.
His heart has clear pronounced for Hector's widow;
He loves her madly. But this heartless widow
Has up to now repaid his love with hate;   *110*
And yet each day he's seen to hazard all
To woo his prisoner or intimidate her.
He utters threats against her son he hides,
And causes tears to flow, he promptly dries.
Hermione herself has often seen   *115*
Her harried lover creep beneath her sway,
And, bringing her the homage of his pleas,
Sigh at her feet less out of love than spleen.
You must not then expect at such a time
A guarantee for his ill-mastered heart: *120*
He might, my lord, he might, in his despair,
To spite his love, wed her he cannot bear.

ORESTES

But tell me how Hermione regards
Her marriage still postponed, her spell ignored?

PYLADES

Hermione, at least in outward show,   *125*
Seems to disdain the fickleness of Pyrrhus,
Imagining, too glad to melt her coldness,
He'll come to beg her to take back his heart.
But she in confidence has wept to me.
She secretly laments her beauty scorned.   *130*
Forever sailing and forever staying,
She sometimes calls Orestes to her aid.

ORESTES

Ah, if I thought it, I would rush, Pylades,
To throw myself . . .

PYLADES

                    Accomplish first your mission.
You await the King. Speak and impress on him,   *135*
The Greeks demand, with one voice, Hector's son.
Far from their capturing his mistress' son,
Their hatred will but aggravate his love.
The more they would embroil them, they'll unite them.
Insist, ask everything, to obtain nothing.   *140*
He's coming.

ORESTES

          Go, urge the cruel girl
To see me, who have come here but for her.

Exit PYLADES

SCENE II

Enter PYRRHUS *and* PHOENIX

ORESTES

Before the whole of Greece speaks through my voice,
Permit me to express, my lord, the honour
And joy I feel to see before me stand   *145*

Achilles' son, and conquerer of Troy.
Just as your father's, we admire your feats:
Hector laid low by him and Troy by you;
And you have shown us by your comely dash
Achilles' son alone could fill his place.   *150*
But what he'd not have done, Greece sees, with pain,
You championing the woes of Trojan blood,
And being moved by an unworthy pity
Maintaining what escaped from such a war.
My lord, can you forget what Hector was?   *155*
Our weakened population still remembers.
Our widows, daughters, shudder at his name;
And in all Greece there's not a family
That does not call to account his wretched son
For husbands, fathers, snatched from them by Hector.   *160*
And who knows what one day this son may dare?
Perhaps we'll see him falling on our harbours,
Setting our ships alight, just like his sire,
And chasing them on the seas with fire and sword.
May I, my lord, avow my inmost thought?   *165*
You should yourself fear how your care's repaid,
Lest perhaps this serpent nurtured in your breast
Might one day sting you for preserving him.
Give satisfaction to the will of Greece,
Assure her vengeance and assure your life;   *170*
Suppress a foe who's dangerous the more
Since he relies on you to fight against her.

PYRRHUS

Greece need not be so anxious for my sake.
I fancied greater cares were troubling her;
And, from so famous an ambassador,   *175*
I had imagined that her plans were grander.
Who would have fancied such an enterprise
Deserved the care of Agamemnon's son;
That a whole nation, famed in victory,
Would deign to plot the death of a mere child?   *180*
To whom, my lord, am I to sacrifice him?
Does Greece still have some right upon his life?

Of all the Greeks am I the only one
Unable to dispose of my own captive?
Yes, when beneath the smoking walls of Troy 185
The bloodstained victors shared out all their spoils,
Fate, whose decrees were at that time obeyed,
Gave me Andromache: with her, her son.
Hecuba[4] took her life beside Ulysses;
Cassandra[5] went to Argos with your father. 190
Have I laid claim to any of their slaves?
Have I enjoyed the fruits of their exploits?
They murmur, Troy one day may rise again,
That Hector's son, if spared, would see me slain.
My lord, such vigilance must importune: 195
I cannot from so far foresee misfortune.
I think on what Troy was, in days gone by,
So rich in heroes, all her ramparts high,
Mistress of Asia; and, in brief, I see
What was the fate of Troy, her destiny. 200
Charred towers I only view and scattered shields,
A river running blood, deserted fields,
A child in chains; let them think what they will,
Can Troy in such state dream on vengeance still?
Bah! if the death of Hector's son was sworn, 205
Why have me put it off for one whole year?
Why was he not undone in Priam's arms?
We should have crushed him by Troy's heaps of
dead.
Then all was proper: old men, suckling babes,
Relied in vain for safety on their weakness; 210
Victory and night more cruel far than we,
Incited us to kill in dire confusion.
My anger showed no mercy to the vanquished.
But must my cruelty survive my wrath?
Must I, despite the pity moving me, 215
Dip my hands leisurely in a child's blood?
No, let the Greeks some other prey enjoy,

---

[4] Hecuba, wife of Priam King of Troy, and mother of Hector and Cassandra.
[5] Cassandra's gift of doleful prophecy foretold her own and Agamemnon's murder. (See Aeschylus' *Agamemnon*.)

And elsewhere hunt what still remains of Troy:
The spate of my hostility is stayed;
Epirus will save henceforth what Troy saved.   *220*

ORESTES

My lord, you know full well how cunningly
A false Astyanax went to the death
That was reserved for Hector's son alone.
It is not Troy but Hector who is hunted.
Upon the son, the Greeks pursue the sire;   *225*
Blood-surfeited, he bought their anger dearly.
Only his blood can drown their living hate;
It may incite them here right to Epirus!
Forestall them.

PYRRHUS

No, no. I agree with joy:
In Epirus let them seek a second Troy;   *230*
Let them confuse their hate, no more distinguish
The blood that made them conquer from the conquered's.
It will by no means be the first injustice
With which Achilles' work has been rewarded.
Hector, himself, great profit from it drew;   *235*
His son, in turn, might some day profit too.

ORESTES

So Greece must find in you a rebel son?

PYRRHUS

To be her slave, have I but fought and won?

ORESTES

Hermione, my lord, will stay your ire:
Her eyes will come between you and her sire.   *240*

PYRRHUS

Hermione may still be dear to me;
I may be hers, but not her father's slave;

Perhaps some day I'll reconcile the needs
Of my own greatness with those of my love.
Meanwhile you may as well see Helen's daughter: 245
I know how near the ties of blood that bind you.
Thereafter I will not detain you more,
And you may tell the Greeks of my refusal.

Exit ORESTES

SCENE III

PHOENIX

So thus you send him to his mistress' feet!

PYRRHUS

They say he has long worshipped the Princess.   250

PHOENIX

What if his flame were to rekindle now?
If he poured out his heart and made her love him?

PYRRHUS

Ah! Phoenix, let them love: let her depart.
Let them both deep in love return to Sparta:
They have the freedom of our ports to sail.   255
How much embarrassment I would be spared!

PHOENIX

My lord . . .

PYRRHUS

Another time I'll tell you all:
Andromache's here.

Exit PHOENIX

SCENE IV

Enter ANDROMACHE *and* CEPHISE

PYRRHUS

Were you seeking me?
Might I permit myself so sweet a thought?

ANDROMACHE

I was going where my son is under guard.   260
Since you allow me once a day to see
The only treasure Troy and Hector left me,
I was about to weep awhile with him;
He has not been embraced by me today.

PYRRHUS

The Greeks, my lady, if I heed their fears,   265
Will give you soon much greater cause for tears.

ANDROMACHE

And what can this fear be that grips their hearts,
My lord? Is there some Trojan spared by you?

PYRRHUS

Their hate for Hector is by no means quenched.
They fear his son.

ANDROMACHE

O such a worthy fear!   270
A hapless child who does not know as yet
Pyrrhus his master is, nor Hector, father.

PYRRHUS

But nonetheless the Greeks demand his death.
The son of Agamemnon comes to press it.

ANDROMACHE

Will you pronounce so cruel a decree?　　　　　275
Do you find him criminal because of me?
You do not fear he will avenge his father,
But that he wipe away his mother's tears.
To me he would have been a father, husband;
But I must lose all, always by your blows.　　　280

PYRRHUS

Your tears have been forestalled by my refusal,
The whole of Greece now threatens me with war;
But even were they to traverse the seas
With a thousand vessels, clamouring for your son;
Were all the blood to flow that Helen shed;　　　285
Were I to see my palace all in ashes,
I will not hesitate, but speed to save him:
I'll shield his life at the expense of mine.
But mid these dangers, that I risk for you,
Will you refuse to look on me less coldly?　　　290
Hated by all the Greeks, on all sides hemmed,
Must I by your reproach be still condemned?
I offer you my sword. Have I some clue
You will accept my heart that worships you?
In fighting for you, may I feel sure, please,　　　295
You'll not be ranged among my enemies?

ANDROMACHE

What are you doing? What will Greece be saying?
Why must so great a heart show so much weakness?
Do you want so fine, so generous a plan,
To be scoffed at as just a lovesick whim?　　　300
Sad captive that I am, weary of living,
Can you indeed be wanting me to love you?
What beauty can you find in my poor eyes
That you have sentenced to eternal tears?
No; to respect an enemy's misfortune,　　　305
To save the wretched, grant my son to me,
Fighting for him against a hundred peoples,
Not make me buy his safety with my heart,

Give him asylum, if need be, despite me:
Such tasks are worthy of Achilles' son.   *310*

PYRRHUS

What, will your anger never run its course?
Can hate and punishment remain eternal?
True, I have caused some suffering, and Phrygia
Has often seen my hands red with your blood.
But how your eyes have taken toll of me!   *315*
How dear they've sold to me the tears they've shed!
Of what remorse have they not made me toy!
I suffer all the pains I caused to Troy.
Vanquished and fettered, penitent I sit,
Seared by a greater flame than e'er I lit,   *320*
My restless tears and all my passion true . . .
Ah! was I ever so unkind as you?
But we have hurt each other quite enough;
Our common enemies should make us one.
My lady, tell me only I may hope,   *325*
I will restore your son and be his father;
Myself I'll teach him to avenge the Trojans;
I'll punish Greece for your wrongs and for mine.
I can dare all, inspired by your eyes:
Your Ilion from its ashes yet may rise;   *330*
In less time than the Greeks took till they won,
I may rebuild its walls and crown your son.

ANDROMACHE

My lord, my heart is far from all this greatness:
We might have dreamt of this had Hector lived.
No, do not hope to see us evermore,   *335*
O sacred walls, my Hector could not save.
My lord, a smaller boon befits the wretched,
My tears ask only you should exile me.
Permit me far from Greece, far even from you,
To hide my son and to lament my husband.   *340*
Your love will kindle too much hate against us:
Return, once more return to Helen's daughter.

PYRRHUS

How can I do so? How you goad my pain!
Can I give back my heart that you retain?
I know I have been pledged to marry her;   *345*
I know she came to be Epirus' Queen;
The Fates have brought you both to Epirus' shores:
You, to obey; and her, to give commands.
Yet have I taken any pains to please her?
Who would not think, finding, on the contrary,   *350*
Your beauty regnant and her charms unseen,
She is the captive here and you the Queen?
Ah! how much joy would but a single sigh
Of mine give her, of all I breathe for you!

ANDROMACHE

And why should she reject your welcome sighs?   *355*
Is she oblivious of your former ties?
Do Troy and Hector stand between you both?
Does duty bind her to her husband's troth?
And what a husband! monstrous memory!
His death alone immortalized your father.[6]   *360*
To Hector's blood his fame entire he owes,
And both of you are known but through my woes.

PYRRHUS

My lady, very well. I must obey you:
I must forget or rather I must hate you.
The tide of my desire has swelled too high   *365*
For it to ebb to mere indifference.
Think well! henceforth my heart, since it no more
Can love intensely, must intensely hate.
I'll stop at nothing in my righteous rage:
The son will answer for his mother's scorn;   *370*
Greece summons him and I will no more put
My fame in jeopardy to save the thankless.

---

[6] Achilles' most famous feat was his victorious duel with Hector. (Depicted in Homer's *Iliad*, XXII.)

ANDROMACHE

Alas! then he will die. His sole defence
His mother's tears, his pretty innocence.
And after all, perhaps, in my sad state,   *375*
His death will mark the end of all my pain.
For his sake I prolonged my wretched life;
Upon his death I'll go to join his sire.
And thus, my lord, the three of us united
By your hands ...

PYRRHUS

            Go, my lady, see your son.   *380*
Perhaps on seeing him, your love, when tried,
Will not still take your anger for its guide.
I'll see you once again to learn our fates.
As you embrace, think, think, he can be saved!

ACT II

SCENE I

HERMIONE

I am obliging you. Yes, he may see me: 385
I'm willing still to let him have that bliss.
Pylades soon will bring him here to me;
But in my heart I know I should not see him.

CLEONE

What is there fatal in your seeing him?
My lady, is he not the same Orestes   390
Whose coming you desired a hundred times,
Whose constancy and steadfast love you missed?

HERMIONE

It is this very love, so ill-requited,
That makes his presence in this place so grim.
What bitter shame for me, what triumph for him,   395
To see his anguish equalled by my ache!
"Is that the proud Hermione?"—he'll say—
"She spurned me once, another jilts her now.
She put so great a price upon her heart,
But now in her turn feels the sting of scorn."   400
Ah, gods!

CLEONE

        Forget such baseless fears:
Your beauty holds him too fast in its power.
Do you think an ardent suitor will offend?

He brings you back a love he cannot hide.
But tell me what your father's orders are.   405

HERMIONE

If Pyrrhus still keeps on prevaricating,
If he refuses to give up the Trojan,
My father orders me to leave at once.

CLEONE

Well then, my lady, listen to Orestes.
Pyrrhus began it, you must make an end.   410
Propriety demands you should forestall him.
Have you not told me that you hated him?

HERMIONE

Do I hate him! My honour is at stake,
After so much affection—all forgotten.
He who was once so dear, and who betrayed!   415
Ah! I have loved him too much not to hate him.

CLEONE

Leave him, my lady, and since you are loved . . .

HERMIONE

Ah! let me have some time to feed my fury
And steel my heart against my enemy.
I wish to leave him weltering in my loathing.   420
He'll do his best to welter—faithless wretch!

CLEONE

Must you still stay to suffer some fresh insult?
To love a captive, love her in your sight,
Is all that not enough to make you loathe him?
After what he has done, what's more to do?   425
No more to make you loathe him, if you could.

HERMIONE

Why must you stir the embers of my anguish?
I fear to face my heart in my sad state.

Try and forget all that you may have seen;
Believe I love no more and praise my will;   430
Believe my heart is hardened in its hate;
Ah! if you can, make me believe it too.
You wish me to depart. Well! nothing stops me:
Let's go, and envy his base love no more.
Upon his mind let her exert her beauty.   435
Come quick—But if he came back to his duty!
If faith within his heart were to return!
If, at my feet, forgiveness he should earn!
If thou, Love, couldst subject him to my will!
If he—But oh! he only wrongs me still.   340
Then let me stay to mar their merriment;
Let me delight in their embarrassment;
Or forcing him to break his solemn pledge,
Let's goad all Greece to brand his sacrilege.
So far I've urged them but the son pursue;   445
I'll make them now demand the mother too.
I'll pay her back the hell she makes me suffer:
Yield him she must or he must be her slayer.

CLEONE

Do you believe her ever tearful eyes
Find any joy in rivalling your own,   450
And that a heart, weighed down by so much care,
Solicited the sighs of her tormentor?
Just see if they at all appease her grief.
Why then the woes in which her soul is steeped?
Why all this pride against a welcome lover?   455

HERMIONE

Alas! I trusted him to my undoing.[7]
I did not hold back anything from him
And freely opened out to him my heart.
I did not shield my eyes with mock reserve;
As my love prompted, so I spoke to him.   460
And who would not have done the same as I

---

[7] Like a character in Chekhov, centuries later, Hermione ignores Cleone's
questions and continues with her own passionate thoughts.

Where love so solemnly was sworn as ours?
Did he look on me then as he looks now?
Do you remember how all spoke for him?
My house avenged; the Greeks ablaze with joy,   465
Our ships weighed down beneath the spoils of Troy,
His father's exploits rivalled by his own,
His fire, that keener even than mine had grown,
My heart, and you too, blinded by his fame,
Before I blame him, you are all to blame.   470
But now enough! Whatever Pyrrhus be,
My heart is moved, Orestes still loves me.
Though yet unloved, at least he knows to woo;
Perhaps he'll teach me how to love him too.
Then let him come to me.

CLEONE

Princess, he's here—   475

HERMIONE

Ah me! I did not think he was so near.

SCENE II

Enter ORESTES

HERMIONE

May I believe, my lord, a trace of love
Has brought you here to seek a sad Princess?
Or should I put down to your duty only
The happy urge that led you here to see me?   480

ORESTES

Such is the fatal blindness of my love.
You know it all too well; Orestes' lot
Prescribes he ever come to worship you,
And swear forever he will never come.
I know your eyes will open all my wounds,   485

With every step towards you I am forsworn:
I know and blush, but call the Gods to witness,
Who saw the anguish of my last good-bye,
That I have sought out climes where my sure doom
Would have fulfilled my vows and stilled my pain.   490
I've begged for death in strange and cruel lands,
Where only human blood appeased their Gods:
Their temple barred to me, these barbarous folk
Fastidiously disdained my lavish blood.
At last I come to you and am reduced   495
To seeking in your eyes elusive death.
My dark despair needs only their indifference:
They have but to forbid the slightest hope,
To expedite the death to which I run;
They've but to say once what they've always said.   500
For one year this alone kept me alive.
Lady, it falls on you to take a victim
The Scythians would have long since snatched from you,
If I had any found as cruel as you!

HERMIONE

Come leave aside, my lord, this mournful talk.   505
Greece has engaged you for more urgent tasks.
Why speak of Scythia and my cruelty?
Remember all the kings you represent.
Must their revenge depend upon your whims?
Is it Orestes' blood they are demanding?   510
Fulfil the mission that has brought you here.

ORESTES

Pyrrhus' refusal puts an end to that.
I'm sent back empty-handed; another power
Makes him embrace the cause of Hector's son.

HERMIONE

The recreant!

ORESTES

Thus, ready to depart,   515

I come to ask you what's to be my fate.
I think I hear already the reply
That secretly your aversion makes against me.

HERMIONE

What's that? Forever gloomily unjust,
Will you forever moan of my aversion?   520
What is this coldness you accuse me of?
I came here to Epirus as commanded:
My father ordered it; but who knows whether
I have not since in secret shared your grief?
Do you think you only fell a prey to fears?   525
That Epirus never saw me full of tears?
In fact, who said to you despite my duty
I did not sometimes wish to see you here?

ORESTES

You, wish to see me! Ah, divine Princess . . .
But are you really saying this to me?   530
Open your eyes: Orestes stands before you,
Orestes, so long object of their scorn.

HERMIONE.

Yes, you whose love, engendered by their spell,
First taught them the full meaning of their power;
You, whose great virtues forced me to esteem you;   535
You, whom I pitied and would like to love.

ORESTES

I understand. Such is my wretched lot:
Your heart for Pyrrhus; wishes for Orestes.

HERMIONE

Do not desire the destiny of Pyrrhus:
I'd hate you far too much.

ORESTES

                      You'd love me more.   540
With what a different eye you'd look on me!
You wish to love me and I cannot please you;

Then love alone enforcing its dominion
Would make you love me though you wished to hate.
O gods! all my esteem and sweet affection . . .   545
How many tongues for me if you'd but hear!
You are today alone Pyrrhus' champion,
Perhaps despite yourself, surely despite him.
He scorns you, does he not? Elsewhere beguiled,
His heart . . .

HERMIONE

       Who said to you he scorns me, Sir?   550
His looks, his speech, have they told you as much?
Do you believe my beauty may be scorned,
That it can kindle but a flickering love?
Others perhaps more highly prize my charm.

ORESTES

Go on; how sweet of you to taunt me thus.   555
Am I the one, you heartless girl, who scorns you?
My constancy has not yet wearied you?
Am I the one, your eyes have failed to move?
The one who scorned them? How they'd love to see
My rival scorn their influence just like me!   560

HERMIONE

His hate or love does not affect me, Sir.
Go, arm the whole of Greece against a rebel:
And let him pay the price of his rebellion;
Let's make Epirus yet another Ilion.
Go—can you now persist I love him still?   565

ORESTES

Do more, my lady, come to Greece yourself.
Do you intend to stay behind as hostage?
Come, let your eyes in every heart strike umbrage.
Let's join our hate to fight him—you and me.

HERMIONE

But, say he were to wed Andromache?   570

ORESTES

What's that?

HERMIONE

Ah, think how deep for us the shame
If husband of a Phrygian he became!

ORESTES

And you hate him? Confess—you but impart
Love's not a passion hidden in the heart!
Everything betrays us, speech, silence, eyes;   575
And flames that are ill-choked but higher rise.

HERMIONE

My lord, I clearly see your partial mind
Injects into my words its murderous poison,
Forever seeks to twist my every meaning,
Believing in me hate is spelt as love.   580
I will be plain; thereafter you may act.
You know my duty brought me to this place;
My duty keeps me here. I cannot sail
Until my sire or Pyrrhus bids me go.
Go, tell him on behalf of Menelaus,   585
No foe of Greece may be his son-in-law:
Between Troy's son and me let him decide;
Which of us two does he intend to hold?
Either he sends me back or gives him up.
Farewell. If he agrees, I'll follow you.   590

Exeunt HERMIONE *and* CLEONE

SCENE III

ORESTES (*Alone*)

Yes, you shall come with me, make no mistake:
I guarantee you now he will agree.
Indeed, I have no fear he will retain her:

His eyes are quite eclipsed by his dear Trojan;
All women else repel him and perhaps   595
He seeks a pretext to be rid of her.
I only have to speak. Enough, what bliss
To snatch from him a prey as sweet as this!
Save all that still remains of Troy, of Hector,
His son, his widow, yet a thousand others,   600
Epirus: as long as Hermione
May never more thy shores nor ruler see.
But soft, he's led here by a chance most kind.
I'll speak. O Love, ordain his eyes stay blind!

SCENE IV

Enter PYRRHUS *and* PHOENIX

PYRRHUS

Ah, there you are my lord! I must confess   605
I brushed aside your arguments too soon;
Reflecting further since I saw you last
I've recognised their force and felt their fitness.
I thought, like you, I might have been untrue
To Greece, to great Achilles, to myself;   610
That I was raising Troy and damaging
All that my father, all that I had done.
No more do I condemn the Greeks' just anger;
Your victim will be soon delivered to you.

ORESTES

My lord, this wise and hard decision—   615
Procures peace at the price of luckless blood.[7a]

PYRRHUS

Yes. But I wish to strengthen it still more:
Hermione's the pledge of lasting peace;

[7a] In deference to Dr. Wheatley's just criticism in her Introduction to Volume II, this should read: "My lord, this wise and hard decision—/It buys peace at the price of luckless blood."

I'll wed her. Such a happy ceremony
Requires but a witness of your rank.   620
There you will represent Greece and her father,
For in you Menelaus beholds his brother.
Go, see her then and tell her that tomorrow
I shall await her hand from you, with peace.

ORESTES

Ah gods!

Exit ORESTES

SCENE V

PYRRHUS

Well Phoenix, is love master still?   625
Will you persist in knowing me so ill?

PHOENIX

Ah, Sire! I find you true; and this fine anger
Has brought you back to Greece and to yourself.
You are no more the toy of a base passion,
But Pyrrhus, son and rival of Achilles,   630
Whom high repute brings back beneath her sway,
Who triumphs over Troy a second day.

PYRRHUS

Say rather that today begins my victory.
From this day only may I vaunt my fame;
And now my heart, as proud as once submissive,   635
Feels it has crushed a thousand foes with love.
Think, Phoenix, from what troubles I escape,
What crowds of ills love carries in its wake,
How many friends and duties sacrificed,
What risks . . . One look would have thrown all aside. 640
All Greece united would have drowned a rebel.
To think for her I ran to meet my death.

PHOENIX

I bless the happy cruelty, my lord,
That makes . . .

PYRRHUS

You've seen how she has treated me.
I thought, when seeing her weep upon her son,   645
She would be forced to give herself to me.
I went to see how her embraces ended:
I found but tears mingled with vehemence.
Grief soured her and made her ever wilder,
A hundred times she moaned the name of Hector.   650
In vain I told her I would save her son:
"He's Hector," she would say embracing him;
"I see his eyes, his mouth, his budding courage;
"Ah! it is you, dear husband, I embrace."
And what does she imagine? Does she hope   655
I'll leave to her a son to feed her love?

PHOENIX

Why certainly. That was her prize for you.
My lord, forget her.

PYRRHUS

I know whence her hope:
Her beauty makes her sure; despite my anger,
She proudly sees me once more at her feet.   660
I'll see her first at mine, quite unconcerned.
She's Hector's widow; I, Achilles' son.
Too deep a hatred separates us two.

PHOENIX

Begin, my lord, by naming her no more.
Go, see Hermione and at her feet   665
Drown in her happiness your very wrath.
Make her consent to marry you, yourself.
Should you rely upon a rival's tongue?
He's deep in love.

PYRRHUS

If I wed her, do you think
Andromache in secret will be jealous?   670

PHOENIX

What? always dreaming of Andromache?
What matters, gods! her joy or jealousy?
What spell, despite you, draws you to her side?

PYRRHUS

No, I have not told her all I should tell:
She did not see my fury in full flow;   675
She does not know how much I am her foe.
Let's go to her. I want to face her straight
And give free rein to my unbridled hate.
Come, see her beauty trampled. It will please
you.

PHOENIX

Yes, my lord, I'll see you on your knees,   680
And swearing to her how you worship her,
Encourage her once more to fresh disdain.

PYRRHUS

Do you imagine, ready to excuse her
My heart runs after her in reconcilement?

PHOENIX

You love her: it's enough.

PYRRHUS

I love the wretch?   685
When love has made her hate but further swell?
With kinsmen none, no hope but me, distraught,
I may despatch her son; perhaps I ought.
A stranger in Epirus, no, a slave,
I offer her, son, kingdom, all I have;   690
And all her false heart grants to me, her suitor,
Is the dark posture of her persecutor!
No, no, I've sworn, my wrath is in full spate:

Let me at least once justify her hate.
I'll yield her son. How many tears will rain!   695
What dire name will she call me in her pain!
What dreadful scenes—to see him in death's jaws!
Phoenix, she'll die, and I shall be the cause.
I should myself be butchering her heart.

PHOENIX

Then why impart aloud such an intent?   700
Why did you not consult your weakness earlier?

PYRRHUS

I understand. Forgive my trace of feeling.
But do you fear my anger's overcome?
It is the last spark of my dying love.
I will be guided by your counsels. Come,   705
Must I yield him? And see Hermione?

PHOENIX

Yes, see her, and, my lord, while still you woo,
Protest . . .

PYRRHUS

All I have promised I will do.

ACT III

SCENE I

PYLADES

Please, please, my lord, calm your extreme distemper.
I do not know you, you are not yourself.   710
May I . . .

ORESTES

       No, no, I want no more advice,
Pylades, I am sick of being calm.
My life is much too drawn out and my anguish:
I must abduct her or else I must die.
It is decided; I must execute it.   725 715
I simply must.

PYLADES

       Well then, let us abduct her:
I am with you. But ponder where you are.
What will they think of you to see you thus?
Dissimulate; control your agitation,
And also make your eyes maintain the secret.   720
These guards, the court, the very air you breathe
Depend on Pyrrhus; Hermione the most.
Above all hide your anger from her eyes.
O gods! in this wild state why did you seek her?

ORESTES

Do I know? Was I master of myself?   725

Carried away by rage, I came perhaps
To threaten both the wanton and her lover.

PYLADES

What was the point of this intemperance?

ORESTES

And who would not be shattered even like me
By such a blow as has just sapped my mind?   730
He says he weds Hermione tomorrow;
To honour me, he'll take her from my hand!
Ah! rather would this hand in his black blood . . .

PYLADES

You blame him, Sir, for this strange turn of fate:
Yet, tortured as he is by his own plans,   735
He's worthy of our pity, just like you.

ORESTES

No, no, I know him, my despair elates him;
Did I not love, he'd scorn Hermione;
Before I loved, her beauty left him cold:
Only to spite me will he marry her.   740
Ah gods! I'd almost won her and she was
About to vanish from his sight forever.
Torn between love and hate she but awaited
A 'no' from him to give her heart to me.
Her eyes were opening and her ear was mine.   745
She pitied me. One word would have sufficed.

PYLADES

You really think so?

ORESTES

What? The hate she swore
Against him . . .

PYLADES

Never did she love him more.

Even if Pyrrhus handed her to you,
Some pretext, ready made, would have detained her.   750
If I were you, sick of her callous charm,
I'd not abduct, but flee from her forever.
You would be burdened with a chafing fury
Who'd curse you and would wish throughout your life,
In bitter recollection of a marriage   755
Almost . . .

ORESTES

          That's why I wish to kidnap her.
Else all would smile for her, and only I
Would be abandoned to a sterile rage.
Must I away from her try to forget?
No, no, this time she'll have to share my torture.   760
Too long I've moaned alone. I'm sick of pity.
The heartless girl must fear me in her turn;
I want her cruel eyes, in constant tears,
To call me all the names I gave to her.

PYLADES

Is this to be your mission's splendid end?   765
Orestes, ravisher!

ORESTES

          What then, my friend?
What if, my task fulfilled should please our peoples?
Will not my tears then please her all the more?
What is the good of Greece's admiration,
If I should be the byword of Epirus?   770
What do you want, my friend? To tell you truly,
My innocence begins to weary me.
I know not why some dark divinity
Forgets the guilty, hunts the innocent.
However I may look upon myself,   775
I see woes only that condemn the Gods.
Let me deserve their anger, earn their hate,

And let crime's fruit precede its punishment.
But why, dear friend, must you deflect on you
An anger that has only me for target?   780
My friendship, far too long, has crippled you:
O shun a wretch, forsake a guilty man.
Dear, dear Pylades, your compassion blinds you.
Leave me my peril, since I seek its fruit.
Take to the Greeks this child that Pyrrhus gives me.   785
Go, go.

PYLADES

We will abduct Hermione.
A generous heart shines best when perils prove;
What cannot friendship do when led by love?
Let's go and prick the zeal of all your Greeks;
Our ships are ready, favourable the wind.   790
I know the dim recesses of this palace:
You see the waves caress its very walls;
Tonight, without fail, brought to you in secret,
Your victim will be carried to your ship.

ORESTES

I take too much advantage of your friendship.   795
Forgive my troubles, you alone have pitied.
Excuse a wretch who loses all he loves,
Whom every man must hate, who hates himself.
Why cannot I in my turn do for you . . .

PYLADES

My lord, dissimulate: that's all I ask.   800
Beware your plan be not too soon disclosed:
Forget meanwhile Hermione is heartless;
Forget your love. I see her coming here.

ORESTES

Answer for her, and for myself I'll answer.

Exit PYLADES

SCENE II

Enter HERMIONE *and* CLEONE

ORESTES

Princess, my efforts have restored your conquest.   805
I've seen Pyrrhus. All's ready for your marriage.

HERMIONE

So I have heard. I've also been informed
You merely wanted me to tell me this.

ORESTES

You wish then to conform with his designs?

HERMIONE

Who would have fancied Pyrrhus was not false?   810
That he would wait so long to show his love
And come to me when I was leaving him?
I wish to think with you he fears the Greeks,
Consults his interests rather than his heart;
That my fond glances meant much more to you.   815

ORESTES

He loves you and I question it no more.
Do not your eyes achieve all they desire?
And doubtless you did not desire to thwart him.

HERMIONE

What can I do, my lord? They pledged my hand.
May I take from him what I have not given?   820
Love does not rule the fate of a princess:
We're only left the honour of obeying.
Yet I was going; and for your sake only
You've seen how far I fell short of my duty.

ORESTES

How well you knew, you cruel . . . But, my lady,   825
Each one is free to love or not to love.
You too were free—I hoped; still you could love
Without your having first to filch from me.
I blame you therefore less than I blame fate.
But why should you be wearied with my plaint?   830
Such is your duty, I confess; and mine
Is to spare you this sorry interview.

Exit ORESTES

SCENE III

HERMIONE

Cleone, did you think he'd be so calm?

CLEONE

A silent grief is to be feared the more.
I pity him all the more deeply since   835
He is himself the author of his anguish.
How very long your wedding was postponed!
He spoke and Pyrrhus instantly agreed.

HERMIONE

You think that Pyrrhus fears? What should he fear?
Men, who for ten years Hector put to flight,   840
Who ten times trembled in Achilles' absence,
And sought asylum in their burning ships,
And whom we still should see, were't not for Pyrrhus,
Demanding Helen of the undaunted Trojans?
Cleone, no, he's not his inward foe;   845
He wills his actions; if he weds, he loves.
But let Orestes blame me for his woes:
Must we forever talk about his tears?
Pyrrhus returns to me, my dear Cleone,
Can you conceive how deep my happiness?   850

Can you appraise his greatness? Have you heard
Tell all his exploits . . . Who can count them all?
Dauntless and shadowed everywhere by victory,
Charming, yes, faithful; the essence of perfection,
Think . . .

CLEONE

   Hush, your rival's coming here in tears   *855*
Doubtless to place her sorrows at your feet.

HERMIONE

Gods! May I not be happy, unintruded?
Let's go, what could I say?

SCENE IV

Enter ANDROMACHE *and* CEPHISE

ANDROMACHE

      Where are you fleeing,
My lady? How you must be gratified,
With Hector's widow weeping at your feet!   *860*
I have not come, a prey to jealous tears,
To envy you a heart your beauty conquers.
A cruel hand cut down before my eyes
The only lover I could ever love.
Hector alone once set my heart on fire;   *865*
I've seen it in his grave with him expire.
But I still have a son. You'll know some day
How strong upon a mother's heart his sway;
But you will never know, may Heaven forbid,
The mortal cares a child can make us suffer,   *870*
When of so many blessings we might taste
He is the sole remaining—and is threatened.
Alas! when weary of ten years of dolour,
The Trojans angrily attacked your mother,
I made my Hector run to be her shield.   *875*

Your power on Pyrrhus is like mine on Hector.
Why fear a child who just survives his sire?
Let me conceal him on some desert isle.
His mother's lessons spell tranquility
And he will only learn to weep with me.   880

HERMIONE

I understand your grief. But duty bids
Me when my father speaks to hold my tongue.
He it is who is hardening Pyrrhus' heart.
To soften Pyrrhus you know best the art!
A long time now your eyes have made him purr.   885
Madam, persuade him: I shall not demur.

Exeunt HERMIONE *and* CLEONE

SCENE V

ANDROMACHE

With what disdain she throws aside my pleas!

CEPHISE

I'd follow her advice and seek out Pyrrhus.
One look from you would rout both her and Greece . . .
But see he comes to you.

SCENE VI

Enter PYRRHUS *and* PHOENIX

PYRRHUS (*To* PHOENIX)

   Where's the Princess?   890
Did you not tell me I should find her here?

PHOENIX

My lord, I did.

ANDROMACHE (*To* CEPHISE)

You see how strong my eyes.

PYRRHUS

What did she say?[8]

ANDROMACHE

Alas! I am forlorn.

PHOENIX

My lord, let's go and find Hermione.

CEPHISE

Why dally, break your obdurate reserve.   895

ANDROMACHE

He's sworn to yield my son.

CEPHISE

He's still not yielded.

ANDROMACHE

No, no, my tears are vain; his death is settled.

PYRRHUS

She does not even deign to look at us.
What haughtiness!

ANDROMACHE

I'll but annoy him further,
Let's go.

PYRRHUS

Come, give the Greeks the son of Hector.   900

[8] The conversations continue aside between the two men, and between the two
ladies, till Andromache's outburst, "Ah! stop, my lord," etc.

ANDROMACHE

Ah! stop, my lord, what are you going to do?
If you will give the son, then give me too.
You swore just now for me your deepest love!
Gods! may I not at least your pity move?
Have you condemned me with no hope of pardon?   *905*

PYRRHUS

Phoenix is witness, I have given my word.

ANDROMACHE

And you were going to brave such perils for me!

PYRRHUS

I was then blind; my eyes are now wide open.
You could have had his pardon for the asking,
But you refused to ask for it at all.   *910*
It is too late.

ANDROMACHE

                Ah! Majesty, you heard
No dearth of sighs, that feared to be repulsed.
Forgive my high and honourable rank
This last reserve that hates to be obtrusive.
As you well know, Andromache would never,   *915*
Were't not for you, embrace a master's knees.

PYRRHUS

No, no, you hate me; deep within your heart,
You fear to be indebted to my love.
This very son you fondle and caress,
If I had saved him, you would love him less.   *920*
Your hatred and your scorn for me increase;
You hate me far more than the whole of Greece.
Delight at leisure in your noble anger.
I'm coming, Phoenix.

ANDROMACHE

                Husband! I am coming.

CEPHISE

Madam . . .

ANDROMACHE

What further could I say to him?   *925*
Author of all my ills, he knows them all.
My lord, behold the state to which you've dragged me.
I've seen my father dead, our walls on fire,
I've seen the slaughter of my house entire,
My bleeding husband draggled in the mud,   *930*
Captive with me, his only living blood.
How far a son will take us! I live, bound!
Still more: at times I found some consolation
My fate had sent me here and not elsewhere;
That lucky in his plight, my royal son,   *935*
Since he was doomed to serve, should be your slave.
I hoped his prison might become his refuge.
Achilles once esteemed defeated Priam:
I thought his son would show yet greater kindness.
Forgive, dear Hector, my believing blindness.   *940*
I could not dream your foe would stoop to crime;
I thought in spite of all he'd prove sublime.
Ah! if he would but leave us by the tomb
Raised by my care to your belovèd ashes,
And ending there his hatred and our pains   *945*
He would unite in death our dear remains!

PYRRHUS

Wait for me, Phoenix.

Exit PHOENIX

SCENE VII

PYRRHUS (*Continues*)

You, my lady, stay.
The son you weep may be restored to you.
Against my will, in moving you to tears,
I give you weapons that you turn against me.   *950*

I thought hard hate within my soul would rise.
But please, dear lady, let me see your eyes:
Just see if mine are those of a strict judge,
Or of an enemy who would distress you.
Why force me, you yourself, to do you wrong?   955
For your son's sake, let's no more hate each other.
Indeed, myself, I beg you now to save him.
Must I forever sigh for you to spare him?
Must I embrace your knees to plead for him?
For the last time, save him and save yourself.   960
I know what binding oaths I break for you,
How many hatreds on my head will rain.
I'll jilt Hermione and on her brow
Place not my crown but an eternal stain.
I'll lead you to the altar decked for her;   965
And place upon your brow her diadem.
But this is not an offer to decry:
I tell you, you must reign or you must die.
Made desperate by a year's ingratitude,
My heart can bear no more incertitude.   970
Too long to hope, fear, groan, intimidate!
It's death to lose you, but it's death to wait.
Think well: I leave you. I will come to take you,
To lead you to the temple, with your son:
And there you'll see me, with no further sighs,   975
Crown you, or slaughter him before your eyes.

Exit PYRRHUS

SCENE VIII

CEPHISE

Did I not prophesy, in spite of Greece,
You would still be the mistress of your fate?

ANDROMACHE

Alas! what was the use of all your talk!
I only had to sentence my own son.   980

CEPHISE

My lady, you've been loyal to your husband.
Too great a virtue might prove criminal.
Hector himself would ask you to agree.

ANDROMACHE

What? Must I give him Pyrrhus as successor?

CEPHISE

His son demands it, whom, else, they would kill.   985
Do you really think his shade would blush at this;
That he'd despise a royal conqueror,
Who'd give you back once more your ancient rank,
Who would in anger stamp upon your victors,
Who would forget Achilles was his father,   990
Who would belie his exploits, nullify them?

ANDROMACHE

Must I forget them, if he'll not remember?
Forget my Hector's loss of funeral rites,
His body dragged defeated round our walls?
Forget his father cast down at my feet,   995
His bleeding body clutching at the altar?
Think, think, Cephise, of that cruel night,
Which doomed a nation to eternal night.
Imagine Pyrrhus, with his glittering eyes,
Entering in the glare of our blazing mansions,   1000
Kicking aside my brothers' mangled corpses,
And slaked in blood inciting to fresh slaughter.
Do you hear the victors' shouts, the wounded's groans,
Choked by the flames or dying by the sword?
Do you see Andromache distraught with horror?   1005
Such is the way I first set eyes on Pyrrhus;
Such are the exploits that have crowned his fame;
Such is the husband you would thrust on me.
No, no, I'll not be party to his crimes;
If he so wills, let's be his final victims.   1010
I'd have to put a curb on all my feelings.

CEPHISE

Then we must see your son being sacrificed:
They but await your word. Why, you are shuddering!

ANDROMACHE

Ah! how your words strike deep into my heart!
What? Must I see my son now also die,   *1015*
My one delight and Hector's very image:
This son he left me as his passion's pledge?
Alas! Can I forget how on the day
He sought Achilles out, or rather death,
He called his son and took him in his arms?   *1020*
"Dear wife," he said to me and wiped my tears,
"I cannot tell how fate will turn this combat;
I leave my son to you, as my love's pledge:
If he should lose me, he will find me in you.
If dear to you is the memory of our marriage,   *1025*
Show to my son how much you loved his father."
Shall I then watch such precious blood being shed?
And, with him, let his ancestors all die?
O savage king, must my crime drag him down?
If I hate you, is he guilty of my hate?   *1030*
Has he reproached you with his father's death?
Has he complained of woes he does not feel?
But still, my son, you die unless I stay
The sword he holds poised just above your head.
I may deflect it—and I'll let it fall?   *1035*
No, no, you shall not die, I cannot bear it.
Let's go to Pyrrhus. But, Cephise, no,
Go find him for me.

CEPHISE

What am I to tell him?

ANDROMACHE

Tell him my mother love is strong enough . . .
Do you think, deep in his heart, he's sworn his death?   *1040*
Can passion push its savagery so far?

CEPHISE

My lady, in a rage he'll soon be back.

ANDROMACHE

Well then, assure him . . .

CEPHISE

What? Of your true faith?

ANDROMACHE

Alas! To promise it, am I still free?
O, husband's ashes! Trojans! O my father!   *1045*
My son, how dear your life is costing me!
Come.

CEPHISE

Where, my lady? What have you decided?

ANDROMACHE

Come to my husband's tomb to seek his guidance.

ACT IV

SCENE I

ANDROMACHE, CEPHISE

CEPHISE

My lady, I am sure it is your husband
Who has achieved this marvellous change in you.   *1050*
He wants Troy's greatness once again restored
By this dear son he wishes you to save.
Pyrrhus has promised, as you have just heard,
My lady. He awaited but your word.
Then trust his passion: certain of your heart,   *1055*
He puts throne, father, allies at your feet.
He makes you sovereign over him, his people.
Is this the victor, worthy of your hate?
Already nobly angry with the Greeks,
He's as concerned as you about your son.   *1060*
His guard protects him to forestall their rage;
He risks his own life to ensure your son's.
All's ready at the temple and you promised.

ANDROMACHE

Yes, I'll be there. But let me see my son.

CEPHISE

My lady, what's the hurry? From now on   *1065*
Whenever you may wish you'll see your son.
Soon you may lavish on him your attentions,
And no more will they count your each embrace.
What joy to rear a child, who's born to grace,

No more as slave raised for his master's scorn,   *1070*
But see with him so many kings reborn!

ANDROMACHE

Come, let me take of him a last farewell.

CEPHISE

What are you saying? Gods!

ANDROMACHE

        Dearest Cephise,
Between my heart and yours I keep no secret.
In my misfortunes you've been staunch and true,   *1075*
But in my turn I thought you better knew
Me. What? Did you think false Andromache
Might fail a husband who still breathes in me?
And that I might revive the bitter pain
Of all our dead, that I in peace might reign?   *1080*
Is such the love I swore his shade so often?
His son was dying and I had to save him.
Pyrrhus, in wedding me, swears to protect him.
It will suffice. I may rely on him.
I know what Pyrrhus is, violent but true;   *1085*
Yes, more than he has promised he will do.
I also may rely on Grecian rage:
Their hate will give my Hector's son a father.
Since it is clear I must be sacrificed,
I'll pledge to Pyrrhus my remaining life;   *1090*
When he makes me his promise at the altar,
I'll bind him to my son with lasting knots,
But prompt thereafter, fatal to me only,
My hand will cut short my unfaithful days,
And, saving thus my virtue, pay my debt   *1095*
To Pyrrhus, to my son, my husband, me.
This is the innocent cunning of my love.
This is what Hector has himself ordained.

Alone I'll join my husband and my sires.
Cephise, you, will have to close my eyes.   *1100*

CEPHISE

Ah, do not reckon I shall live beyond . . .

ANDROMACHE

Cephise, I forbid you follow me.
To you I leave the care of my one treasure:
If you once lived for me, live now for him.
Sole guardian of the final hope of Troy,   *1105*
Think, how so many monarchs need your aid.
Stand watch on Pyrrhus, make him keep his faith:
And if you must, I let you mention me.
Make him esteem our solemn marriage vows;
Tell him before I died, I was his wife,   *1110*
That he should let his injured feelings fade,
In leaving him my son, I proved my trust.
Let my son know the heroes of his race;
Lead him as far as possible in their trace.
Tell him by what great deeds they won their fame,   *1115*
Rather than what they were, what they became;
Speak of his father's virtues constantly,
And sometimes also speak to him of me.
But do not let him ever dream of vengeance:
He's left a master and should humour him.   *1120*
Make sure he's not too proud of his high lineage:
His blood is Hector's, but it is the last drop;
And for this drop in one day I have had
To sacrifice my blood and hate and love.

CEPHISE

Alas!

ANDROMACHE

Remain behind if at the prospect,   *1125*
You cannot hold your tears in silent check.

Someone is coming. Hide your tears, remember
That my immortal hope is in your hands.
It is Hermione. Let's shun her fury.

Exeunt ANDROMACHE *and* CEPHISE

SCENE II

Enter HERMIONE *and* CLEONE

CLEONE

Your silence, lady, leaves me wonderstruck.   *1130*
You still refuse to speak, has not his scorn
Provoked your temper in the very least?
You suffer calmly such a savage blow,
You who would shudder at her very name,
Who could not bear the thought without despair   *1135*
That he should deign to cast a glance at her?
He marries her, he gives her, with his crown,
The vows he has just pledged to you yourself,
And still your lips, despite these insults, sealed,
Refuse to open in his accusation!   *1140*
How much I fear this fatal calm, my lady!
And how much better . . .

HERMIONE

Is Orestes coming?

CLEONE

Yes, yes, my lady, and you may be sure
You will soon see him at your feet once more.
Ready to serve you with no hope of gain,   *1145*
He's sure to be enchanted by your glance.
But here he is.

SCENE III

Enter ORESTES

ORESTES

My lady, is it true
For once I see you at your own behest?
Is it perhaps some false hope flattering me?
Have you indeed desired me to be here?   *1150*
Am I to think, no more averse to me,
You wish . . .

HERMIONE

I wish to know if you still love me.

ORESTES

If I still love you? Gods! my vows, false oaths,
My flight, return, esteem and all my wrongs,
My dark despair, my eyes forever wet,   *1155*
If you do not heed them, what will you heed?

HERMIONE

Avenge me, I heed all.

ORESTES

At once, my lady:
Let's set the whole of Greece once more on fire:
Let's take, in citing your name and my arm
You, Helen's place and Agamemnon's, me.   *1160*
To Epirus let us bring Troy's misery,
And let them speak of us as of our sires.
Let's go, all's ready.

HERMIONE

No, my lord, let's stay:
I will not take such wrongs so far away.

What, must I crown the insolence of my foes   *1165*
By waiting elsewhere for a slow revenge?
Must I postpone it to the battle's chance
That in the end may not at all avenge?
Epirus, when I leave, with tears must shower.
If you'll avenge, avenge me in an hour.   *1170*
All your delays, I read as mere refusals.
Run to the temple. You must kill . . .

ORESTES

                              Whom?

HERMIONE

                                        Pyrrhus.

ORESTES

Pyrrhus, my lady?

HERMIONE

                    What? Your hatred wavers?
Go, run, and fear lest I may call you back.
Do not assert his claims I would forget;   *1175*
And you should not be pleading for him yet.

ORESTES

I plead for him? My lady, all your favours
Have carved too deep his crimes upon my soul.
Let's take revenge, but in some other way.
Let's be his enemies, not his assassins: *1180*
By right of conquest let us see him dead.
Must I, as answer, take the Greeks his head?
Have I been vested with the State's high order,
Merely to mark my mission with a murder?
Let Greece proclaim his crime, in Heaven's name,   *1185*
And let him die deluged in public shame.
Remember that he reigns, that a crowned head . . .

HERMIONE

Is't not enough for you I wish him dead?
And not enough for you, my pride offended
Demands a victim, but for me intended?   *1190*
That I'm the prize of a base tyrant slain,
That I detest him; nay, I loved him once?
I do not hide it, I once loved the knave,
Whether my heart or father ordered me
Does not avail; but you should give it heed.   *1195*
Despite my faith so shamefully betrayed,
Despite my deep revulsion at his crime,
As long as he's alive, fear my forgiveness,
As long as he's alive, my hate's unsure:
If he's not dead today, I may tomorrow   *1200*
Love him once more.

ORESTES

                Then I must murder him
And stop his pardon; I must; what must I?
How can I serve your wish so speedily?
What way to take my blows up to his person?
I've hardly set my foot upon Epirus,   *1205*
And here you're wanting me to shake the State;
You want the King to die; to punish him
You give me but a day, an hour, a minute.
I have to murder him before his people!
Let me accompany him to the altar,   *1210*
I'm willing now; I only wish to go
And reconnoitre where to strike him down.
Tonight I'll serve you and tonight he'll die.

HERMIONE

But yet today he'll wed Andromache.
The throne is all prepared within the temple;   *1215*
My shame is sealed and his base crime complete.
What are you waiting for? His head's exposed:
Without a guard he will approach the altar;
Round Hector's son he has arrayed his men;

He's bare to any arm that would avenge.   *1220*
Will you, in spite of him, protect his life?
Arm, with your Greeks, all those who came with me;
Incite your friends; all mine are at your call.
He has betrayed, deceived, despised us all.
Indeed, their hate already equals mine: *1225*
To spare a Trojan's consort they decline.
Speak, speak: he cannot possibly escape,
You've but to see him fall into their trap.
In such a splendid rage, be last or first,
Come back all dripping with his blood accursed;   *1230*
Then go now: in this state be sure of me.

ORESTES

But think, my lady . . .

HERMIONE

                    Ah! this is too much.
So many arguments affront my anger.
I wished to furnish you the means to please me,
To satisfy you; but I clearly see   *1235*
You always must complain and merit nothing.
Be off: and elsewhere boast your constancy.
And leave me here the care of my revenge.
My heart's confounded at my craven kindness,
I've been rebuffed too often in one day.   *1240*
I'll go alone to where their marriage beckons,
Where you dare not approach to earn my love.
There, I will somehow thrust myself upon him;
I'll pierce the heart that I have failed to touch;
And with my bloody hands cut short my life,   *1245*
Uniting thus our fates in his despite;
And traitor though he is, far less I'll rue
To die with him than to live on with you.

ORESTES

No, I'll deprive you of that dismal glee,
My lady: he'll not die except by me.   *1250*

I'll be the one to sacrifice your foe,
And if you wish, you'll pay me what you owe.[9]

HERMIONE

Hurry and trust your destiny to me,
And take care all your ships are set to sail.

Exit ORESTES

SCENE IV

CLEONE

You're rushing to your ruin; you should think . . .   *1255*

HERMIONE

Let me be ruined, I only think revenge.
I am not sure, even though he's promised me,
I should rely on others for fulfilment.
To him the cad's less guilty than to me,
And my blows would strike surer home than his.   *1260*
What pleasure to avenge my wrongs myself,
To draw my arm out dyed in his false blood,
And to increase my pleasure and his pain,
To screen my rival from his dying gaze!
What if Orestes in his execution   *1265*
Spare him the sting, he dies because of me!
Go, find him: bid him clearly tell the traitor
My hate it is that slays him, not the State.
Cleone, run. My vengeance would be vain
Should he not, dying, know by me he's slain.   *1270*

CLEONE

I shall obey. But what is this I see?
Gods! who'd have thought it, lady? Here's the King.

---

[9] After the 1676 edition Racine wisely suppressed four somewhat insipid (lover's) lines that Orestes uttered further, in the manner of the first two plays, and which detracted from the high gravity of the dramatic situation.

HERMIONE

Run, run, Cleone, and inform Orestes
He should restrain his hand until he see me.

Exit CLEONE

SCENE V

Enter PYRRHUS *and* PHOENIX

PYRRHUS

Madam, you weren't expecting me; I see   *1275*
My coming here has caused you some concern.
I do not come, bristling with false pretence,
To veil my baseness with a show of right:
It is enough, my heart softly condemns;
And I would ill urge what I do not think.   *1280*
I wed a Trojan: yes and I confess
I promised you the troth I now pledge her.
Another man would say to you in Troy
Our fathers, without us, arranged our match,
And that without consulting you or me,   *1285*
We were affianced, loveless, to each other;
But it's enough for me I gave consent;
And my ambassadors pledged you my troth;
Far from disclaiming them, I wished fulfilment;
And I received you with them in Epirus;   *1290*
And though another's conquering eye already
Had then forestalled the power of your eyes,
I still refused to let this love deter me;
I wished at any cost to play you true,
I gave you royal honours; till today   *1295*
I thought my vows could take the place of love.
But now love triumphs; by a blow of fate,
Andromache enslaves a heart she hates.
Dragged each by other, we run to the altar

To pledge, despite ourselves, immortal love.   *1300*
So now, my lady, burst upon a traitor,
Who's false with pain and yet who would be false.
Far from restraining such a righteous wrath,
It will relieve me more perhaps than you.
Hurl on me all the perjurer's names you choose: *1305*
I fear your silence more than your abuse;
And, in my heart, a thousand secret tongues
The more will shout, the less you voice your wrongs.

HERMIONE

My lord, in this avowal stripped of guile,
At least I see you true to your own self,   *1310*
And that, in mind to break your solemn bond,
In crime you wallow like a criminal.
Of course it is not right a conqueror
Stoop to the servile law of keeping faith.
Why, is not faithlessness a field to conquer?   *1315*
You only search me out to boast of it.
What? Undeterred by oath or yet by duty,
You seek me out, a Greek, and love a Trojan?
You leave me, take me back and go once more
From Helen's daughter back to Hector's widow?   *1320*
You crown in turn the princess and the slave,
Down Troy for Greece and Greece for Hector's son?
Such is the conduct of a mastermind,
A hero, never slave of his mere word.
To please your bride you would perhaps be forced   *1325*
To lavish your pet names of perjurer, traitor.
You came to scan the pallor of my face,
To laugh at my distress in her embrace.
You wish me weeping in her chariot's lee;
But this for one day would be too much glee;   *1330*
And why seek elsewhere further borrowed honours,
Are not your bloody exploits fame enough?
Hector's old father with dejected heart
Lamenting loud the death of all his sons,
The while your savage arm deep in his breast   *1335*
Scoops out his feeble blood congealed by age?

All Troy plunged burning in her streams of blood;
Polyxena, [10] your very hand had slaughtered
In front of all the frowning, outraged Greeks:
Can anyone say no to such a hero?   1340

PYRRHUS

I know too well to what excessive rage
Revenge for Helen's sake seduced my heart:
To you I may make grievance of the blood
I've had to shed, but will forget the past.
I thank the high Gods, your indifference   1345
Shows I may innocently woo my love.
I was too quick to show you my regret,
I should have known you well, myself still better.
My deep remorse has deep offended you;
One must be loved before one is untrue.   1350
You never dreamt to hold me in your chains;
I feared to wrong you, perhaps I'm serving you.
Our hearts were never made to love each other;
I did my duty and you heeded yours.
Indeed you were in no way bound to love me.   1355

HERMIONE

Not love you, dearest?[11] What else have I done?
For you I've spurned the sighs of all our princes;
I've sought you out myself deep in your realm;
And here I still am, false though you have been,
And though my leniency has shamed my Greeks.   1360
I ordered them to hush up my betrayal,
I longed in secret for my knave's return;
I fancied soon or late, restored to duty,
You'd bring me back the heart that was my due.
I loved you false; how would I love if true!   1365

[10] See last footnote to Racine's First Preface (page 140).
[11] It is almost impossible to translate satisfactorily the French noun *cruel* here, marking the first time that Hermione addresses Pyrrhus with the intimate *tu* to convey the wounded tenderness of her naked heart exposed by the rapier thrust of Pyrrhus' last remark. "Dearest" conveys the intimate tenderness, but hardly the reproach.

And at this very time your cruel lips
So calmly have pronounced to me my death,
Ingrate, alas! I think I love you still.
But if you must, my lord, if Heaven in anger
Has given other eyes magnetic power,   *1370*
Well marry her, I say, but then at least
Do not compel my eyes to witness it.
For the last time perhaps I speak to you:
Postpone it by a day; tomorrow act.
Still no reply? Ah villain, I see clear   *1375*
Each moment spent with me you count too dear!
Impatient to return to your loved Trojan,
You cannot bear another's company.
For her your heart cries out, your eyes seek her.
I will not keep you longer, now be gone.   *1380*
Go, swear to her the faith you swore to me,
Go and profane the Gods' high majesty.
The Gods, most just Gods, will not have forgotten
By these same pledges you were bound to me:
Upon the altar your base heart lay bare,   *1385*
Go, run. But fear to find Hermione there!

Exit HERMIONE

SCENE VI

PHOENIX

You've heard, my lord. Beware of overlooking
An angry lover thirsting for revenge.
She has too many followers in this place:
The Grecian cause with hers is now united;   *1390*
Orestes loves her still; perhaps is won . . .

PYRRHUS

Andromache awaits me. Guard her son.

ACT V

SCENE I

HERMIONE (*Alone*)

What have I done? What must I further do?
I am consumed by passion, torn by doubt.
I wander, aimless, buffeted by fate,   *1395*
Shall I know never if I love or hate?
How cruelly his callous eyes dismissed me,
With neither pain nor pity, even assumed!
Was he at all distressed and moved to mercy?
Could I extract a single groan from him?   *1400*
Dumb to my moans, indifferent to my fears,
Did he show any interest in my tears?
And still I pity him? O wretched whim,
My heart, my craven heart still pleads for him?
I quake at the mere thought he shall not live?   *1405*
And, ready to revenge, I still forgive?
No, no, I'll not revoke my dread decree:
Let him die! Since he no more lives for me—
The traitor triumphs, laughing at my anger,
He thinks he'll see my fury melt in tears;   *1410*
He thinks forever weak, with wavering heart,
With one arm I'll repel the other's dart.
He fancies I must be, as ever, kind.
But perhaps quite other thoughts fill his false mind.
In triumph at the temple, does he care   *1415*
If, here, we wish to see him live or die?
He leaves me to decide this dreadful doubt.
No, for the last time, let Orestes act.
Yes, let him die, since he should have foreseen it,
And since he has compelled me now to wish it!   *1420*

To wish it? What? Am I to order it?
Must all my love end in my darling's death?
This prince of men whose exploits formerly
I used to hear recounted with such joy,
To whom in secret I had linked myself   *1425*
Before our fatal marriage was arranged?
Have I then crossed so many seas and lands
But to come here so far to plan his death?
To kill, to murder him? Ah! let me first . . .

SCENE II

Enter CLEONE

HERMIONE

What have I done, Cleone? What is it?   *1430*
What's Pyrrhus doing?

CLEONE

He is at his peak,
The proudest and the most in love of men.
I've seen him lead towards the festive temple
His latest conquest, like a conqueror;
With eyes all sparkling, full of joy and hope,   *1435*
Intoxicated with her sight he strode.
Andromache, through a thousand cries of joy,
Right to the very altar dreams of Troy,
Still powerless to love or yet to hate,
Joyless and voiceless seems but to obey.   *1440*

HERMIONE

The villain? Was he criminal to the end?
Did you, Cleone, closely scan his face?
Is he enjoying calm and perfect bliss?
Did he not cast one glance towards the palace?
Tell me, you pressed yourself upon his sight?   *1445*

Did the knave blush on recognizing you?
Did his distress avow his faithlessness?
Did he maintain his arrogance to the end?

CLEONE

My lady, he recks nothing. His own safety
And reputation are like you forgotten.   *1450*
Unmindful who may follow, friend or foe,
He's only bent upon his love's pursuit.
He has placed his guard around the son of Hector,
And thinks it's he alone whom danger threatens;
Phoenix, himself in charge, has taken him   *1455*
To a fortress far from temple, far from palace.
Such is the amorous Pyrrhus' sole concern.

HERMIONE

The traitor! He shall die. What did Orestes say?

CLEONE

Orestes, with his Greeks, is in the temple.

HERMIONE

Well, is he all prepared for my revenge?   *1460*

CLEONE

I do not know.

HERMIONE

            You do not know? What's that?
Orestes, too, betrays?

CLEONE

            He worships you.
But torn asunder by a deep remorse,
He hesitates between his love and duty.
In Pyrrhus he reveres the sacred crown,   *1465*
Reveres Achilles, Pyrrhus too reveres:
He fears Greece, and an outraged world he fears,
But most of all, he says, he fears himself.

He'd love to bring his head to you as conqueror:
The name of murderer terrifies and stops him.   *1470*
So he has entered, unsure in his heart
Whether he'll come out guilty or mere witness.

HERMIONE

No, no, he'll put no hindrance to their triumph:
He'll take good care not to disturb the show.
I know full well what awe restrains his hand: *1475*
The coward fears to die, that's all he fears.
Just think of it! without a single prayer,
My mother's cause made all Greece spring to arms!
For her fair eyes alone, ten years of war
Saw twenty kings, strangers to her, expire!   *1480*
And I, who only seek a recreant's death,
And charge a lover to avenge my insult,
A lover who may win me at this price,
I give myself and still am not avenged?
Away! I will rely on me alone   *1485*
For justice; let the temple ring with groans;
Let me disrupt their fatal marriage ties,
And see they are united but a while.
In my mad frenzy I will all pursue:
All shall be Pyrrhus—yes, Orestes too![12]   *1490*
Though I shall die—revenged, in death I'll wallow.
I will not die alone, someone shall follow.

SCENE III

Enter ORESTES

ORESTES

My lady, it is over. You are served:
Pyrrhus, the traitor, is dying at the altar.

[12] With this fine stroke, which Eugene O'Neill seeks to emulate in *Mourning Becomes Electra*, Racine, at twenty-seven, shows he instinctively understood the subconscious, centuries before Freud.

HERMIONE

He's dead?

ORESTES

　　　He's dying; and our angry Greeks　　　　　*1495*
Have drowned his faithlessness in his own blood.
I promised you to do it; and though my qualms
Had made me dread the whole conspiracy,
I hastened to the temple, where our Greeks
Were merged among the throng right to the altar.　　*1500*
Pyrrhus took note of me. But, quite unblushing,
It seemed he was emboldened by my sight,
As though Greece, dared in her ambassador,
Had but to underline his nuptial splendour.
To cap it all he took his crown with joy　　　　　*1505*
And placed it on her head with his own hands.
He said: "I give you crown and loyalty:
Andromache, Epirus rule and me.
I pledge your son a father, in men's view;
I call the Gods to witness, swear it you.　　　　　*1510*
I here proclaim his enemies my own
And recognize him as the Trojan's Crown."
These words that were applauded by the people,
Provoked a cry of anger from our Greeks;
The traitor was surrounded on all sides　　　　　*1515*
And I could find no place to strike at him.
Each sought the honour of being first to fell him.
I saw him struggling in their hands awhile,
All bloody, seeking to escape their blows;
But in the end he slumped before the altar.　　　　*1520*
I passed right through the terror-stricken throng
To come to take my sweet princess away,
And reach the port where very soon our friends
Will join us dripping with his promised blood.

HERMIONE

What have they done?

ORESTES

      Forgive their hastiness: *1525*
They have, I see indeed, betrayed your vengeance.
You wished the first blow to be struck by me,
That he should feel in dying you had killed him;
But my zeal it is that has spurred them on,
For you alone, I dragged them to the temple,   *1530*
My lady; and you justly may delight in
A death, but executed by their arms.
You alone, launched the blows . . .

HERMIONE

              Scoundrel, be silent,
And bear yourself your craven regicide.
Go to your Greeks at home and boast your rage: *1535*
Go, I denounce it, loathe the sight of you.
What have you done, barbarian? Why cut short
So furiously so beautiful a life?
How could you, monsters, murder him today
Without your whole blood crying out for him?   *1540*
Speak, man, who made you master of his fate?
For what? And by what right, assassinate?
Who told you to?

ORESTES

      O Gods! What? Did you not
Yourself, but now, in this place, tell me to?

HERMIONE

Ah! should you have believed a maddened lover?   *1545*
Ought you not to have read my inmost thought?
And did you not see in my raving temper
How all the time my heart belied my mouth?
Even had I wished it; should you have obeyed?
Ought you not to have made me say it again   *1550*
And again a hundred times, consulting me before
The deed and coming back to me once more,
Or rather never showing me your face?

Why not leave me the care of my revenge?
Why must you thrust yourself where you are shunned?
This is the accursèd fruit of all your love;   *1555a*
Your black fate, villain, you have brought to me.
It's you, whose mission, fatal to us both,
Made him, to his undoing, choose my rival.
Else he would still be here, on both attending;
Perhaps loving me, or at the least pretending.   *1560*
Good-bye. Be off. I stay here in Epirus:
Greece, I renounce, and Sparta, and her Empire,
And all my kin; for it's enough for me
To see a freak like you, their progeny.

Exeunt HERMIONE *and* CLEONE

SCENE IV

ORESTES (*Alone*)

Was that Hermione whom I just heard?   *1565*
For whom does all the blood I've just shed flow?
I am, if I heard right, a murderous traitor.
Is't Pyrrhus who dies? Am I indeed Orestes?
I strangled deep down my divinest conscience;
I forced myself to kill a king I reverenced;   *1570*
In one day I infringed the rights of sovereigns,
And of ambassadors and all mankind,
Even sacred right of altar where he fell;
And am become a murderer and blasphemer.
For whom? For an ungrateful wretch I promised,   *1575*
Who would not see me more unless he died,
Whose fury I espoused. And when I served her,
She asks me to restore his blood and life!
She loves him! and I am a raving freak!
I see her vanish evermore from me!   *1580*
And, as she flees, the wretch leaves as my prize
All the fell names I earned to charm her eyes!

LAST SCENE

Enter PYLADES, *Soldiers of* ORESTES

PYLADES

My lord, it's time we went. Let's leave this palace,
Or else make up our minds to leave it never.
Our Greeks are masters of the gates here still,   *1585*
But all the people armed are after us.
Andromache is now in sole command;
They treat her as their queen and us as foes.
And she herself, once so perverse to Pyrrhus,
Now gives him all a faithful widow's dues,   *1590*
Orders he be avenged, and perhaps on us
Wants to avenge Troy and her Hector still.
Let's go and not wait till we are surrounded:
Our Greeks will join us; while Hermione
Detains around her all the gaping crowd,   *1595*
Our way lies open, let us go in safety.

ORESTES

No, I must follow, friends, Hermione.
After her latest sentence let me die.
Farewell: I did the crime. Let me atone.

PYLADES

Hermione, my lord? You must forget her.   *1600*
What? Must you, tool and object of her frenzy,
Seek some fresh outrage in the realms of death?
And must you die merely because she's dead?

ORESTES

What did you say? She's dead?

PYLADES

        Did you not know it?
In coming here we met her on the way,   1605
Running towards the temple, dazed, distraught.
She found dead Pyrrhus carried by his soldiers,
Incited by his blood to avenge his death.
This sight must have deprived her of her senses;
For from the gateway's top we saw her bending   1610
Over her Pyrrhus' corpse, dagger in hand,
Raise eyes to Heaven, stab herself and fall.

ORESTES

The Gods be thanked for my surpassing misery.
Yes, Heaven, I praise thy high tenacity.
Upon my punishment relentless bent,   1615
Thou'st made me drink the dregs of chastisement.
Thy hatred loved to fill my wretched chalice;
I was but born as instance of thy malice,
To be misfortune's model ultimate.
Be it so! I die content, fulfilling fate.   1620
Where are that loving pair? My joy to crown,
In their blood, in my own, I now must drown;
Both him and her in dying I must see;
Let us unite three hearts that couldn't agree.
But what thick mists around me sudden flow?   1625
How to get out? Why do I shudder so?
What horror rends me? Thank Heaven, I break clear—
Gods! streams of blood are gushing round me here!

PYLADES

My lord!

ORESTES

        What? Pyrrhus, must I meet you still?
Must I find everywhere your form to kill?   1630
Struck down by such blows how did you come through?
There, there, that is the blow I kept for you.
But what do I see? Hermione kiss his brow?
She comes to snatch him from the threatening blow?

Ah gods! what vampire looks she hurls on me!   *1635*
What fiends, what serpents in her company?
Ye hellish daughters, come, tear me in shreds!
See, see, those serpents hissing round your heads!
For whom do you bring these engines of affright?
Do you come to drag me down to eternal night?   *1640*
Then, torturing, come, and take Orestes' life;
But no, hold back, let Hermione still the strife:
Far better she can tear my limbs apart;
To make an end, let her devour my heart.

PYLADES

He loses consciousness. Friends, let us hurry: *1645*
Let's make the most of this unhappy seizure.
Let's save him quick. Our efforts would be vain,
If once more, conscious, he became insane.

THE END

❧❧❧

THE LITIGANTS

A Comedy

To the Reader

When I read *The Wasps* of Aristophanes, I hardly dreamt that I was some day to write *The Litigants*, based on it. I confess that it amused me greatly, and that I found in it a number of jests which tempted me to let the public share them; but I intended to put them into the mouths of the Italian players where they were destined as of full right. The judge who jumps from the window, the delinquent dog and the tears of his progeny, seemed to me just the incidents worthy of Scaramouche's gravity. The departure of this actor interrupted my plan, and gave birth to the desire in the minds of some of my friends to see upon our stage a sample of Aristophanes. I did not fall in with the first suggestion they made to me. I told them that however witty I thought that author, I was not disposed to take him for model, if I had to write a comedy; and that I would much prefer to follow the regularity of Menander or of Terence than the licence of Plautus and Aristophanes. They replied that they did not ask of me a comedy, but merely wished to see if the quips of Aristophanes would go down well in our language. Thus, half encouraging me, half themselves taking a hand at the job, my friends made me begin a play which did not take long to complete.

However, most people care not a fig for the intention or the diligence of authors. My trifle was straightway scrutinised as closely as a tragedy. Even those who had laughed the loudest trembled lest they had not laughed according to the rules, and took it ill that I had not thought more earnestly of the proper way to make them laugh. Others fancied that it was correct for them to be bored, and that the affairs of the Law Courts could not possibly furnish fit matter for the amusement of the nobility. The play was soon after performed at Versailles. There the highest in the land did not hesitate to laugh; and those who had imagined it to be disreputable to laugh in Paris, were perhaps compelled to laugh at Versailles to save their reputations.

They would be wrong, indeed, if they reproached me for having wearied their ears with too much legal quibbling. It is a jargon which is more alien to me than to anybody, and I have only made use of a few barbarous words of it which I picked up in the course of a lawsuit which neither my judges nor myself have ever quite understood.

If I am at all afraid, it is because serious-minded persons may treat as drivel the prosecution of the dog and the antics of the judge. But, in fact, I am translating Aristophanes, and it should be remembered that his audiences were pretty exacting. The Athenians well knew what was Attic salt, and they were very sure when they had laughed at something that they had not laughed at poppycock.

As for me, I find that Aristophanes was right to push matters beyond the probable. The judges of the Areopagus* would not perhaps have relished his noting in a natural way their cupidity, the tricks of their secretaries, and the rantings of their lawyers. It was fitting to caricature the characters a little to prevent them from recognising themselves. The public did not fail to distinguish the truth through the absurd; and I am convinced it is better to have spent the irrelevant eloquence of two orators over an accused dog, than if a real criminal had been put in the dock and the interest of the audience engaged in the life of a man.

However that may be, I may say that our age has not been any gloomier than his, and that if the aim of my comedy was to arouse laughter, never has a comedy better attained its aim. It is not that I expect some great honour for having entertained society for quite a while. But I am pleased to have done it without it costing me a single of those dirty equivocations and those improper jokes which nowadays cost so little to most of our writers, and which make the theatre fall once more into the turpitude from which our cleaner authors had rescued it.

---

* The administrative and judicial Council in ancient Athens, meeting on the hill of that name just below the Acropolis, crowned by the Parthenon.

THE LITIGANTS

First performed in October or November, 1668, at the Hôtel de Bourgogne; first edition, 1669.

CHARACTERS

DANDIN	*A judge*
LEANDER	*Son of Dandin*
WRANGLER	*A burgher*
ISOBEL	*Daughter of Wrangler*
THE COUNTESS	
SMALL JOHN	*A porter*
RESPONDENT	*A clerk*
THE PROMPTER	

The scene is in a town of lower Normandy.

ACT I

SCENE I

SMALL JOHN (*Dragging a sack bulging with case records*)

SMALL JOHN

Bah! on the future let but fools rely:
Who laughs on Friday shall on Sunday cry.
A judge, since last year, has employed me hard,
I came from Amiens to be his Swiss guard.
These bastard Normans hooted like an owl;   5
But with the wolves one soon learns how to howl.
An honest knave, though Picard I began,
I cracked my whip as well as any man.
The stoutest lords addressed me, bowing low,
"Sir Small John," they cajoled, stout as a cow!   10
But honour without cash can scarce hold water:
I was reduced to acting the theatre porter:[1]
In vain they doffed their hats and rushed the sentry,
Until they greased my palm, no hope of entry!
No tip, no Swiss, and so my door stayed shut.   15
It is quite true my master had his cut:
We kept accounts. I took it in my stride
The house with hay and candles to provide:
I took care not to lose. For come what may,
I knew to get the straw and scarcely pay.   20
A pity to his job he held so fast;
Always the first in court, and always last,
And often all alone: he'd love to stay
There without food or drink all night and day.

[1] In the seventeenth century, theatres in Paris employed strapping porters to make sure none entered without payment.

"Master Dandin," to him I sometimes said,   25
"Too early every day you leave your bed.
He who would travel far must spare his jade.
First of all drink, eat, sleep, then ply your trade."
He paid no heed. So long, all work, no play,
That he has more than one screw loose, they say!   30
He wants to sit in judgment on us all
And always from his lips lets mumblings fall,
Above my head, insisting willy nilly
To sleep in robes and wig, however silly.
One day he cut his cock's head off, irate,   35
For having woken him a little late;
He said some litigant, whose case fared ill,
Had bribed the poor bird not to be too shrill.[2]
In vain, since this wise sentence, the old man chides;
To speak to him of law his son forbids.   40
He makes us guard him day and night in short;
Or else he would be bolting straight to court.
To give us the slip God knows if he is quick!
With no sleep, I've become thin as a stick.
A shame. I stretch myself and only yawn.   45
Let him watch who will. I will nod till dawn.
Tonight I simply must have this small treat;
It harms nobody, sleeping in the street.
Let's sleep.

SCENE II

Enter RESPONDENT

RESPONDENT

Small John! Small John!

---

[2] Racine owes this delightful touch, among others in the play, to Aristophanes'
The Wasps, which he acknowledges in his foreword, To the Reader. The whole
idea of the domestic trial (in Acts II and III) is taken from Aristophanes, where
the accused dog has swallowed Sicilian cheese instead of Maine capon, as in Racine.

SMALL JOHN

Respondent, steady!
He is afraid I shall catch cold already.   *50*

RESPONDENT

So early in the street? Why, what the deuce!

SMALL JOHN

And must one always cool one's heels, you goose,
Guard a man always, always hear him shout?
Ah, what a throat! A wizard, without doubt.

RESPONDENT

Good!

SMALL JOHN

I told him I would sleep, with great submission   *55*
Scratching my head: "Then put in your petition,
How you would sleep," he said in all his glory.
I fall asleep just telling you the story.
Good-night.

RESPONDENT

What's this, good-night? The devil take
Me if . . . But what sound does the silence break?   *60*

SCENE III

DANDIN (*At the window*)

Small John! Respondent!

RESPONDENT (*To* SMALL JOHN)

Hush!

DANDIN

I am alone; that clod,
My guard, has given us the slip, thank God.

If I grant him time, he may appear, the stump!
To discharge myself, from window let me jump.
Out of court.

RESPONDENT

Whew! he jumps!

SMALL JOHN

I've got you, Sir.   65

DANDIN

Thief! thief!

SMALL JOHN

Soft, soft, from here you shall not stir.

RESPONDENT

No use your shouting.

DANDIN

Help, help! Murder! Spies!

SCENE IV

Enter LEANDER

LEANDER

Quick there, a torch! I hear my father's cries.
What, Dad, at this small hour to leave your lodging?
Why run out in the dark?

DANDIN

I'm going ajudging.   70

LEANDER

Judging whom? Everyone's asleep.

SMALL JOHN

No sleep for me!

LEANDER

Why all these many sacks down to the knee?

DANDIN

Three months I plan to stay away in session
And so, with sacks and suits I've made provision.

LEANDER

And who will feed you?

DANDIN

The bar is my resource.   75

LEANDER

But, Dad, where will you sleep?

DANDIN

Why, on the Bench, of course.

LEANDER

Come, Dada, will you not hear our appeals?
Sleep safe at home, at home take all your meals.
Allow your reason to persuade you still;
And for your health's sake . . .

DANDIN

No, I will be ill.   80

LEANDER

Please, rest. You are already too far gone.
Why, you are but a bag of skin and bone.

DANDIN

Rest? What? Must I be then, like you, you clown?
Do you think a judge must only go to town,
Strutting the streets with a string of popinjays,   85

Dancing all night, gambling away your days?
I earn my money, not by pounds but pence.
Each of your ribbons costs me a sentence.
My robes make you blush, you, son of a judge.
You ape the nobleman and hard work dodge.   90
Look at the Dandins' portraits in my room,
Does not the judge's wig on each head bloom?
Your fathers all were wise. Their Christmas swag
Would put ten marquis' presents in the bag.
Wait till December's golden days shall dawn.   95
What use your duke? except at court to fawn.
How many of the tallest have been seen
Puffing upon their cold hands, while they preen
Themselves in my court, hands in pocket prancing,
Nose-cloaked, to keep warm in attendance dancing!   100
That's how I treat them. Ah, my son and brother,
Is this the lesson of your deceased mother?
My poor Babonnette! My loss is past bearing!
To think she never missed a single hearing!
Alas! she never left me, not one day;   105
And Heaven knows the things she brought away!
Why, with the barman's napkins she'd be stranded,
Rather than leave the courthouse, empty-handed.
That's how good households should be run. Don't hold
Me, foolish boy.

LEANDER

                You'll catch your death of cold,   110
Father. Small John, take back to bed your master.
Make fast each door and every window faster;
Go, barricade the lot, 'twill keep him warmer.

SMALL JOHN

Why not grill it all up, even the dormer?

DANDIN

What? With no order back in bed to creep?   115
Obtain a writ to tell how I must sleep.

LEANDER

Now you must go to bed, Dad, by injunction.

DANDIN

I'll go, but madden you without compunction;
I will not sleep.

LEANDER

Ah! very well, then play!
Don't leave his side, Small John. Respondent, stay.   *120*

Exeunt DANDIN *and* SMALL JOHN

SCENE V

LEANDER

With you a moment I must speak alone.

RESPONDENT

Must I guard you?

LEANDER

You've hit the nail, I own.
I have my madness like my father here.

RESPONDENT

What? you too want to judge?

LEANDER

Let us be clear.
You know that house.

RESPONDENT

I understand at last: *125*
Love's got you up and cracking pretty fast.

You wish to speak of Isobel I'm sure,
Who, as I've often said is sweet, demure;
But Mr. Wrangler, you must not forget,
Will spend in lawsuits all his fortune yet.   *130*
Whom does he not sue? He will drag to court
The whole of France yet if his life's not short.
Adjacent to his judge he's come to lodge:
One must for ever sue, the other judge.
And it's a toss up if he'll give her to you   *135*
Before he sues the curate, notary, you too.

LEANDER

Like you I know him. But in spite of all
I die for Isobel.

RESPONDENT

She's at your call.
You need but speak, she's waiting to be wed.

LEANDER

The affair moves not as quickly as your head.   *140*
Her father is a boor whom I make pale; if
One is not sergeant, attorney or bailiff,
No seeing his daughter; poor Isobel,
Imprisoned, pines at home as if in hell.
Sadly she sees her youth fade with her health,   *145*
My love in smoke, in lawsuits all her wealth.
He'll ruin her if he is left alone.
Is not some honest trickster to you known
Who'll do his friends a service, for a fee;
Some bumptious bailiff?

RESPONDENT

Yes, of course, there be!   *150*

LEANDER

But where?

RESPONDENT

If only my poor father were
Still living, he'd be your very man, Sir.
Earned more a day than we in half a year:
On his lined brow his deeds were graven clear.[3]
He would have seized for you a prince's coach;   *155*
And by his own hand; and, without reproach,
If in the district twenty whips would crack,
My father shouldered nineteen as his whack!
But what's to do? Aren't I the master's son?
I'll serve you.

LEANDER

You?

RESPONDENT

Better than anyone.   *160*

LEANDER

You'll serve her pa a false summons?

RESPONDENT

Like a shot.

LEANDER

You'll give the daughter a love note?

RESPONDENT

Why not?
I'll ply both trades.

LEANDER

Come quick, I hear him cry.
Let's elsewhere think this matter out.

Exeunt LEANDER *and* RESPONDENT

[3] A parody, by almost exact quotation, of a line in Corneille's *Le Cid*.

SCENE VI

Enter WRANGLER

WRANGLER (*Going to and fro*)
                    Ho! Fry,
See, they guard the house; I'll soon be back, but   *165*
Make sure the way upstairs is firmly shut:
And that this letter the Maine post will catch;
And fetch three fat wild rabbits from my hatch.
Take them to my attorney's, rain or shine,
And if his clerk comes, see he tastes my wine.   *170*
Ah! give him the sack at my window hanging.
Let me see! If some tall dry man comes banging
To see me—he often serves as witness
And swears for me, whatever the unfitness—
Let him wait. It will soon strike four o'clock.   *175*
I fear my judge go out. Then let me knock.

SMALL JOHN (*At the door ajar*)
Who goes there?

WRANGLER
May one see his Honour?

SMALL JOHN (*Shutting the door*)
                    No.

WRANGLER
May one speak to his secretary?

SMALL JOHN
                    No.

WRANGLER
Or to his porter?

SMALL JOHN

That is me!

WRANGLER

Then please
Drink to my health, Sir.

SMALL JOHN

May God give you ease!   *180*
But come tomorrow.

WRANGLER

My cash, before you shut!
The world, to tell the truth, is now a slut.
There was a time when lawsuits I could cozen.
Six crowns would win for me a good half-dozen.
Alas! today I fancy all my wealth   *185*
Would not suffice to win a porter's "health."
But I see the Countess of Pimposh appear.
For a most urgent business she comes here.

SCENE VII

Enter the COUNTESS

WRANGLER

Madam, there's no going in.

COUNTESS

It is too bad!
To tell the truth my valets drive me mad.   *190*
To get them up in time, in vain I scold;
Daily I must awake my whole household.

WRANGLER

He now insists on hiding from our gaze.

COUNTESS

I could not speak to him for two whole days.

WRANGLER

I have a strong opponent, who may gain . . .   *195*

COUNTESS

After what I've gone through, you can't complain.

WRANGLER

Ah yes, indeed I can.

COUNTESS

Sir, what decrees!

WRANGLER

I'll take your word for it. Now listen, please.

COUNTESS

If only, Sir, their perfidy, you knew.

WRANGLER

It is a trifle.

COUNTESS

Sir, let me tell you . . .   *200*

WRANGLER

Here are the facts. Some fifteen years ago,
A certain ass's foal crossed my meadow
And did great damage rolling in the sludge.
Prompt I complained before the village judge.
The ass was seized; the expert designated,   *205*
The damage, two hay bundles estimated.
At last the sentence, twelve months late, revealed
My suit had been dismissed. I prompt appealed.

While fighting still the lower court's decrees—
Pay great attention, Madam, if you please—   *210*
Our friend, Drolichap, who is some magician,
Obtained, for cash, an order on petition
In a higher court of first instance and won.
My foe contests the execution:
Another incident. While we appealed,   *215*
My opponent lets his poultry peck my field.
The court called for a survey that should weigh
The hay a hen could swallow in one day:
This too was tacked onto the suit, and all
Suspended stayed till the case came on call,   *220*
The fifth or sixth of April, fifty-six.
I asked for more costs; put down all my tricks,
Plaints, written statements, new facts, requisitions,
Experts' reports, inspections and commissions,
Three provisional orders, a little forgery,[4]   *225*
And loud complaints imputing perjury.
Fourteen adjournments, processes some seventy,
Exhibits twenty-six, and stays but twenty.
At last the great decree. My case I lost,
And quite a thousand crowns or so it cost.   *230*
Do you call that law? Is that the way to judge?
After some twenty years! I will not budge;
A civil suit is open still to me,
I won't give in. But you too, as I see,
Fight on.

COUNTESS

Pray God!

WRANGLER

I'll leave no stone unturned.   *23.*

ʃCOUNTESS

I . . .

---

[4] "Forgery" is not in the original.

WRANGLER

For two hay wisps, a thousand pounds I've burned.

COUNTESS

Sir, all my suits were on the point of ending;
But four or five small causes were still pending:
Against my father and my husband's name,
Against my children. Ah, the final shame!   240
I do not know the shifts and slants they feigned,
Nor everything they did; but they obtained
An order, by which, with full maintenance due,
I was for life forbidden, Sir, to sue!

WRANGLER

To sue?

COUNTESS

          To sue.

WRANGLER

                    Indeed, a scurvy trick!   245
I am amazed.

COUNTESS

          And I, Sir, am quite sick.

WRANGLER

To bind the hands of persons of your state!
But tell me, Madam, is your pension great?

COUNTESS

I'd manage, Sir, to live quite decently,
But living without suing is to die!   250

WRANGLER

Shall adversaries gnaw our souls away
And shall we nothing say? But, Madam, pray,
Since when have you been suing?

COUNTESS

Let it pass;

For thirty years at most.

WRANGLER

Not much.

COUNTESS

Alas!

WRANGLER

How old are you? You seem in the very pink.   255

COUNTESS

Some sixty years.

WRANGLER

The best age, I should think,

For suing.

COUNTESS

We shall see; they have not won.

I'll sell my petticoat; have all or none.

WRANGLER

Madam, hear me. This is what you must do.

COUNTESS

Yes, Sir, like my own father, I hear you.   260

WRANGLER

I'd go and find my judge.

COUNTESS

Yes, Sir, I'll go.

WRANGLER

Throw myself at his feet.

COUNTESS

Yes, I shall throw
Myself, I am resolved.

WRANGLER

But listen, please.

COUNTESS

You treat the matter with consummate ease.

WRANGLER

Have you finished, Madam?

COUNTESS

Yes.

WRANGLER

I'd go straight
To find my judge.

265

COUNTESS

Alas! How well you state . . .

WRANGLER

If you must always speak, I'll hold my tongue.

COUNTESS

How kind of you! I hope I did no wrong.

WRANGLER

I'd go and find my judge and say . . .

COUNTESS

Yes.

WRANGLER

See.
And say to him: Sir . . .

COUNTESS

Yes, Sir.

WRANGLER

Ah, bind me . . .   *270*

COUNTESS

I'll not be bound.

WRANGLER

Tell that to the marines!

COUNTESS

I will not be.

WRANGLER

Why must you make such scenes?

COUNTESS

No.

WRANGLER

You do not know what I am driving at.

COUNTESS

I'll sue, Sir, sue, I tell you and that's that.

WRANGLER

But . . .

COUNTESS

But I'll not be bound, Sir, as I've said.   *275*

WRANGLER

When once a mad thought hits a woman's head.

COUNTESS

Mad yourself.

WRANGLER

Madam!

COUNTESS

Why should I be bound?

WRANGLER

Madam . . .

COUNTESS

You see, familiar he would sound.

WRANGLER

But, Madam . . .

COUNTESS

This mean quibbler, who's so crass,
Dare give me counsel!

WRANGLER

Madam!

COUNTESS

With his ass!   *280*

WRANGLER

You rouse me.

COUNTESS

My good man, look to your hay.

WRANGLER

I boil.

COUNTESS

The fool.

WRANGLER

For witnesses I pray!

SCENE VIII

Enter SMALL JOHN

SMALL JOHN

A splendid witches' sabbath at our door,
Go further, pray, and all your tempests pour.

WRANGLER

Sir, be witness . . .

COUNTESS

That the man is a sot.   285

WRANGLER

You heard her, Sir: that word, pray, forget not.

SMALL JOHN

Madam, you should not utter words so bad.

COUNTESS

Indeed: and he, of course, may call me mad!

SMALL JOHN

Mad! You are wrong. Must you the lady wound?

WRANGLER

I'm giving her advice.

SMALL JOHN

Oh!

COUNTESS

To be bound!   290

SMALL JOHN

Oh! Sir.

WRANGLER

Why won't she hear me to the end?

SMALL JOHN

Oh! Madam.

COUNTESS

I? His manners let him mend!

WRANGLER

A shrew!

SMALL JOHN

Soft. Soft.

COUNTESS

A crooked quibbler!

SMALL JOHN

Stop!

WRANGLER

Who dares no longer sue!

COUNTESS

Will you not hop
It, abominable trickster, heap of evil,   295
Shuffler, thief, toad?

WRANGLER

That's great, why what the devil!
Sheriff! Sheriff!

COUNTESS

Bailiff! Bailiff!

SMALL JOHN

To cover!
When judge and lit'gants, all, must be bound over.

ACT II

SCENE I

LEANDER, RESPONDENT

RESPONDENT

On me alone do not make all dependent,
Since I'm the bailiff, you can be the sergeant.   *300*
You only have, dressed up, to tread my heels:
You'll have all means to make her your appeals.
Change your blond wig for one of swarthy trim.
Do litigants care a fig you're in the swim?
When they rush to your father, court to pay,   *305*
You hardly know whether it's night or day.
But are you not amazed at this countess,
Whom fortune sends me with such readiness?
A writ on Wrangler, falling in my net,
She storms, as soon as eyes on me she set,   *310*
Accusing him of letting fall some bad
Expressions saying she was raving mad:
Mad to be bound it seems; and such like scorn
And blasphemies that ever suits adorn!
But you say nothing about all my wrappings?   *315*
Do I look the very bailiff in these trappings?

LEANDER

Indeed.

RESPONDENT

    I don't know why, but since this morning,
My soul and back's gone harder without warning.
No matter. Here's your letter and the writ.

The letter gets to her, I promise it.   *320*
But to make sure this contract too is signed,
Upon my steps you must not lag behind.
You will pretend to make enquiries. Rather,
You will make love in presence of her father.

LEANDER

Do not exchange the summons for the note!   *325*

RESPONDENT

The summons for papa; on whom you dote,
The billet-doux.

Exit LEANDER

SCENE II

Enter ISOBEL

ISOBEL

Who knocks?

RESPONDENT

Isobel! Friend.

ISOBEL

Do you want someone, Sir?

RESPONDENT

Miss, I pretend
To bring this little summons to your view,
Begging the honour of serving it on you.   *330*

ISOBEL

Excuse me, Sir, I nothing know of it.
My father will come soon and scan the writ.

RESPONDENT

Then he is not at home?

ISOBEL

No.

RESPONDENT

Ah, for shame!
The summons, Miss, is made out in your name.

ISOBEL

You take me for another without doubt:
I know what lawsuits cost, so leave me out;   *335*
And, if one went to court as much as I,
Your kind would soon need other fish to fry.
Good-bye.

RESPONDENT

Permit, Miss . . .

ISOBEL

I shall not permit.

RESPONDENT

It is no summons.

ISOBEL

Pshaw!

RESPONDENT

A little chit.   *340*

ISOBEL

Still less.

RESPONDENT

But read.

ISOBEL

In vain you wave it aloft.

RESPONDENT

It's from Mr. . . .

ISOBEL

Good-bye.

RESPONDENT

Leander.

ISOBEL

Soft.

It's from Mr. . . .?

RESPONDENT

You're driving me to death
To get myself heard. I'm all out of breath.

ISOBEL

Respondent! Pardon my amazement but—   345
Give.

RESPONDENT

In my face the door you rushed to shut.

ISOBEL

Who could have known you, dressed up in that way?
But give.

RESPONDENT

To good men is that all you say?

ISOBEL

Do give it to me.

RESPONDENT

Pest . . .

ISOBEL

Then do not give.
Go back with it, lucky to be alive!   *350*

RESPONDENT

Take, and next time be not so quick to scream.

SCENE III

Enter WRANGLER

WRANGLER

Yes? I'm a sot, a thief, in her esteem?
A bailiff is enjoined a writ to bear,
And I'll serve her a dish of my own fare.
To have to brew it once more I should burst,   *355*
And sooner if she summoned me the first.
But a man's talking to my daughter here.
She reads a note? Some lover, it is clear!
Draw nearer.

ISOBEL

Seriously, can I set store
On't.

RESPONDENT

Like your father he now sleeps no more.   *360*
He is in torment; he (*Seeing* WRANGLER) will show
    you plain,
In forcing him to law you'll nothing gain.

ISOBEL

My father! Really, you may tell the quack,
That if we're sued, we know how to fight back.
There, that is what I think of all your pleading.   *365*

WRANGLER

Was it, indeed, a summons she was reading?
Darling, the family honour you shall crown:
You shall defend your wealth. Come, child, my own![5]
I'll buy for you *The Law and Whom It Fits*.
But what the deuce, you must'nt tear up writs.   *370*

ISOBEL

Go tell the rabble I am not afraid
And challenge them to do their worst. I've said.

WRANGLER

Soft, do not storm.

ISOBEL

Good-bye, Sir.

Exit ISOBEL

SCENE IV

RESPONDENT

What a way!
But let's report.

WRANGLER

Excuse her, Sir, I pray.
She's not adept; and so, if you'll permit   *375*
I'll paste once more the pieces of your writ.

RESPONDENT

No.

WRANGLER

I'll read it with ease.

[5] Another parody of Corneille's *Le Cid*.

RESPONDENT

I am not spiteful:
I have a copy on me.

WRANGLER

How delightful!
And yet the more I see you, Sir, the less
I can recall your face and your address.   *380*
I know no end of bailiffs.

RESPONDENT

Then note me:
I do my duty with great industry.

WRANGLER

Good. Who has sent you, Sir?

RESPONDENT

A worthy lady,
Who honours you, and who is still quite ready
To see you on my summons straight appear   *385*
And make her sweet amends in language clear.

WRANGLER

Amends? Why, I have harmed nor flesh nor blood.

RESPONDENT

I well believe it, Sir, you're much too good.

WRANGLER

What do you ask?

RESPONDENT

She wishes, Sir, that you
In front of witnesses give her her due   *390*
And call her wise, and not extravagant.

WRANGLER

My countess, to be sure.

RESPONDENT

Your humble servant.

WRANGLER

I'm at her service.

RESPONDENT

How obliging, Sir!

WRANGLER

Yes, you may tell her that an officer
Is on the way to take her all my homage.   *395*
Why what the deuce? Should victims pay the damage?
Let's hear her tune.
            "Sixth January. Ground.
For having falsely said she must be bound,
Being led to this with intent to wrangle,
The high and mighty Lady Yolande Wangle,   *400*
Countess of Pimposh, All bosh," et cetera:
"Be it said on the spot he must make her a
Full redress at the lady's lodge: in clear
Voice, with four witnesses and a lawyer,"
Ah, tush, "the said Jerome will loud declare   *405*
He deems her judgment wise, beyond compare.
Le Bon." Indeed, is that your Lordship's name?

RESPONDENT

Your servant, Sir. (*Aside*) Let's play a brazen game.

WRANGLER

Le Bon? On writs this name is not in vogue.
Mr. Le Bon!

RESPONDENT

Yes, Sir?

WRANGLER

You are a rogue.   *410*

RESPONDENT

Sir, pardon me, I am an honest man.

WRANGLER

The veriest rogue from Caen to Milan.

RESPONDENT

What, Sir? You may continue to defy me:
You'll have the goodness to indemnify me.

WRANGLER

Indemnify? In cuffs.

RESPONDENT

        You are too good: *415*
You'll pay me well.

WRANGLER

        Rascal, you rouse my blood.
Take that, as payment.

RESPONDENT

        One cuff! Let us write:
"The said Jerome, bristling throughout with spite,
Proceeded to assault and battery
Upon my bailiff's cheek, whereat my finery
Fell flopping in the mud; to wit my hat."   *420*

WRANGLER

Add that.

RESPONDENT

        Good, that is ready cash, and that
I badly need. "And this defiant start
Repeated with his foot." Take courage, heart!
"And furthermore the aforementioned did try
This same report in temper to destroy."   *425*
Come, my dear Sir, that will make quite a bag.
Do not relax.

WRANGLER

Away, you scalliwag.

RESPONDENT

Good Sir, one word more. Should it not displease,
A little cudgelling and I'm at my ease.

WRANGLER

I'll make sure he's a bailiff.

RESPONDENT (*In the position of writing*)
                    Dear back, harden!
Strike quick: I have four babes to feed.

WRANGLER
                              Ah! pardon!   *430*
I could not find in you a bailiff's tongue;
But still the cleverest man is sometimes wrong.
I'll make amends for this outrageous doubt.
Yes, you are bailiff, Sir, bailiff throughout.
There shake my hand. With your kind I would sup: *435*
And, my late father always brought me up
In the fear of God and bailiffs, above all.

RESPONDENT

No, quite so cheap you can't beat great or small.

WRANGLER

No more suits, Sir!

RESPONDENT

                    Your servant. What, to spurn
The law, raise cane, cuff, kick!

WRANGLER
                    Pray, in return   *440*
Give blow for blow.

RESPONDENT

                    You've beaten me. Enough!
Not thousand crowns could raise from me a cuff.

SCENE V

Enter LEANDER

RESPONDENT

My officer has come here just in time.
Your presence, Sir, in this place is of prime
Importance. He has put me in this flap,   *445*
Giving as meagre gift a great fat slap.

LEANDER

To you, Sir?

RESPONDENT

To me, speaking to my person.
Cuffs, kicks and blows, why everything but arson.

LEANDER

Have you a witness?

RESPONDENT

Ah, Sir, rather feel:
The slap upon my cheek is quite warm still.   *450*

LEANDER

Flagrante delictu,[6] a criminal case.

WRANGLER

I care a fig.

RESPONDENT

His daughter, in my face,
Has paper mine with thirty scraps requited.
Protesting she was glad, indeed delighted
To defy us.

[6] I.e., caught in the act.

LEANDER

Go, fetch the daughter here.   *455*
This family's contumacy is clear.

WRANGLER

Some witch must surely have my senses tangled:
If no one now I know, let me be strangled.

LEANDER

What's that? To beat a bailiff! Here she is.

SCENE VI

Enter ISOBEL

RESPONDENT (*To* ISOBEL)

Do you not recognise him?

LEANDER

What's this, Miss!   *460*
So it is you who said you did not care
And snapped your furious fingers in the air?
Your name?

ISOBEL

Isobel.

LEANDER (*To* RESPONDENT)

Write it. And how old?

ISOBEL

Eighteen.

WRANGLER

A few more I should say, all told.
But never mind.

LEANDER

In state of matrimony? 465

ISOBEL

No, Sir.

LEANDER

You laugh? Write down she thinks it funny.

WRANGLER

Don't speak of matrimony, Sir, to maids:
Why, that is prying into family shades!

LEANDER

Record, he interrupts.

WRANGLER

No, I obey.
Take care, my child, of every word you say. 470

LEANDER

There, there, be not afraid. Answer at ease.
We would do nothing here that might displease.
Did not this officer just now hand you
A certain document?

ISOBEL

Yes, Sir.

WRANGLER

True, true.

LEANDER

Did you destroy the document, unread? 475

ISOBEL

I read it, Sir.

WRANGLER

Good.

LEANDER

Write on, what she said.
And why did you destroy it?

ISOBEL

I was worried,
Lest at the business Father might be flurried,
And lest on reading it he burst in fury.

WRANGLER

And you, not sue? Sheer loss to judge and jury!   480

LEANDER

You did not in a temper tear it then,
Nor in contempt of those who did it pen?

ISOBEL

I have for them, Sir, neither rage nor scorn.

LEANDER

Write.

WRANGLER

I said, from her father she was born!
She answers very well.

LEANDER

And yet you've shown   485
A clear contempt for wearers of the gown.

ISOBEL

A gown before had always shocked my sight;
But this aversion now is very slight.

WRANGLER

My poor, dear child! I'll wed you to your hero
Upon the spot, so long it costs me zero. *490*

LEANDER

You will obey then, all the law decrees you.

ISOBEL

Sir, I shall do my very best to please you.

RESPONDENT

Sir, make her sign.

LEANDER

When you are called upon,
Will you maintain what you have said and done?

ISOBEL

Sir, be assured that Isobel is true. *495*

LEANDER

Sign. Justice has been done. Now that will do.
Will you not sign, Sir?

WRANGLER

Gladly, let me write.
I'll sign all she has said, with eyes shut tight.

LEANDER (*To* ISOBEL)

All's going well. The outcome's sweet to me:
He signs a contract drawn up properly, *500*
And will be called soon to account for it.

WRANGLER

What is he saying? He admires her wit.

LEANDER

Good-bye, and be as good as you are fair.
All will end well. Take her home, Officer.
And you, Sir, march.

WRANGLER

Where, Sir?

LEANDER

You follow me.   505

WRANGLER

But where?

LEANDER

March, in the King's name. You'll soon see.

WRANGLER

What's this?

Exeunt ISOBEL *and* RESPONDENT

SCENE VII

Enter SMALL JOHN

SMALL JOHN

Stop there! Has no one seen my master?
Which way hopped he? Through door or window faster?

LEANDER

Moonshine!

SMALL JOHN

Into the son I have not bumped.
The father's where the devil has him dumped.   510
He clamoured nonstop for his condiment
And so I rushed into the pantry basement
To fetch the pepper pot. While I was gone,
He vanished.

SCENE VIII

Enter DANDIN *and* RESPONDENT

DANDIN

Silence, silence, everyone.

LEANDER

Great God!

SMALL JOHN

There he is, up in the eaves, whew![7]   515

DANDIN

What men are you? What matters bring me you?
Who are these men in gowns? Your advocates?
Proceed.

SMALL JOHN

Now you shall see him judging cats!

DANDIN

About your case have you yet seen my clerk?
Go ask him if I'm seized, or in the dark.   520

LEANDER

I must go up and drag him from the skies.
Upon your prisoner, Bailiff, keep your eyes.

SMALL JOHN

Ho! Ho! Sir.

[7] As in Aristophanes.

LEANDER

        Shut your mouth and follow me,
You fool.

Exeunt LEANDER *and* SMALL JOHN

SCENE IX

Enter the COUNTESS

DANDIN

Make haste. Your petition, allow me.

WRANGLER

Without your Honour's order I'm held static.   *525*

COUNTESS

My God! I see his Honour in his attic.
What is he up to?

RESPONDENT

        Madam, he holds court.
The field is open to you.

WRANGLER

        Sir, in short,
I've been assaulted and insulted. To you
I come complaining.

COUNTESS

        Complaining, I come too.   *530*

WRANGLER, COUNTESS

You see before you my opponent stand.

RESPONDENT

Jove! I should also like to take a hand.

RESPONDENT, WRANGLER, COUNTESS

Your Honour, for a summons I apply.

WRANGLER

Let's turn by turn to tell our grievance try.

COUNTESS

His grievance? Only falsehood trips his tongue.   *535*

DANDIN

What have they done to you?

WRANGLER, RESPONDENT, COUNTESS

Tremendous wrong.

RESPONDENT (*Continuing*)

I cap them with a slap and kicks a dozen.

WRANGLER

One of your nephews, Sir, is my third cousin.

COUNTESS

Sir, Father Cordon knows about my case.

RESPONDENT

Your Honour, I am bastard without trace.   *540*

DANDIN

Your station.

COUNTESS

Countess.

RESPONDENT

Bailiff.

WRANGLER

Townsman true.

DANDIN

Keep talking all: I'll hear the three of you.

WRANGLER

Your Hon . . .

RESPONDENT

He's given us the slip and vanished.

COUNTESS

Alas!

WRANGLER

The hearing, what, already finished?
I scarce had time my next word to release.   545

Exit DANDIN

SCENE X

Enter LEANDER, *without gown, etc.*

LEANDER

Come, gentlemen, pray leave us now in peace.

WRANGLER

Sir, may one enter?

LEANDER

No, within my power!

WRANGLER

Why not? I shall have done in scarce an hour.
Or at the most, in two.

LEANDER

I'll have no caller.

COUNTESS

Well done, to slam the door on such a bawler;   *550*
But I . . .

LEANDER

No callers, Madam, I adjure you.

COUNTESS

I will, Sir, enter.

LEANDER

Perhaps.

COUNTESS

I assure you.

LEANDER

Then by the window.

COUNTESS

By the door.

LEANDER

We'll see.

WRANGLER

Even if till night a fixture here I be.

SCENE XI

Enter SMALL JOHN

SMALL JOHN (*To* LEANDER)

They will not hear him though his lungs be spent.   *555*
Whew! I have bundled him into our basement,
Next the wine cellar.

LEANDER

In a word I say,
You shall not see my father.

WRANGLER

Yet, today,
I simply must see him about my case.

(DANDIN *appears through an air hole*)

But what see I? Heaven sends him face-to-face.   560

LEANDER

What? Through the air hole?

SMALL JOHN

The devil's biting him.

WRANGLER

Sir . . .

DANDIN

Knave! I would be out were't not for him.

WRANGLER

Sir . . .

DANDIN

Off with you, my man, I think you dotty.

WRANGLER

Sir, will you please . . .

DANDIN

Away, you drive me potty.

WRANGLER

Sir, I have ordered . . .

DANDIN

Hold your tongue, you whale!   565

WRANGLER

They take to your house . . .

DANDIN

Take him off to gaol.

WRANGLER

A certain cask of wine.

DANDIN

I'm not so base.

WRANGLER

A splendid muscatel.

DANDIN

Unfold your case.

LEANDER (*To* RESPONDENT)

Upon them we must rivet all our eyes.

COUNTESS

He's going to regale you, Sir, with lies.   *570*

WRANGLER

I speak the truth.

DANDIN

For God's sake, let her be.

COUNTESS

Pray, listen, Sir.

DANDIN

You're suffocating me.

WRANGLER

Sir.

DANDIN

You are strangling me.

COUNTESS

Then turn my way.

DANDIN

She's strangling me! Ah!

WRANGLER

You're dragging me away!
Take care, I'm falling.

SMALL JOHN

They are, on my word,   575
Both bottled in the cellar.

LEANDER

Quick as a bird,
Fly to their aid. But I'll at least take care
That Mr. Wrangler, since he's lodged in there,
Emerges not today. Respondent, guard!

RESPONDENT

You guard the air hole.

LEANDER

Quick, go; I'll keep guard.   580

Exeunt WRANGLER, SMALL JOHN *and* RESPONDENT

SCENE XII

COUNTESS

The wretch! He's gone to prejudice his mind.

(*Through the air hole*)

No grain of truth in all he says, you'll find;
He has no witness; liar!

LEANDER

Not so fast:
Why badger them? Perhaps they breathe their last.

COUNTESS

He'll make him, Sir, believe his every slant.   585
Allow me to go in.

LEANDER

Oh no! You shan't.

COUNTESS

Sir, I see well the muscatel has won
The approval both of father and of son.
But patience! as is fitting, I'll unmask,
In higher quarters, both the judge and cask.   590

LEANDER

Then do go; and stop shrieking in the street;
What a den of madmen! What a toothsome treat!

Exit the COUNTESS

SCENE XIII

Enter DANDIN *and* RESPONDENT

RESPONDENT

Where are you running, Sir? It's risky trudging.
And you are limping too.

DANDIN

I'm going a-judging.

LEANDER

Why, Father? One leg seems a trifle short.   595
A surgeon, quick.

DANDIN

Let him appear in court.

LEANDER

Come, stop now, Dad . . .

DANDIN

　　　　　　　Ha! I see how it is:
You think you can do with me what you please;
Respect or deference for me you have none:
I can't pronounce a sentence—no not one.　　　　　　　*600*
Finish, take this bag, take quick.

LEANDER

　　　　　　　　　　　Ah! gently,
Dad. We must solve the problem evidently.
If, without judging, life for you's a quandary,
If you are itching to judge all and sundry,
On that account you need not leave your home;　　　　*605*
Show here your genius, judging all who come.

DANDIN

Do not mock justice, though I show forbearance:
I will not be a judge but in appearance.

LEANDER

A judge without appeal, you'll leave your trace,
Judge both of civil and of criminal case.　　　　　　*610*
Why, you may hold two sessions every day:
On every matter you may have your say.
If a butler fail to hand a glass that's clean,
Condemn him to a fine, or if he's seen
Allowing it to slip from him and crash,
Why in that case, condemn him to the lash.

DANDIN

It's something, certainly, and may be fun.　　　　　*615*
But my vacations, who will pay me? None?

LEANDER

You may take as collateral each one's wage.

DANDIN

He speaks, one must confess it, like a sage.

LEANDER

Against one of your neighbours . . .

SCENE XIV

Enter SMALL JOHN

SMALL JOHN

Stop, stop, catch!

LEANDER

No doubt, my prisoner's bolted through the hatch!   620

RESPONDENT

No, no, fear nothing.

SMALL JOHN

All is lost . . . and Citron . . .
Your filthy cur has just devoured a capon.
Nothing is safe from him. He paws and pounces.

LEANDER

Good! Here's a case for Dad. Help, help, you dunces!
Quick, after him. Run.

DANDIN

Softly all of you,   625
No noise, hush! A secret arrest will do.

LEANDER

Dad, you must make a positive example:
Severely judge this roving, thieving sample.

DANDIN

Punctiliously let me pontificate.
Let both the parties have their advocate;   630
We've none.

LEANDER

Ah well! Let's manufacture some.
Your porter and your clerk, see, here they come:
You'll shape them into splendid lawyers, Sir;
They are quite ignorant.

RESPONDENT

Sir, I demur.
I'll make his Honour sleep as well as any.   635

SMALL JOHN

Sure, I know nothing. I am two a penny.

LEANDER

Your first case will be made out. Don't be daunted.

SMALL JOHN

But, Sir, I cannot read.

LEANDER

You will be prompted.

DANDIN

Let's prepare. Gentlemen, no gerrymander!
We'll shut our eyes to gifts, our ears to slander.   640
You, Master Small John, will be prosecuting;
And you, Master Respondent, be defending.

ACT III

SCENE I

WRANGLER, LEANDER *and the* PROMPTER

WRANGLER

Yes, that is how, Sir, I became defendant.
I neither knew the bailiff nor the sergeant.
I'm telling the whole truth.

LEANDER

        It's plain to me.   645
But if you heed me, you will let them be.
Take my advice and rest upon your oars.
To sue them would mar less their peace than yours.
Three quarters of your wealth has gone awry
In swelling sacks of papers stacked on high: 650
And in an action, where with loaded dice . . .

WRANGLER

Indeed, you give to me most sound advice,
Of which I'll take advantage by and by:
But put in a word, I beseech you try.
Since Master Dandin's going on the Bench,   655
I'll hither fetch with speed my filial wench.
She may be questioned; truth from her will shine:
And her replies are better even than mine.

LEANDER

You shall have justice: go and come back quick.

PROMPTER

What a man!

Exit WRANGLER

SCENE II

LEANDER

  I've recourse to a strange trick;   *660*
But father is a man to drive one mad;
And with a juicy case he must be had.
Besides I have my plan; and he must sentence
This fool who brings all down to court attendance.
But here come trooping in our reprobates.   *665*

SCENE III

Enter DANDIN, RESPONDENT *and* SMALL JOHN

DANDIN

What are you, there?

LEANDER

  They are the advocates.

DANDIN

You?

PROMPTER

  I support their failing memory.

DANDIN

I follow: And you?

LEANDER

I am the gallery.

DANDIN

Then let's begin.

PROMPTER

Gentlemen . . .

SMALL JOHN

                    Not so proud.
No one will hear me if you prompt so loud.   670
Gentlemen . . .

DANDIN

    Hat!

SMALL JOHN

Oh! My . . .

DANDIN

        Hat on, I say.

SMALL JOHN

Oh! Sir, I know the deference I should pay.

DANDIN

Then leave your hat.

SMALL JOHN (*Putting on his hat*)

    Gentlemen . . . (*To the* PROMPTER) You, don't screech.
What I know best is just my opening speech.
Gentlemen, when I see with exactitude   675
The changing world and its vicissitude;
When I see mid so many different men
No constant star, but spheres that turn again;
When I the Caesars see and all their fortune;
When I the sun see, when I see the moon;   680

When I see the realms of the Babibonians[8]
Transferred from the Serpeans[9] to the Nacedonians,[10]
When I the Morons[11] see from State depotic[12]
Pass to the demotic,[13] then to monarchic;
When I see Japan. . .

RESPONDENT

When will he've seen all!   685

SMALL JOHN

Why has he butted in and made me fall?
I'll say no more.

DANDIN

Counsel irreverend,
Why did you not let him his period end?
I sweated blood to see if, safe at home,
He, from Japan, would to his capon come,   690
And you must interrupt with frivolous word.
Counsel, proceed.

SMALL JOHN

I've lost the thread, my lord.

LEANDER

Go on, Small John. 'Twas very well begun.
But why hang stiff your arms as though you've done?
You stand there, like a statue on your feet.   695
Relax. Take heart. Acknowledge no defeat.

SMALL JOHN (*Waving his arms*)

When . . . I see . . . when . . . I see

LEANDER

Say what you see.

---

[8] Babylonians. [9] Persians. [10] Macedonians. [11] Romans. [12] despotic. [13] democratic. [Racine's note].

SMALL JOHN

Oh, hang it all! Two things at once? Not me!

PROMPTER

One reads . . .

SMALL JOHN

One reads . . .

PROMPTER

In the . . .

SMALL JOHN

In the . . .

PROMPTER

Metamorphoses

SMALL JOHN

What's that?

PROMPTER

That the metem . . .

SMALL JOHN

That the metem . . .

PROMPTER

'psychosis . . .   *700*

SMALL JOHN

'Psychosis . . .

PROMPTER

Ho! The horse!

SMALL JOHN

And the horse . . .

PROMPTER

Go on.

SMALL JOHN

Go on . . .

PROMPTER

The dog!

SMALL JOHN

The dog!

PROMPTER

The lout!

SMALL JOHN

The lout . . .

PROMPTER

A plague on this counsel!

SMALL JOHN

On you a plague!
Look at that one, as dismal as a morgue!
Go to the devil!

DANDIN

You, come to the facts. Hush!   705

SMALL JOHN

Must one forever beat about the bush?
They make me mouth words longer than my arms,
Great, big, fat words, stretching from here to Worms.
I do not know why all this hue and howl,
To say a mastiff's pounced upon a fowl: 710
That there is nothing which this cur'll not catch,
That he has swallowed capon, house and thatch,
And that the next time that he shows his face,
I'll bash his head in, and so close his case.

LEANDER

Proud peroration that the exordium fits!   *715*

SMALL JOHN

It's pretty plain; so let them show their wits.

DANDIN

Call the witnesses.

LEANDER

He would if he could,
But witnesses are costly even when good.

SMALL JOHN

Yet we have some that cannot challenged be.

DANDIN

Let them approach.

SMALL JOHN

They're clinging here to me;   *720*
Here in my pocket, capon's head and claws.
See them and judge.

RESPONDENT

Object!

DANDIN

Under what laws?

RESPONDENT

From Maine, your Worship, they are said to come.

DANDIN

True, dozens from Le Mans I have at home.

RESPONDENT

Gentlemen . . .

DANDIN

Tell me if you will be long.   *725*

RESPONDENT

I cannot say.

DANDIN

That means he's going strong.

RESPONDENT (*In a tone rising to falsetto*)

Gentlemen, all, that the guilty may confound,
All, that to human fears must give most ground,
By chance seem to be gathered for our shame:
Intrigue I mean and eloquence. The fame   *730*
Of the deceased on the one hand appals me;
While Master Small John, on the other, enthrals me
With his shattering eloquence.

DANDIN

Advocate,
In your turn, pray, your shattering tone abate.

RESPONDENT (*In the grand manner*)

Bless you, I've several . . . But to whatever dismay   *735*
The aforesaid eloquence makes us give way,
And the aforesaid fame, Gentlemen, none the less
The anchor of your goodness comforts us: yes,
Before great Dandin innocence breathes free;
Before this Cato of our Normandy,   *740*
This sun of righteousness that rules the sky
Victrix causa diis placuit, sed victa Catoni.[14]

DANDIN

Truly, he pleads well.

RESPONDENT

Without further fear,

[14] The victorious cause was favoured by the gods, but the vanquished by
Cato (Lucan).

I come to my defence and let all hear,
Aristotle, *primo, peri Politicon,*   *745*
Says well . . .

DANDIN

Counsel, the case concerns a capon,
Not Aristotle and his *Politics.*

RESPONDENT

Yes, but the weight of the *Peripatetics*
Would prove that good and evil . . .

DANDIN

I must hold
That Aristotle here would leave me cold.   *750*
To the facts.

RESPONDENT

Pausanias, in Corinthians, claims . . .

DANDIN

The facts.

RESPONDENT

Rebuffe . . .

DANDIN

The facts, I say.

RESPONDENT

Great James . . .

DANDIN

The facts, the facts.

RESPONDENT

Harmenopulos, Greek . . .

DANDIN

I shall pass judgment.

RESPONDENT

Hi! You're pretty quick!

(*Speaking quickly*)

Here are the facts. A dog enters a kitchen   755
And finds a capon luscious as a bitch. In
Short my client by hunger is consumed;
While his opponent struts around deplumed;
Thus, he for whom I speak, takes, on the sly,
Him whom I speak against. A hue and cry: 760
He's caught; and counsel on both sides bespoken;
Day fixed. I am to speak, I speak, I've spoken.

DANDIN

Tut, tut, tut! a fine handling of his case!
He rides the irrelevent at steady pace,
But when he reaches facts, gallops like mad.   765

RESPONDENT

The good part is the former.

DANDIN

                          No, the bad.
Has any ever argued with like passion?
What says the gallery?

LEANDER

He's in the fashion.

RESPONDENT (*In a vehement tone*)

What happens, gentlemen? They come. In what wise?
They chase my client and a house they prise.   770
Which house? Our judge's; and all helter-skelter,
They force the storeroom where we've taken shelter!
They charge us, both with robbery and theft!

They drag us to our accusers, where we're left
With Master Small John, gentlemen. I attest: *775*
Who does not know law *Si quis canis*, Digest,
De Vi, paragraph, gentlemen, *Caponibus*
Is plainly contrary to this abuse?
And were it even true, Citron, my client,
Had eaten all, or rather the more pliant   *780*
Portion of the said capon, be it recalled
All we have done before this case was called!
When was my client ever warned before?
Who was it that kept watch beside your door?
When have we failed to bark at all the thieves?   *785*
Witness those three attorneys whose wide sleeves
The said Citron snapped. The shreds may be heeded.
In our defence are documents still needed?

SMALL JOHN

Master Adam . . .

RESPONDENT

Be off!

SMALL JOHN

Respondent . . .

RESPONDENT

Off.

SMALL JOHN

Is hoarse.

RESPONDENT

Be off with you!

DANDIN

Your headgear doff   *790*
And end.

RESPONDENT (*In a heavy tone*)

Since, we are allowed, to take breath,
Forbidden, to stretch out, on pain of death,
I shall, without prevarication, state,
In full detail compendiously dilate,
Unfold to you the idea universal   795
Behind my case, and facts now, in a nutshell.

DANDIN

He would far sooner tell all twenty times
Than leave out any. Man, or imp that mimes,
Devil, conclude or suffer Heaven's scorn!

RESPONDENT

I finish.

DANDIN

        Ah!

RESPONDENT

Before the world was born . . .   800

DANDIN (*Yawning*)

Come, Counsel, skip on to the Flood.

RESPONDENT

                                        Before
The world was born, and fashioned furthermore,
The world, the universe, all nature, all
Was buried in the heart of the material.
And all the elements, earth, air, fire, water,   805
Were sunk and piled up, like a monstrous slaughter,
A formless mass, and the most crass confusion,
Disorder, chaos, and a vast profusion:
Unus erat toto naturae vultus in orbe,
Quem Graeci dixere chaos, rudis indigestaque moles.[15]   810

---

[15] Nature throughout the universe offered a uniform aspect, what the Greeks called *chaos*, a mass of crude confusion (Ovid, *Metamorphoses*).

LEANDER

What a fall, my Father!

SMALL JOHN

Sir, sleepyhead!

LEANDER

Father, wake up.

SMALL JOHN

Your Worship, are you dead?

LEANDER

Father!

DANDIN

Well? Well? What's it? Ah! what a man!
I sensed my soundest sleep when he began!

LEANDER

Father, pass judgement.

DANDIN

To the galleys.

LEANDER

                                        A dog.   *815*

To the galleys!

DANDIN

Bless me! my mind's a fog:
My brain is reeling with the world, with chaos.
End, man!

RESPONDENT (*Handing up puppies*)

Come, progeny, all plunged in pathos;
Come, babes, whom they would orphan quite today:
Come, to your infant pleadings give full play.   *820*
Yes, gentlemen, you see our misery:

Orphans are we, pray set our father free.
Our father, from whose fertile seed we sprout,
Our father, who . . .

DANDIN

A plague on you, out, out.

RESPONDENT

Our father, gentlemen . . .

DANDIN

     Out, what a din!   *825*
They've pissed all over.

RESPONDENT

Sir, our tears begin.[16]

DANDIN

What, I already feel moved by compassion!
How very apt to reach the height of passion!
I'm at a loss. By justice I am pressed.
The crime is proved: he has himself confessed. *830*
But if he's sentenced, the outcome how unwelcome:
How many mites put to a foundlings' home.
But I am busy and will no one view.

LAST SCENE

Enter WRANGLER *and* ISOBEL

WRANGLER

Sir . . .

DANDIN

Do you think the hearing's but for you?
Good-bye. But tell me, who is that child there? *835*

[16] This very intimate touch by the author of *Athalie* and the *Cantiques Spirit-uels* is not in Aristophanes, although it might well have been!

WRANGLER

She is my daughter, Sir.

DANDIN

Quick, call her here.

ISOBEL

But you are busy.

DANDIN

I—why, I'm quite free.
That you her father were, why keep from me?

WRANGLER

Sir . . .

DANDIN

She knows your case better than you do.
Speak. She is pretty and can ogle too!   *840*
My girl, that is not all, you must be good.
I'm overjoyed to see your youthful blood.
D'you know I was a gay dog in my day?
Much talked of.

ISOBEL

Ah Sir! Why, of course, I'd say.

DANDIN

Tell me, which party do you want to lose?   *845*

ISOBEL

None.

DANDIN

For you I'd do anything. Then choose.

ISOBEL

You are, Sir, much too kind. I'm in your debt.

DANDIN

Have you seen no one put to torture yet?

ISOBEL

No; and would not as long as I may live.

DANDIN

Come, dear, the heart for it to you I'll give.   *850*

ISOBEL

Can one a wretch's pains with pleasure view?

DANDIN

Yes, it will while away an hour or two.

WRANGLER

Sir, I have come here to tell you . . .

LEANDER
                                But Father,
In two words let me tell it to you rather:
It is about a marriage, you may guess   *855*
All are agreed, it rests for you to bless.
The girl is willing, while her lover pants,
And what his daughter wants her father wants.
You must pass judgment.

DANDIN (*Taking his seat once more*)
                                Marry on the spot.
Tomorrow, if you wish; today, if not.   *860*

LEANDER

Your father-in-law seated there, come, Miss,
Salute.

WRANGLER

        What's that?

DANDIN

What mystery then is this?

LEANDER

What you have said is followed to the letter.

DANDIN

Since I've passed judgment, I can do no better.

WRANGLER

His daughter none can give without the bride.   865

LEANDER

Quite so. Let charming Isobel decide.

WRANGLER

It is some scurvy trick, have you not sensed it?
Speak.

ISOBEL

Father, I dare not appeal against it.

WRANGLER

But I appeal.

LEANDER

This writing here is sure.
Will you appeal from your own signature?   870

WRANGLER

What did you say?

DANDIN

It is a binding contract.

WRANGLER

I see I've been deceived. I'll not be sidetracked:
Of more than twenty suits this will prove source.
He's got the girl, but shall not get the purse.

LEANDER

Who asked for anything? Your teeth why gnash?   875
Leave me your daughter and conserve your cash.

WRANGLER

Ah!

LEANDER

Are you satisfied, Dad, with the session?

DANDIN

Indeed. Let suits follow in quick succession,
And let me pass my latter days with you.
Let counsel be in future briefer too.   880
And our accused?

LEANDER

Let there be only joy:
Ah, pardon, Father.

DANDIN

He's discharged, my boy,
And dear daughter-in-law, to mark your graces.
Let's now relax in pastures of fresh cases.

THE END

�֍֍֍

BRITANNICUS

A Tragedy

To His Grace the Duc de Chevreuse*

Your Grace,

You will perhaps be amazed to see your name at the head of this work; and if I had asked your permission to dedicate it to you, I doubt whether I should have received it. But it would have smacked of some ingratitude to hide any longer from the world the kindnesses with which you have always honoured me. How would it look if a man who ever strives for glory were to remain silent about a patronage as glorious as yours? No, Your Grace, it is altogether to my profit that it should be known that your attention extends even to my friends, that you interest yourself in all my works and that you have procured for me the honour of reading out this one to a man whose every hour is precious. You were witness with what deep insight he judged of the economy of the play, and how far beyond my conception ranged his idea of what constitutes an excellent tragedy. Your Grace need not fear that I commit myself further, and that not daring to praise him openly I address myself to you in order more fully to praise him. I know that it would be dangerous to weary him with praises; and I make bold to say that this very modesty which you share with him is not the least of the bonds which unite you to each other.† Moderation is only a commonplace virtue when it is come across with commonplace qualities. But that, with all the qualities of heart and head, with a judgment which, it seems, could only have been the fruit of several years' experience, with a thousand intellectual embellishments which you cannot hide from your intimate friends, that you should still have that wise restraint which everyone admires in you, is certainly a virtue rare in an age in which the most trivial matters are vaunted. But I am allowing myself to slip imperceptibly into the temptation of speaking of you.

* Head of one of the great families of France, favourable to the Jansenists of Port-Royal, whose protection Racine, as a pupil of Port-Royal, continued to enjoy even when his theatrical career earned him the reproach of his Port-Royal mentors.

† The Duc de Chevreuse, six years Racine's junior, had married the daughter of Colbert (Minister of Finance) to whom Racine is referring. Racine's next play, *Bérénice*, is dedicated to Colbert.

The temptation must indeed have been violent, since I have not been able to resist it in a letter in which I had no other aim than to testify to you with what great respect I am,
Your Grace,.
Your very humble and
very obedient Servant,
RACINE

First Preface*

Of all the works I have given
to the public none has brought me more applause nor more
critics than this. Whatever care I may have taken in fashioning
this tragedy, it seems that the more I have striven to make it good,
the more some people have striven to decry it. There is no intrigue
to which they have not had recourse, no criticism of which they
have not made use. There are some indeed who have even sided
with Nero against me. They have said that I made him too cruel.
As for me, I always thought that the very name Nero conjured
up something worse than cruel. But perhaps they wish to draw
distinctions about his history and to maintain that he was a good
man in his first years. One need only have read Tacitus to know
that if he was for a while, a good emperor, he always was a very
wicked man. My tragedy does not deal with outside matters.
Nero is here depicted as an individual and in the bosom of his
family. And they will spare me the necessity of bringing to their
notice all the passages which would quickly prove to them that I
have no apology to make him.

Others have said, on the contrary, that I had made him too good.
I confess that I had never conceived of Nero as a good man. I
have always thought of him as a monster. But here he is a budding
monster. He has not yet set fire to Rome. He has not killed his
mother, his wife, his tutors. But apart from that it seems to me
that he lets through enough cruelties to prevent anyone from
mistaking his character.

Some have sided with Narcissus and have complained that
I portrayed him as a very wicked man and the confidential adviser
of Nero. One passage is enough to refute them. "Nero," says
Tacitus, "chafed at the death of Narcissus, because that freedman

* Printed in Racine's lifetime only in the first edition, of 1670.

had a marvellous conformity with the still-hidden vices of the
Prince: *Cujus abditis adhuc vitiis mire congruebat.*" Others have
been shocked that I should have chosen so young a man as
Britannicus to be the hero of a tragedy. I have stated to them,
in the preface of *Andromache*, Aristotle's views on the tragic
hero; and that very far from being perfect, he must always have
some defect. But I shall tell them once again here that a young
prince of seventeen years of age, full of spirit, full of love, full of
frankness and full of credulity, the usual qualities of a young man,
has seemed to me very capable of arousing pity. I do not require
more of him. But, they say, this Prince had only entered his
fifteenth year when he died. He is made to live, he and Narcissus,
two years longer than they did live. I would not have mentioned
this objection if it had not been made with asperity by a man†
who himself took the liberty of making an emperor reign twenty
years who in fact reigned only eight, although this alteration is
much greater in chronology, where time is reckoned by the reigns
of the emperors.

Junia, too, does not lack critics. They say that out of an old
coquette called Junia Silana I have made a very good young lady.
What would they have to reply to me if I said to them that this
Junia is an invented character like the Emilia of *Cinna*, like the
Sabina of *Horace*?‡ But I may tell them that if they had read
their history well, they would have found a Junia Calvina, of
Augustus' family, sister of Silanus, to whom Claudius had promised Octavia. This Junia was young, beautiful, and as Seneca says,
festivissima omnium puellarum.§ She loved her brother dearly;
"and their enemies," says Tacitus, "accused them both of incest,
although they were only guilty of a little indiscretion." If I depict
her more restrained than she was, I have not heard it said that we
were forbidden to modify the manners of a character, especially
an unknown one.

Some have found it strange that she appears on the stage after
the death of Britannicus. The delicacy is certainly great, not
to wish her to say in four fairly moving lines that she is going

---

† Corneille. The play in which Corneille took this chronological liberty is
Héraclius, where Phocas is represented as reigning for twenty years.
‡ Plays by Corneille.
§ "The most fetching of all maidens."

to Octavia. But they maintain that it was not worth the trouble of bringing her back once more. Someone else might have mentioned it for her. They do not know that one of the rules of the theatre is not to make a recital except of those events that cannot take place on the stage; and that all the ancients often bring on the stage actors who have nothing else to say except that they come from one place and are going back to another.*

All that is useless, say my critics. The play is ended with the account of Britannicus' death, and one should not listen to the rest. None the less one does listen to it and even with as much attention as the end of any tragedy. For my part, I have always understood that tragedy being the imitation of a complete action, in which several persons take part, this action is not ended until one knows what situation it leaves these same persons. This is Sophocles' practice almost throughout. This is how in the *Antigone* he takes as many lines to describe Haemon's frenzy and the punishment of Creon after that princess's death, as I have taken to depict the curses of Agrippina, the retreat of Junia, the punishment of Narcissus and the despair of Nero, after Britannicus' death.

What would one have to do to please such difficult judges? It would be easy enough to do so if one were prepared to betray common sense. It would only be necessary to deviate from the natural and plunge into the extraordinary. Instead of a simple plot burdened with little matter, such as a plot that takes place in only one day must be, a plot which progresses step by step to its end, which is only sustained by the interests, the sentiments, and the passions of the characters, it would be necessary to fill this very plot with a heap of incidents, which could take place only in a month, with a great number of theatrical tricks, all the more surprising for being less probable, with countless declamations in which actors are made to say precisely the contrary of what they should say. It would, for example, be necessary to portray some drunken hero, who would wish to make his mistress hate him out of pure lightness of heart, a chatterbox Lacedemonian, a conqueror uttering nothing but maxims of love, a woman

---

* This somewhat specious justification did not prevent Racine from vindicating his critics by suppressing later this peccant scene of Junia's reappearance, Act V Scene 6 of the first edition (1670).

giving lessons in pride to conquerors.* Such no doubt are the
ways to make all these gentlemen shout 'bravo'. But then what
would the few wise men, I strive to please, say? What face, so to
speak, would I dare to turn to those great men of antiquity whom
I have chosen as models? For, to quote an Ancient's thoughts,
those are the true audiences whom we should bear in mind and
we should ceaselessly ask ourselves: "What would Homer and
Virgil say if they were to read these lines? What would Sophocles
say, if he saw this scene enacted?" However that may be, I have
never dreamt of preventing people from speaking against my
works. It would have been useless to have so dreamt: *Quid de te
alii loquantur ipsi videant*, says Cicero, *sed loquentur tamen.*†

I only beg the reader to pardon me this little preface, which I
have written to justify my tragedy to him. There is nothing more
natural than to defend oneself, when one believes one has been
unjustly assailed. I see that Terence himself appears to have
written prologues merely to justify himself against the criticisms
of an evil-intentioned old poet, *malevoli veteris poetae*, who came
to canvass voices against him up to the very hour his comedies
were performed.

> *. . . Occepta est agi;
> Exclamat, etc.*‡

One might have raised an objection which has not been made.
But what might have escaped an audience, may be detected by
readers. It is that I make Junia enter the order of the Vestal
Virgins, where according to Aulus Gellius, no one was received
below six years of age nor over ten. But the people take Junia
under their protection here—and I have believed that in consideration of her birth, her virtue and her misfortune they could
dispense with the age prescribed by the laws, as they dispensed

---

* Racine refers here to Corneille's Attila (drunken hero); Agésilas (chatterbox
Lacedemonian); and to Julius Caesar (a conqueror uttering nothing . . .) and
Cornelia (a woman giving lessons . . .) in Corneille's *La Mort de Pompée*.

† Cicero, *Republic*, VI, XVI: "What others prattle of you is their business; but
they will still prattle."

‡ Terence, *Eunuch*, Prologue, v. 22—"The performance was beginning; he
cries out." This and the previous paragraphs are Racine's counterattack on
Corneille and his dramatic practice. Corneille and his supporters were much put
out by *Britannicus* where Racine, for the first time, challenged Corneille on his own
ground of political tragedy, and at least equalled, if not surpassed, the old master.

with the age requirements of the consulate in the case of so many great men who had deserved this privilege.

Finally, I am very conscious that many other criticisms may be levelled at me, about which I can do no more than profit from them in the future. But I greatly pity the misfortune of a man who works for the public. Those who see our faults most clearly are those who are most eager to hide them. They forgive us the portions that have displeased them for the sake of those that have delighted them. On the other hand, nothing is more unjust than an ignoramus. He always imagines that to admire is the lot of persons who know nothing. He condemns a whole play because of a scene which he dislikes. He even attacks the most brilliant portions to give an impression of intellect; and if we show the slightest resistance to his views he deems us presumptuous persons who listen to nobody, and never dreams for a moment that he sometimes derives more vain satisfaction from a downright bad piece of criticism than we derive for having created a pretty good play.

*Homine imperito numquam quidquam injustius.**

---

* Terence, *Adelphi*, v. 99—"Nothing is more unjust than an ignoramus."

Second Preface*

This is, of all my tragedies, the one over which I may say I have most laboured. Yet I confess that its success did not at first correspond with my hopes. It had hardly appeared on the stage when it aroused a number of criticisms which seemed bent on destroying it. I myself thought that its fate in future would be less fortunate than that of my other tragedies. But finally there happened to this play what will always happen to works of some merit. The criticisms vanished, the play remained. It is now the one of my plays which the Court and the public see more than once most willingly; and if I have created something solid which is worthy of some praise, most connoisseurs are in agreement that it is this very *Britannicus*.

In truth I had worked on models which had helped me enormously in the picture I wished to paint of the court of Agrippina and Nero. I had copied my characters from the greatest painter of antiquity, namely from Tacitus. And, I was at the time so immersed in the pages of that excellent historian, that there is hardly a brilliant stroke in my tragedy of which he has not given me the idea. I had intended to include in this collection an extract of the finest passages I have tried to imitate; but I found that this extract would take up almost as much space as the tragedy. Thus the reader will be content to be referred to that author, who moreover is accessible to everybody; and I will limit myself to indicating here some of his passages on each of the characters that I have brought on the stage.

To begin with Nero; it must be remembered that he is here in the first years of his reign, which have been happy, as is known. Thus I was not at liberty to portray him as wicked as he later became. I do not however portray him as a virtuous man which he

* This second Preface replaced the first from the edition of 1676 onwards.

never was. He has not yet killed his mother, his wife, his tutors: but he has in him the seed of all his crimes. He begins with wanting to throw off the yoke. He hates them one and all, and, hides his hate under false caresses: *Factus natura velare odium fallacibus blanditiis.** In short he is here a budding monster, but who does not yet dare to declare himself and who seeks to colour his wicked deeds: *Hactenus Nero flagitiis et sceleribus velamenta quae sivit.*† He could not bear Octavia, a princess of exemplary goodness and virtue: *Fato quodam, an quia praevalent illicita; metuebaturque ne in stupra feminarum illustrium prorumperet.*‡

I give him Narcissus as confidential adviser. I have followed Tacitus in that, who says that Nero chafed at the death of Narcissus because this freedman had a marvellous conformity with the yet hidden vices of the Prince: *Cujus abditis adhuc vitiis mire congruebat.* § This passage proves two things: it proves both that Nero was already vicious, but that he hid his vices, and that Narcissus encouraged him in his evil inclinations.

I have chosen Burrhus to oppose a man of honour to that pestilential courtier; and I have chosen him rather than Seneca. Here is the reason. They were both tutors of Nero's youth, one for arms, the other for letters; and they were famous; Burrhus for his experience in arms and for the strictness of his morals, *militaribus curis et severitate morum*; Seneca for his eloquence and his agreeable turn of mind, *Seneca praeceptis eloquentiae et comitate honesta.*** Burrhus after his death was deeply lamented on account of his virtue: *Civitati grande desiderium ejus mansit per memoriam virtutis.*††

Their whole aim was to resist the pride and violence of Agrip-

---

* Tacitus, *Annals*, XIV, LVI—"Born with the talent of hiding his hatred under false caresses."

† Ibid., XIII, XLVII—"Up to this moment Nero had sought to hide his licentiousness and his crimes."

‡ Ibid., XIII, XII—"By a kind of fatality or by the all powerful pull of illicit voluptuousness; and it was feared that he might be carried to corrupt illustrious women."

§ Ibid., XIII, I.

** Ibid., XIII, II—"By his military knowledge and by the austerity of his ways"; "Seneca by the art of teaching eloquence and by the graces he mingled with virtue."

†† Ibid., XIV, LI—"This great man left long regrets to the empire mindful of his virtue."

pina: *quae, cunctis malae dominationis cupidinibus flagrans, habebat in partibus Pallantem.** I say only this one word about Agrippina, for there would be too much to say of her. It is she that I have striven above all to depict well; and my tragedy is not less the fall of Agrippina than the death of Britannicus. That death was a thunderbolt for her, and it was clear, says Tacitus, from her terror and from her consternation that she was as innocent of that death as Octavia. Agrippina lost in him her last hope and this crime made her fear a still greater one: *Sibi supremum auxilium ereptum, ut parricidii exemplum intelligebat.*†

The age of Britannicus was so well known, that I was not at liberty to portray him other than a young prince who was full of spirit, full of love and full of candour, the usual qualities of a young man. He was fifteen years old and is said to have shown much promise, whether it be true or whether his misfortunes gave rise to that belief, without his really having shown signs of it: *Neque segnem ei fuisse indolem ferunt; sive verum, seu periculis commendatus retinuit famam sine experimento.*‡

One must not be surprised if he has to guide him only a man as wicked as Narcissus; for orders had been passed a long time back that there were to be near Britannicus, only men without faith or honour: *Nam ut proximus quisque Britannico neque fas neque fidem pensi haberet olim provisum erat.*§

It remains for me to mention Junia. She must not be confused with an old coquette who was called Junia Silana. This is another Junia whom Tacitus calls Junia Calvina, of the family of Augustus, sister of Silanus to whom Claudius had promised Octavia. This Junia was young, beautiful, and as Seneca says: *festivissima omnium puellarum* (the most fetching of all maidens). Her brother and she loved each other dearly; and their enemies says Ticitus, accused them both of incest, though they were guilty only of a little indiscretion. She lived on into the reign of Vespasian.

I make her enter the order of the Vestal Virgins although

---

* Tacitus, *Annals*, XIII, II—"Agrippina, consumed by all the fires of a selfish ambition, was supported by Pallas."
† Ibid., XVI—"She saw her last resource snatched from her and well apprehended that it was the rehearsal for matricide."
‡ Ibid., XII, XXVI—"He was said not to have lacked merit, whether he really had it, or whether he owed this reputation to the prestige of his misfortune without having had to justify it."
§ Ibid., XIII, XV.

according to Aulus Gellius, no one was ever received in it below the age of six nor above ten. But the people take Junia under their protection here. And I imagined that in consideration of her birth, her virtue and her misfortune, they could exempt her from the age prescribed by the laws, as they exempted from the age requirements of the consulate so many great men who had deserved this privilege.

BRITANNICUS

First performed on December 13, 1669, at the Hôtel de Bourgogne; first printed in 1670.

CHARACTERS

NERO	*Emperor, son of Agrippina*
BRITANNICUS	*Son of the Emperor Claudius*
AGRIPPINA	*Widow of Domitius Enobarbus, father of Nero and, by a second marriage, widow of the Emperor Claudius*
JUNIA	*In love with Britannicus*
BURRHUS	*Tutor of Nero*
NARCISSUS	*Tutor of Britannicus*
ALBINA	*Lady-in-waiting to Agrippina*

Attendants

The scene is in Rome, in a room of Nero's palace.

ACT I

SCENE I

AGRIPPINA, ALBINA

ALBINA

What, Madam, does this mean? While Nero sleeps,
Must you stand waiting here for him to wake?
And wandering through the palace, unattended,
Must Caesar's mother watch beside his door?
Return, my lady, to your own apartments.   5

AGRIPPINA

I cannot go, Albina, even a moment.
I must await him here. The anxieties
He causes me will hold me while he sleeps.
All I've foretold is sure to happen now:
Against Britannicus he takes his stand;   10
No longer will he suffer any brake;
Weary of men's love, he demands their fear.
Britannicus impedes him and each day
I feel I stand, in my turn, in his way.

ALBINA

What? You, to whom he owes the air he breathes,   15
Who summoned him to Empire from so far;
Who, disinheriting the son of Claudius,
Let Caesar's mantle fall upon Domitius?[1]
Why, everything, my lady, speaks for you.
He owes you love.

[1] Domitius was Nero's name (after his father's house) before he was adopted
by Claudius.

AGRIPPINA

Indeed, he owes it to me: 20
If he be noble everything prescribes it;
But if he's base, all speaks to him against me.

ALBINA

If he is base, Madam! Why, all his acts
Denote he has a high sense of his duty.
For three whole years, what has he said, what done,   25
Not warranting to Rome a model Emperor?
For two years, Rome, beneath his careful sway,
Believes herself ruled once more by her Consuls:
He governs like a father. Nero, young,
Has all the virtues of Augustus old.   30

AGRIPPINA

No, no, my interest does not jaundice me.
True, he begins where great Augustus ended;
But fear, lest future blotting out the past,
He end just how Augustus has begun.
In vain he shams: I read upon his face   35
The dark, wild humours of his savage sires,
Uniting with their fierce and stubborn blood
The pride of all the Neros born of me.
Sweet are the first fruits of a tyrant's reign:
Caligula[2] delighted Rome awhile;   40
But his feigned goodness, turning into madness,
Made cruel havoc soon of Rome's delight.
What matters it to me if, after all,
Nero, more persevering in his good,
Should one day leave behind a model rule?
Have I placed in his hands the helm of State   45a
To steer it as the Senate's whim directs?
Let him be, if he must, the people's father;
But let him not forget I am his mother.
And yet, in what terms may we designate

---

[2] Caligula was the third Roman Emperor, after Augustus and Tiberius. He was
succeeded by his uncle, Claudius, Nero's predecessor.

The violence the dawn has just unveiled?   *50*
He knows, for all the world's aware of it,
Britannicus has lost his heart to Junia,
And this same Nero, bent on doing right,
Drags Junia here, arrested at midnight.
What does he want? What drives him? Hate or love?   *55*
Or does he but delight to do them harm?
Or rather is it not perhaps his spite
To punish them, because I lend them aid?

ALBINA

You lend them aid, my lady?

AGRIPPINA

Stop, Albina,
I know, I have alone hastened their downfall;   *60*
That, through me, from the throne he should have won
By right of blood, Britannicus was hurled;
Through me alone, foiled of Octavia's hand,[3]
Silanus, Junia's brother, took his life,
Silanus, on whom Claudius cast his eyes,   *65*
And who could count as ancestor, Augustus.
Nero enjoys it all: for my reward,
Between them and him I must hold the balance,
So that some day, by means of this same law,
Between my son and me, Britannicus   *70*
May hold it.

ALBINA

What a plan!

AGRIPPINA

My dear Albina,
I must prepare a haven for the storm.
Nero will cut adrift, if not thus tied.

---

[3] Octavia, the Emperor Claudius' daughter and Britannicus' sister, was married by Agrippina to Nero to further his prospects to Claudius' succession.

ALBINA

Why make, against a son, such needless safeguards?

AGRIPPINA

I would soon have to fear him, were he not
To fear me any more.

ALBINA

           Perhaps, my lady,
A baseless terror is alarming you.   *75b*
But if his duty towards you is impaired,
At least he lets us see no trace of this,
And these are secrets between him and you.
Whatever further laurels Rome accords him,
There's none he does not mete out to his mother.   *80*
His lavish love holds nothing back from you.
Your name in Rome is sacred as his own.
One hardly hears the sad Octavia mentioned.
Your sire Augustus honoured Livia less.
Nero has been the very first to let   *85*
The fasces, laurel-crowned, precede his mother.
What further gratitude could you desire?

AGRIPPINA

A little less respect and greater trust.
Albina, all these gifts arouse my gall:
I see my honours rise, my credit fall.   *90*
No, no, gone is the time when Nero, young,
Sent me the prayers of an adoring Court;
When he left all affairs of State to me,
When at my word the Senate would assemble
Within the palace, where, behind a veil,   *95*
Invisible and present, I became
The almighty spirit of that mighty body.
At that time still unsure of Rome's support,
Nero was not yet drunken with his greatness.
Ah! how can I forget that sorry day,

When Nero, himself dazzled by his glory,   *100*
Received the envoys of a hundred kings,
Come to salute him emperor of the world.
I was about to mount the throne with him.
I do not know what hint urged my disgrace;
But Nero, from the moment he beheld me,   *105*
Showed his displeasure plainly on his face.
Deep in my heart I felt the dreaded omen.[4]
Gilding his insult with a false respect,
The wretch stood up and, with a swift embrace,
Barred me the throne I was about to mount.   *110*
And, ever since that fatal blow, my power
Slides each day, avalanching to its doom.[5]
Only its shade abides; men now invoke
The name of Seneca or the aid of Burrhus.

ALBINA

Ah, if your soul is plagued with such suspicions,   *115*
Why nourish in your heart the murdering poison?
At least let Caesar plainly know your views.

AGRIPPINA

No more does Caesar speak to me alone.
In public and at fixed times I have audience.
His answers, even his silences, are prompted.   *120*
Two geniuses preside, his and my masters,
One or the other, over all our meetings.
But I shall cling the more he seeks to escape.
Albina, I must profit from his conflict.
I hear them opening doors. Let's go in quick   *125*
And ask him how he justifies her capture.
Let's try to pierce the secrets of his soul.
What's this? Already Burrhus comes from him?

---

[4] The astrologers had foretold to Agrippina that Nero would become Emperor but would kill his mother, to which she had replied, "Let him kill me, provided he becomes Emperor!" (Tacitus, *Annals*, XIV, IX.)

[5] Racine skilfully conveys, without mentioning it, the impression of an avalanche by alliteration in *ch*, and onomatopoeia.

SCENE II

Enter BURRHUS

BURRHUS

Madam, Caesar directed I impart
To you an order that at first might vex you,   *130*
But which is only prompted by precaution
That Caesar wished me to explain to you.

AGRIPPINA

Let's go in then. He will explain it better.

BURRHUS

Caesar, I fear, is occupied awhile.
Already both the consuls, by a door   *135*
Less open to the public, have forestalled you,
My lady. But permit me to return . . .

AGRIPPINA

I do not wish to trouble his high converse.
Yet, none the less, for once, may we speak straight
And without false pretences to each other?   *140*

BURRHUS

You know how Burrhus always hated falsehood.

AGRIPPINA

How long do you intend to hide the Emperor?
Am I to see him never but by begging?
Have I then raised your fortune to this height
To put a bar between my son and me?   *145*
Can you not leave him to himself a moment?
Must Seneca and you fight for the honour
Who will be first to wipe me from his mind?

Have I entrusted him to you for this?
That in his name you both should rule the State?   *150*
The more I think, the less I can conceive
How you could dare to reckon me your tool,
You, whose ambition I might well have left
To rust in the dim honours of some legion,
And me, who have been born to sit on thrones,   *155*
Wife, sister, daughter, mother of your masters![6]
What then are your pretensions? Do you think
My voice has made one emperor to have three?
Nero is child no more. Should he not reign?
How long must he tread limping in your train?   *160*
Must he see nothing except through your eyes?
Has he not then his ancestors for guides?
Let him Tiberius choose, Augustus rather,
Or, if he can, Germanicus my father.
To such heroic heights I dare not reach;   *165*
But there are virtues I myself can teach.
At least I could instruct him what reserve
Between himself and subjects to preserve.

BURRHUS

I had not thought at this time to do more
Than to explain one action of the Emperor,   *170*
But since, instead of hearing my report,
You make me guarantor of all his life,
I shall, my lady, answer with a soldier's
Freedom that knows not how to gild the truth.
You have entrusted to me Caesar's youth,   *175*
This I admit and will remember ever.
But, did I promise to betray your son,
To make of him a puppet Emperor?
No, no more should I render you account.
He's no more son, but master of the world.   *180*
I must account for him to all the Empire

---

[6] Wife of the Emperor Claudius, sister of the Emperor Caligula, daughter of the Commander-in-Chief Germanicus (himself father and brother of Caligula and Claudius respectively), and mother of Nero.

That deems its weal or woe within my hand.
Ah! if he had to grow in ignorance,
Could Seneca and I alone misguide him?
Why did you drive all flatterers from his side?   *185*
Need you have sought corrupters but in exile?
The court of Claudius, with its crowd of slaves,
Could have presented thousands, not just two,
All plotting for the prize of ruining him.
They would have made him grow old, still a child.   *190*
Then, Madam, why complain? We reverence you.
We swear by Caesar and his mother too.
The Emperor, true, no more comes every dawn,
To place the Empire at your feet and fawn.
But should he, Madam? Should his gratitude   *195*
Shine clearly only in his servitude?
Must Nero always humble, always tame,
Not dare to be a Caesar but in name?
Shall I speak plainly? Rome approves it thus.
For so long subject to three freedmen,[7] Rome,   *200*
Now breathing free at last from their fell yoke,
Reckons her freedom from the reign of Nero.
Indeed: it seems that virtue were reborn.
The Empire is no more her master's prey.
In the Campus Martius judges are elected;   *205*
The soldiers designate their chiefs to Caesar;
Thrasea in the Senate, Corbulo
In th' army are unscathed, despite their name;
The wilderness, once full of senators,
Is peopled now alone by their detractors.   *210*
What matters it if Caesar heeds our counsels,
Provided they are servants of his fame;
Provided that throughout a glorious reign
Rome's ever free and Caesar without stain?
But, Madam, Nero is his only law.   *215*
I but obey and do not claim to teach him.
He only has to follow his forefathers:
To prosper, he need only be himself:

---

[7] Callistus, Narcissus and Pallas, who exercised great influence in Claudius'
reign (Callistus, indeed, even in the preceding reign of Caligula).

Happy if, one to other chained, his virtues
Draw out the promise of his earliest years!   220

AGRIPPINA

So, not daring to leave the future free,
You think without you, Nero would be lost.
Well, tell us, you, pleased with your handiwork,
Who have just praised to us his qualities,
Why Nero in the guise of ravisher,   225
Orders the abduction of Silanus' sister.
Is he but burning to humiliate.
My forbears' blood that sparkles in her veins?
Of what does he accuse her? And what crime
Makes her so suddenly a State offender?   230
A girl who reared in lowliness till then,
Would not have seen him, were she not abducted,
And who might well have counted as a grace
The happy freedom never to see his face!

BURRHUS

I know she is suspected of no crime;   235
But up till now, my lady, Caesar has not
Condemned her. She is put to no constraint;
She's in a palace rich with ancestors.
You know, by right of her imperial rank,
Her husband may become a rebel prince;   240
And Caesar's blood may not ally itself
Except to such as Caesar may accept.
And you yourself must say it is not right
Augustus' niece should wed unknown to Nero.

AGRIPPINA

I see: so Nero tells me through your voice   245
Britannicus may not lean on my choice.
In vain, to lure him from his misery,
I've fed his love with hopes of Junia's hand.
To spite me, Nero wishes all to see
His mother's promises exceed her power.   250
Rome has the fondest notions of my credit:

He wants this insult to enlighten her,
To frighten all the world into remembering
No more to think the Emperor is my son.
Well, let him. Yet I dare to tell him still   255
He should first strengthen his imperial sway,
And that, in forcing on me the dread need
Of testing my weak power against his power,
He must expose his own, and in the balance
My name may heavier weigh than he imagines.   260

BURRHUS

My lady, why suspect his deference still?
Can he do nothing you do not take ill?
Can Caesar think you are on Junia's side?
Or with Britannicus you are allied?
Do you espouse the quarrel of your foes   265
To find a pretext to bewail your woes?
At the least word that causes you to chide
Will you still haste the Empire to divide?
Must you still fear each other and for ever
With explanations your embraces sever?   270
Forget the sad task of eternal censor,
And show a mother's love that's fond, intenser;
Bear some neglect without too much ado,
And do not warn the Court to slink from you.

AGRIPPINA

And who would count upon my aid at all   275
When Nero himself loud proclaims my fall?
When he appears to shun me more and more?
When Burrhus dares to bar me from his door?

BURRHUS

I clearly see it's time to hold my tongue,
And that my free speech has begun to irk you.   280
My lady, Grief's unjust, and every reason
That does not please her, strikes as out of season.
Here comes Britannicus; I leave him to you,

Leave you to hear and pity his misfortune,
And blame perhaps for it the advice of those   *285*
Whom the Emperor has consulted least, Heaven knows!

Exit BURRHUS

SCENE III

Enter BRITANNICUS *and* NARCISSUS

AGRIPPINA

Ah! Prince, where are you running? Why this haste
To throw yourself so blindly mid your foes?
What do you seek?

BRITANNICUS

       What do I seek? Ah, gods!
All I have lost, my lady, is hidden here.   *290*
Surrounded by a thousand brutish soldiers,
Junia's been basely dragged into this palace.
Alas! at this strange spectacle, what horror
Must have amazed her shy and gentle spirit!
So she's been torn from me. A harsh decree   *295*
Must part two hearts linked by their misery.
We must not share our grief, commands our foe,
In case we lighter make each other's woe.

AGRIPPINA

Enough, I feel your insults just like you.
My protests have preceded your complaints;   *300*
But I do not rely on empty anger
To keep my word to you and save my promise.
I speak no more. If you will hear me further,
At Pallas's you'll find me. There I'll wait.

Exeunt AGRIPPINA *and* ALBINA

SCENE IV

BRITANNICUS

Narcissus, should I trust her? At her word,   *305*
Take her as judge between her son and me?
Speak. Is she not the very Agrippina
Whom once my father married, to his[8] ruin,
And who, so you have said, with wicked haste
Cut short his days, too long for her designs?   *310*

NARCISSUS

No matter. Like you she is feeling outraged.
She's pledged herself to give you Junia.
Unite your troubles; bind your interests.
In vain this palace echoes with your sighs:
As long as, with a thin and plaintive voice,   *315*
You scatter here complaints instead of fears
And all your indignation melts in tears,
So long, you may be sure, you'll still complain.

BRITANNICUS

You are aware, Narcissus, if I mean
Eternally to hug my present chain;   *320*
Aware if, dazed forever by my fall,
I'll yield the Empire and my forbears' call!
But I am still alone. My father's friends
Are but obscure men, my misfortune numbs;
My very youth keeps distant from me still   *325*
All those who in their hearts would do my will:
And as for me, since my scant year's experience
Has given me sad knowledge of my fate,
Whom do I see around save friends suborned,
Who watch assiduously my every step,   *330*

[8] Some editions of Racine have "my" (*ma ruine*) instead of *sa ruine*. (Pléiade Edition.)

Who, picked by Nero for this sneakish art,
Traffic with him the secrets of my heart?
Narcissus, in this way I'm daily sold:
He learns my plans, my every word he's told;
Like you he knows what passes in my soul.   *335*
What do you think, Narcissus?

NARCISSUS

        Who so foul . . .
Sir, you must see your allies are discreet
And not speak freely to each one you meet.

BRITANNICUS

Well said, Narcissus. And yet, this distrust
Is the last wisdom of a noble heart,   *340*
Though oft betrayed. But still, I must believe you,
Or rather swear none to believe but you.
My father, I remember, trusted you.
Alone of all his freedmen you've been true;
Your eyes, forever open for my guidance,   *345*
Have saved me from a thousand hidden shoals.
Go, find out if the news of this fresh storm
May have aroused the courage of our friends.
Their eyes examine, listen to their speech;
Find, if I may expect his aid, from each.   *350*
Above all, note with cunning how securely
Nero guards the princess within the palace.
Learn if she has recovered from her peril
And whether I am still allowed to see her.
Meanwhile, I'll seek out Nero's mother at   *355*
The house of Pallas, like you, father's freedman.
I'll see, incite and follow her, and try,
Under her wing, higher than she to fly!

ACT II

NERO, BURRHUS, NARCISSUS, GUARDS

NERO

Burrhus, you may be sure: despite her taunts,
She is my mother. I'll ignore her whims.   360
But I will not ignore nor suffer more
The insolent official who dares feed them.
Pallas has poisoned her with his advice.
He daily leads Britannicus astray.
He is their only guide; who follows them   365
Is sure to find them at the house of Pallas.
It is too much. I'll tear him from them both.
For the last time, let him away, away:
I wish, I order it. Make sure, by sunset,
He is no more in Rome or in my Court.   370
Go now. This order touches the Empire's safety.
Narcissus, come nearer. And you, retire.

Exit BURRHUS; GUARDS *retire*

SCENE II

NARCISSUS

Thank Heaven, my lord, fair Junia in your power
Assures to you today the rest of Rome.
Your enemies, denied their modest hope,   375

Have powerless gone to Pallas's to mope.
And yet I find you restless and dumbfounded,
More agitated than Britannicus.
What may portend your sad, secretive air
And these dark glances wandering here and there,   *380*
When Fortune smiles upon you from above?

NERO

At last it's happened—Nero is in love.

NARCISSUS

You?

NERO

But a moment, yet for all my life.
I worship Junia. She must be my wife.

NARCISSUS

Junia?

NERO

Stirred by a curious desire,   *385*
Last night I watched her brought into the palace,
Her sad eyes, wet with tears, to Heaven raised,
Sparkling through all the glittering arms and torches:
Beautiful, unadorned and simply clad,
Befitting beauty just borne off from sleep.   *390*
Indeed, I do not know if this undress,
The shadows, torches, cries and midnight silence,
And the wild aspect of her bold abductors,
Enhanced the frightened sweetness of her eyes.
However that may be, by all entranced,   *395*
I wished to speak to her, but lost my voice:
I stood there rooted, as though wonderstruck,
And let her pass beyond to her apartments.
I passed into my own. There, all alone,
In vain I sought to drive her image from me.   *400*
Obsessed with her, I thought to soothe her woe;
I loved the very tears I caused to flow.

Sometimes, but too late, I expressed regrets;
I had recourse to sighs and even threats.
And that is how, plunged in my latest passion,   405
With sleepless eyes I waited for the dawn.
But perhaps too sweet a picture I have drawn;
I may have seen her at too great advantage.
What do you say to this?

                               NARCISSUS

                    Who would believe
She could conceal herself so long from Nero?   410

                                 NERO

You know she did: and whether out of anger
That blamed me for her brother's suicide,
Or out of the austere pride of her heart
That would not let us see her budding beauty,
Staunch in her grief and in the shadows cloistered,   415
She shut herself up even from her fame.
It is this virtue, novel at my Court,
Whose shy persistence high inflames my love.
What? While there's not in Rome another woman
Not honoured and made vainer by my love,   420
Who, trusting in the power of her eyes,
Would not come to essay on Caesar's heart,
Junia alone, hid shyly in her palace,
Regards such honours as an ignominy;
Flees me, and does not care perhaps to know   425
If Caesar's worth the loving or can love?
Tell me, Britannicus loves her?

                               NARCISSUS

                      Not love her?

                                 NERO

How can he, so young, know his heart perchance?
Or the deep poison of a magic glance?

NARCISSUS

Love often comes before the age of reason.　　　430
You may be sure he loves her. Well apprised
By such great beauty, tears oft fill his eyes.
He knows to bow before her least desires
And in her heart already fans love's fires.

NERO

What's that? Upon her heart he has some sway?　　　435

NARCISSUS

I cannot say. But what, my lord, I can say
Is that I've seen him sometimes haste from here,
His heart full of an anger hid from you,
Weeping the treachery of a fickle Court,
Sick of your greatness and his servitude,　　　440
By trepidation and impatience rent:
He'd visit Junia and return—content.

NERO

All the more wretched if she favoured him.
Narcissus, he should rather seek her anger.
Nero will not be jealous unavenged.　　　445

NARCISSUS

What, you, my lord? And what need Nero fear?
Junia might pity him and share his woe:
His are the only tears she has seen flow.
But now, my lord, that her wide-opened eyes,
Observing close the splendour of your throne,　　　450
Will see around you kings, who've lost their own,
Merged in the crowd, her lover too with them,
All vying for the honour of a glance
That you may deign to cast on them by chance;
When from this pinnacle of glory, she　　　455
Beholds you come to sigh her victory;
Lord of a heart, be sure, already moved,
Command she love you and you will be loved.

NERO

Ah! for how many troubles I am heading!
And what vexations!

NARCISSUS

What can you be dreading,   460
Sire?

NERO

All, Octavia, Agrippina, Burrhus
And Seneca, all Rome, my three good years.
Not that the slightest trace of love for Octavia
Unites me to her bed or moves my pity.
Weary, a long time now, of her caress,   465
I rarely deign to stay and see her tears:
Most happy to throw off, by her divorce,
A fetter they imposed on me by force!
Why, Heaven itself condemns her secretly:
In vain, for four years, she has prayed to Heaven.   470
Her virtue fails to have impressed the Gods:
To honour her with child they will not deign:
The Empire still demands an heir in vain.

NARCISSUS

Then why delay, Sire, to repudiate her?
The Empire and your heart condemn Octavia.   475
Your ancestor Augustus longed for Livia:
To wed each other both divorced their consorts;
And to this blest divorce you owe the Empire.
Tiberius, who by marriage was his son,
Dared, in his face, divorce Augustus' daughter.   480
You only, thwarting still your own desires,
Dare not divorce, to light fresh nuptial fires.

NERO

Do you not know the angry Agrippina?
My anxious love already pictures her
Leading Octavia to me and attesting,   485

With flaming eyes, her sacred marriage rights;
And, striking sharper blows upon my soul,
Telling long tales of my ungrateful role.
How could I listen to this tedious moan?

NARCISSUS

Are you not, Sire, her master and your own?   *490*
Must you for ever cower beneath her tutelage?
Live for yourself and reign. Why reign for her?
Are you afraid? But, Sire, you're not afraid;
You have just exiled Pallas, in his pride,
Whose impudence you realise she sustains.   *495*

NERO

Safe from her eyes, I threaten, I command,
I heed your counsels and I dare approve them;
I rage against her and I try to brave her.
But—I am laying bare to you my soul—
As soon as, by ill-luck, I'm in her sight,   *500*
Whether I dare not yet deny the power of
Those eyes, where I have so long read my duty;
Or whether, mindful of so many boons,
I tender her in secret all she's given,
My strength against her I in vain assemble: *505*
My startled Genius before hers must tremble.[9]
And so, to free me from this servitude,
I shun her everywhere, am even rude,
From time to time inciting her to rancour,
So that she may avoid me as I shun her.   *510*
But too long I detain you. Go, Narcissus:
Britannicus might charge you with deceit.

NARCISSUS

No, no, Britannicus completely trusts me;
He thinks, my lord, I see you on his order,

[9] Plutarch, in his *Life of Antony*, describes how Antony's genius was similarly destined to quail before Octavius', a feature of which Shakespeare made use in *Antony and Cleopatra*.

To take note here of all concerning him,   *515*
And wishes me to tell him all your secrets.
Above all, chafing still to see his love,
He hopes my service will procure this boon.

NERO

Agreed. Go, you may give him this sweet news:
He shall see her.

NARCISSUS

Sir, banish him from her.   *520*

NERO

I have my reasons, and you may be sure
I'll sell him dear the joy of seeing her.
Meanwhile, boast of your happy ruse to him:
Tell him, for his sake, I am being deceived,
Without my order he is seeing her.
The door is opening. Hush now, here she comes.   *525a*
Go, find your master and conduct him here.

Exit NARCISSUS

SCENE III

Enter JUNIA

NERO

My lady, you grow pale and show surprise,
Do you read some sad foreboding in my eyes?

JUNIA

My lord, I cannot hide from you my error:
I wished to see Octavia, not the Emperor.   *530*

NERO

I know, my lady, and must say I envy
Your dear concern for fortunate Octavia.

JUNIA

What you, my lord?

NERO

                    You fancy in this place
Octavia's eyes alone may know your grace?

JUNIA

And whom else would you have me beg, my lord?   535
Who else could name my crime, I do not know?
You, who are punishing it, you must know.
My lord, pray, tell me what is my offence.

NERO

My lady, is it then a minor crime
To hide yourself from me so long a time?   540
Has Heaven endowed you with such priceless beauty
So that to bury it you deem your duty?
Happy Britannicus!—in peace to see grow
Far from our eyes, his love, your beauty's glow.
Why, banished from this glory till today,   545
Have you so ruthlessly kept me away?
My lady, he has dared, so they observe,
To tell his love and you show no reserve.
I cannot think, without consulting me,
To this my modest Junia would agree,   550
Nor that to love or be loved she'd resort,
Without my knowing it but by report.

JUNIA

My lord, I'll not deny his loving sighs
Have oft confirmed the message of his eyes.
He has not spurned to welcome as his spouse   555
This remnant of a once illustrious house.

Perhaps he still remembers, formerly
His father destined me his bride to be.
He loves me and obeys his Emperor—father,
And he obeys your mother or you, rather.   560
Your wishes ever correspond with hers . . .

NERO

My mother has her plans and I have mine.
Enough of Claudius and of Agrippina:
I do not by their choice make up my mind.
My lady, I alone will speak for you,   565
And I myself for you your lord will find.

JUNIA

Ah! Sire, remember, any other marriage
Would shame the Caesars who have given me birth!

NERO

My lady, no. The husband I select
May join your ancestors with his, unshamed: 570
You may, without a blush, agree to wed him.

JUNIA

And who then is this husband, my lord?

NERO

I.

JUNIA

You?

NERO

I would name to you a greater hero,
If any name stood higher here than Nero.
To make a choice to which you may consent,   575
My eyes have scoured the Court, Rome and the Empire.
The more I've searched, my lady, and the more
I still search in whose hands to place this treasure,
The more I see that only Caesar's worthy

To be the happy guardian of your love, 580
And worthily to him alone can give you
Whom Rome has given the empire of the world.
Yourself, look back upon your earliest years;
Claudius had destined you to wed his son;
But this was at a time when he expected 585
Some day to name him heir of all the Empire.
The gods have since pronounced. You, therefore, should
Bow to their will and choose both love and Empire.
They would have showered this gift on me in vain,
If you were not to be a part of it; 590
If all were cares not sweetened by your charms;
If while I give to vigils and alarms
Days ever to be pitied, ever envied,
I cannot sometimes linger at your feet.
You need not let Octavia stand between us. 595
Apart from me, Rome gives you her support,
Repudiates Octavia and unties
A marriage knot that Heaven declines to bless.
Then think, my lady, and weigh carefully
This choice that's worthy of a prince who loves you, 600
That's worthy of your eyes too long imprisoned,
That's worthy of the world which calls for you.

JUNIA

My lord, I think I'm right to stand amazed.
Within a single day, I find myself
Dragged to this palace like a criminal; 605
And when in terror I appear before you,
And I can hardly trust my innocence,
You sudden offer me Octavia's place.
And yet I dare to say I've not deserved
Either this too great honour or this shame. 610
And can you wish, my lord, to see a girl
Who as a child lost all her nearest kin,
Who nursing her misfortunes in the shade,
Has aimed at virtues that befit her woes,
Pass sudden from this deep obscurity 615
Into a rank exposed to all the world,

Whose brilliance I may not at all sustain,
Indeed, whose majesty another fills?

NERO

I've said, already, I repudiate her.
Be less afraid and be less modest too.   *620*
Do not imagine now my choice is blind;
I'll speak for you: you've only to agree.
Be worthy of the blood from which you've sprung,
And to the solid glory of the honours
That Caesar would bestow, do not prefer   *625*
The empty glory of a rash refusal
You may regret.

JUNIA

         Heaven knows my inmost thoughts.
I do not dream of an insensate glory:
I know full well the greatness of your offer;
And yet the more the splendour shed on me,   *630*
The more this rank would shame me and throw light
On the dark crime of stealing it from her.

NERO

You are indeed most careful of her interests,
My lady; friendship can no further go.
But let us speak out plain and drop the veil;   *635*
Her brother not his sister most concerns you:
And for Britannicus . . .

JUNIA

         He made me love him;
And I have not, Sire, tried to keep it secret.
Such truthful speaking is perhaps absurd;
But through my lips my heart is ever heard.   *640*
Far from the Court, I do not think it meet
To train myself, Sire, in the art of deceit.
I love Britannicus; to him was pledged
When the Empire was to follow on our marriage.

But now these very woes that have unthroned him, 645
His spectral honours and deserted palace,
The absent Court his fall has scared away,
Are all so many bonds that Junia tie.
To meet your needs, all hasten, high and low;
Your ever rosy days in pleasures flow. 650
The Empire is for you their quenchless source;
Or if, perchance, some trouble checks their course,
The whole world, anxious to restore the flood,
Hastens to remove it from your mind and mood.
Britannicus is lonely. In his state, 655
He finds no one but me to share his fate,
And has, for sum of pleasure, a few tears
That sometimes while away his woes and fears.

NERO

These tears are just the pleasures that I covet,
For which all else but him would pay the forfeit. 660
But I will play the prince a sweeter tune.
My lady, he'll be here to see you soon.

JUNIA

Ah, Sire! I ever counted on your goodness.

NERO

Well might I have forbidden him to see you,
But wish, my lady, to prevent the danger 665
In which his temper might entangle him.
I do not wish to crush him. It is better
He should be told his fate by your sweet mouth.
If his young life is dear to you, dismiss him
Without the least hint Nero may be jealous. 670
Take on yourself the odium of the breach;
And whether by your silence or your speech,
At least by coldness, to him clear impart
He now must elsewhere bear his hopes and heart.

JUNIA

I, stand and speak until his heart is torn! 675

My mouth a thousand times my love has sworn.
Even if I were to speak so treacherously,
My eyes would stop him from obeying me.

NERO

Concealed near by, I'll watch you from the start,
Entomb your love deep down within your heart.   *680*
You'll have no language secret from my ear;
The glances you think dumb I'll overhear;
And, without fail, his doom shall be the fees
Of any sign or gesture meant to please.

JUNIA

Alas! if I may still some boon implore,   *685*
My lord, permit I see him nevermore!

SCENE IV

Enter NARCISSUS

NARCISSUS

Britannicus, my lord, seeks the princess.
He's coming.

NERO

Let him come.

JUNIA

Ah, Sire!

NERO

I leave you.
His fate depends on you much more than me.
Remember, when you see him, I too see.   *690*

SCENE V

JUNIA

Ah! dear Narcissus, run and tell your master;
Tell him . . . Alas! I'm lost, for here he comes.

SCENE VI

Enter BRITANNICUS

BRITANNICUS

My lady, what good fortune brings me to you?
To think I have so sweet an interview.
But with this joy what trouble is in store!   695
Alas! May I still hope to see you more?
Must I, in stealth and like a thievish knave,
Seek out a happiness you daily gave?
Heavens, what a night! Your tears, your innocence,
Could not disarm their cruel insolence?   700
Where was your lover? And which jealous sprite
Refused to let me die, pierced in your sight?
Alas! all terror-stricken as you were,
Did not your heart against me secret stir?
My Princess, did you deign to long for me?   705
Ah! could you conjure all my misery?
Still no reply? How icy is your welcome!
Is this the way your eyes console my woe?
Speak. We are all alone. Misled, our foe
Is elsewhere busy while I speak to you.   710
Let's make the most of his auspicious absence.

JUNIA

You're in a place full of his mighty presence.

These very walls, my lord, perhaps have eyes;
And never is the Emperor without spies.

BRITANNICUS

Since when, my lady, have you grown so timorous?   *715*
What, will you let your heart be taken prisoner?
Where is your loving promise, once so zealous,
Of our love even Nero would be jealous?
But, dearest, put aside these futile fears.
Faith is not yet extinct in every heart;   *720*
All seem to approve my anger with their eyes,
Why, even Nero's mother is on our side.
And Rome herself, disgusted at his conduct . . .

JUNIA

Ah! Sir, you do not purport what you say.
You have, yourself, told me a thousand times   *725*
How Rome was all united in his praise;
You always paid some tribute to his goodness.
No doubt, your language has been soured by grief.

BRITANNICUS

Your words, I must admit, leave me amazed.
I did not come to you to hear him praised.   *730*
To tell to you the grief consuming me
I hardly steal a moment favouring us,
When this dear moment is, my lady, spent
In praising him, the foe by whom I'm rent!
What makes you so perverse, within one day?   *735*
What? Must your very glances nothing say?
What do I see? You fear to meet my eyes?
Has Nero charmed you? Is it I you despise?
Ah! if I were to think . . . for God's sake, lady,
Clear up the darkness that engulfs my soul.   *740*
Speak. Ah! have I been blotted from your mind?

JUNIA

Away, my lord, the Emperor is coming.

BRITANNICUS

Narcissus, after this, on whom to count?

Exit BRITANNICUS

SCENE VII

Enter NERO

NERO

My lady . . .

JUNIA

Sire, I cannot listen further.
You've been obeyed. Let me at least shed tears   745
Now that his eyes no longer will be witness.

Exit JUNIA

SCENE VIII

NERO

Narcissus, you have seen the violence
Of their love. It stood out even in her silence.
She loves my rival, as I'm full aware;
But I will seek my joy in his despair.   750
I keep a charming picture of his smart,
And I have watched him doubt his lover's heart.
I'll follow her. My rival waits for you.
Go, run and plague him with suspicions new.
And while, before me, she for him will moan,   755
Make him pay dear his happiness unknown.

Exit NERO

NARCISSUS (*Alone*)

A second time, Narcissus, Fortune smiles.
Why hesitate before her wanton wiles?
Come, to the bitter end, her favours cherish;
To make me happy, let poor wretches perish!   *760*

ACT III¹⁰

SCENE I

NERO, BURRHUS

BURRHUS

Pallas obeys, my lord.

NERO

And tell me how
My mother took her arrogance brought low?

BURRHUS

You may be sure, my lord, this blow strikes home;
That soon her pain will break out in reproaches.
Her indignation is about to burst: 765
Ah, would she were to stop at useless cries!

NERO

What? So you think her capable of plotting?

BURRHUS

Sire, Agrippina still should make you fear.
Rome and your soldiers too her sires revere;
They see in her Germanicus, her father.   770
She knows her power—and you know well her courage;
And that which makes me fear her all the more
Is, you yourself are bolstering her anger
In furnishing her arms against yourself.

  ¹⁰ Louis Racine, in his *Memoires on the Life and Work of Jean Racine*, recounts
how his father suppressed, on Boileau's advice, before *Britannicus* was given to
the players, a scene between Burrhus and Narcissus (intended as Act III, Scene 1).

NERO

I, Burrhus?

BURRHUS

Sire, this love that holds you fast . . .   775

NERO

Burrhus, I understand: the ill's past cure.
My heart has told me more than you can tell.
Take it I must love her.

BURRHUS

So you imagine,
My lord, and satisfied with some resistance,
You fear an ill that's feeble at its birth.   780
But if your heart, still steadfast in its duty,
Would not compact with its seductive foe;
If you looked back upon your first years' fame;
If you, my lord, could deign to call to mind
Octavia's virtues that deserved not this,   785
And her chaste love that conquered your disdain;
Above all, if avoiding Junia's eyes,
You would, a few days, stay away from her:
Be sure, however much one seems to love,
One loves not if one wishes not to love.   790

NERO

I shall believe you, when amid alarms
I must enhance the glory of our arms;
Or when, in Senate seated, I dictate
In time of peace the fortunes of the State.
I'll have full faith in your experience.   795
Believe me, love's a very different science,
Burrhus; and it perhaps would be unfair
Right down to it to drag your virtue rare!
Farewell. I suffer too much, far from Junia.

Exit NERO

SCENE II

BURRHUS (*Alone*)

Burrhus, Nero lays bare his inmost soul.   *800*
This savagery you thought you might control
Is ready to break loose from your weak bond.
To what excesses it may spread beyond!
O gods! What course to take in this mischance?
And Seneca, whose counsels might go home,   *805*
Knows not this peril, far detained from Rome.
If I could but rouse Agrippina's love,
I might . . . she comes . . . may Fortune gracious prove![11]

SCENE III

Enter AGRIPPINA *and* ALBINA

AGRIPPINA

Well, Burrhus, did I err in my suspicions?
What splendid lessons you are teaching him!   *810*
He exiles Pallas, perhaps whose only crime
Is having raised your master to the Empire.
You know it well. Without his counsel, never
Would Claudius, whom he ruled, have named my son.
Further, you find a rival for his wife   *815*
And wish to free him from his nuptial ties.
A worthy task for you, the foe of flatterers,
Chosen to put a brake upon his passions,
To flatter them yourself and make his heart
Disdain his mother and forget his wife!   *820*

[11] Literally: My good luck sends her to me.

BURRHUS

It is, my lady, still too soon to accuse.
Caesar's done nothing one may not excuse.
Blame only Pallas for his fitting exile:
His pride, for long, has called for this reward;
And the Emperor only executes, unwilling,   *825*
What all the Court was secretly demanding.
The other is an ill that may be met:
We may succeed in drying Octavia's tears.
But calm your temper. By a gentler path
You may restore her husband's former ardour.   *830*
Threats and rebukes will make him all the harder.

AGRIPPINA

In vain you seek to make me hold my tongue.
I see my silence but provokes your scorn;
It is too much to fawn on him I've made.
Be sure my power is not removed with Pallas: *835*
Heaven leaves me force enough to avenge my fall.
The son of Claudius shows he now resents
The crimes that to me only bring regrets.
Make no mistake. I'll show him to the Army,
Bewail his mournful childhood to the soldiers,   *840*
Make them, at my example, rue their error.
On one side they shall see an Emperor's son,
Claiming the faith they swore his dynasty,
And they shall hear Germanicus's daughter;
On the other, they shall see Domitius' son,   *845*
Supported but by Seneca and Burrhus,
Who both, recalled from exile by myself,
Before my very eyes share supreme power.
I'll take good care to tell our common crimes:
They'll learn the devious paths by which I've led him.   *850*
To make more odious both his power and yours,
I shall avow the most injurious rumours.
I shall tell all, exiles, assassinations,
Even poison . . .

BURRHUS

They will not believe you, Madam.

They'll know how to reject the unfair dodge   855
Of an angry, self-incriminating witness.
For me, who was the first to aid your plans,
Who even made the Army pledge him faith,
Repent, I do not, of my candid zeal.
He is a son who follows on his father.   860
Adopting Nero, Claudius, by his choice,
Made equal both his son's and your son's claims.
Rome had free choice. Thus, legally, she chose
Tiberius, whom Augustus had adopted;
And young Agrippa, stemming from his blood,   865
Was left, excluded from the rank he claimed.
Broadbased on such foundations, Nero's power
Can be no longer shaken even by you;
And if he hears me still, his goodness soon
Will make you, Madam, lose all wish to do it.   870
I have begun. I go now to pursue it.

Exit BURRHUS

SCENE IV

ALBINA

To what lengths will your passion push you, Madam?
Pray Heaven the Emperor does not hear of this!

AGRIPPINA

Ah! would he were to come before me now!

ALBINA

For Heaven's sake, my lady, hide your anger.   875
What? Must you sacrifice your days' repose
For the interests of the sister or the brother?
Will you thwart Caesar even in his loves?

AGRIPPINA

Can you not see how far I am abased,
Albina? Upon me he foists a rival.   880

If I do not soon snap this fatal bond,
My place is filled and I become a cipher.
Till now Octavia, with her empty title,
Powerless at Court, could be ignored by it.
Rewards and honours, showered as I saw fit,   885
Drew to me all the selfish prayers of men.
Another woman captures Caesar's love:
She'll wield the influence both of wife and mistress.
The fruit of all my cares, great Caesar's chance,
Will soon become the prize of her one glance . . .   890
All flee my presence . . . I'm alone . . . distraught . . .
Albina, no, I cannot bear the thought.
Even if I hastened Heaven's most dread decree,[12]
My thankless son . . . His rival comes to me.

SCENE V

Enter BRITANNICUS *and* NARCISSUS

BRITANNICUS

Our common foes are not invincible;   895
Our miseries find sympathetic hearts.
Your friends and mine, my lady, hid till now,
While we lost time in frivolous regrets,
Fired by the anger that oppression kindles,
Have to Narcissus just avowed their pain.   900
Nero does not yet hold, in calm possession,
The wretched girl he loves despite my sister.
If you are still moved by my sister's wrong,
We may bring back the faithless to his duty.
Half of the Senate now is on our side: 905
Sulla, Piso, Plautus . . .

[12] The astrologers' prophecy that Nero would kill his mother (see footnote 4, p. 303). Racine most skilfully wins some sympathy for the unlovable Agrippina by depicting her haunted by her doom throughout the play—he makes her refer to it thrice more (Act IV, line 1281; Act V, lines 1675–6 and line 1700).

AGRIPPINA

What are you saying?
Sulla, Piso, Plautus! Rome's leading men?

BRITANNICUS

I see too well this news, my lady, pains you,
And that your weak and trembling anger fears
Already to obtain what it desired.   *910*
No, you have made too certain of my fall;
You need not fear the pluck of any friend.
I have no more a friend; your wise precautions
Have long since suborned or removed them all.

AGRIPPINA

To your suspicions pay less heed, my lord: *915*
Our safety hangs upon our understanding.
I've promised. That's enough. Despite your foes,
I take back nothing of what I have promised.
In vain the guilty Nero flees my wrath:
Sooner or later he must hear his mother.   *920*
I will in turn try menacing and pleading,
Or else, with me myself your sister leading,
I'll plant, all round, her sorrows and my fears
And every heart win over by her tears.
I'll harass Nero from all sides. Good-bye!   *925*
If you'll take my advice, avoid his eye.

Exeunt AGRIPPINA *and* ALBINA

SCENE VI

BRITANNICUS

Have you not flattered me with a false hope?
Can I rely at all on your account,
Narcissus?

NARCISSUS

Yes, my lord. But I must not
In this place further clarify this riddle.   *930*
Let us away. What are you waiting for?

BRITANNICUS

What am I waiting for? Alas! Narcissus.

NARCISSUS

Explain yourself.

BRITANNICUS

If by your stratagem
I might once more see . . .

NARCISSUS

Whom?

BRITANNICUS

I blush to say.
Yet with a calmer heart I'd meet my fate.

NARCISSUS

In spite of all I've said, you think her true?   *935a*

BRITANNICUS

No. I believe her criminal and false!
That I should hate her; none the less I feel
That I believe it much less than I ought.
In spite of her betrayal, my staunch heart
Excuses, justifies and worships her.   *940*
I wish to put an end to all my doubt
And wish to hate her in complete composure.
And who would think a heart so outward noble,
From childhood hostile to a faithless Court,
Would yield such honour and would promptly hatch   *945*
Such perfidy, unheard of even at Court?

NARCISSUS

And who knows if the wanton, from her cloister,
Did not contrive to trap the Emperor?
Too sure her beauty could not stay unsought,
Perhaps she fled in order to be caught,   *950*
To tempt the Emperor with the glorious sin
Of conquering where none else dared to win.

BRITANNICUS

I cannot see her then?

NARCISSUS

                    My lord, just now
She is accepting her new lover's vows.

BRITANNICUS

Then let us go, Narcissus . . . Junia—see!   *955*

NARCISSUS

Gods! I must warn the Emperor instantly.

Exit NARCISSUS

SCENE VII

Enter JUNIA

JUNIA

Away, away, my lord, and flee an anger
My obstinacy has inflamed against you.
Nero is much enraged. I have escaped
A moment while his mother has detained him.   *960*
Farewell: do not defame my love: one day
You'll see it vindicated full of joy.
Your image is for ever in my heart
And nothing can efface it.

BRITANNICUS

So that's it!
You seek my absence to ensure your prize,   965
To have a free field for your latest sighs.
No doubt, at sight of me, a secret shame
Pours in your cup of joy a drop of blame.
Ah well! let me away.

JUNIA

Without imputing . . .

BRITANNICUS

You should at least have fought a little longer.   970
I do not grumble that a vulgar love
Should lean upon the side that Fortune favours,
That pomp of Empire should have dazzled you,
That at my sister's cost you wish to rule;
But that, while wanting all this like another,   975
You seemed to me so long to have despised it:
No, I confess it still, my desperate heart
To face this one mishap was unprepared.
I've seen injustice rise upon my ruin;
I've seen Heaven privy to my persecutors.   980
So many shocks had not appeased its wrath,
By you to be forgotten still remained.

JUNIA

If times were happier, my deserved impatience
Would make you soon repent of your distrust.
But Nero threatens: in this pressing peril,   985
My lord, I've other cares than to afflict you.
Away, have faith and do not still complain.
Nero, while listening, ordered me to feign.

BRITANNICUS

The scoundrel . . .

JUNIA

Witness of our interview,
He scanned my face with fixed severity,   990

Ready to make you pay most savagely
For any gesture that betrayed my love.

BRITANNICUS

Nero was listening! But alas! my lady,
Why could your eyes not feign and undeceive me?
They might have named the author of this outrage.   *995*
Is love then dumb, or has it but one tongue?
Ah! how much anguish might one look have spared me!
You should . . .

JUNIA

                    I should have dumb remained and saved you.
Alas! how many times, since I must tell you,
I was about to blurt out my distress!   *1000*
And cutting short my sighs, how many times,
I could not meet your eyes I ever sought!
What agony to greet one's love with silence,
To hear him groan and torture him oneself,
When by a single look one might console!   *1005*
And yet what tears this look would cause to flow!
Ah! terror-stricken by this worrying thought,
I felt I had not played the part enough.
I feared the pallor of my frightened brow;
I thought my looks were too full of my grief;   *1010*
I felt unceasingly, the furious Nero
Might burst on me for pleasing you too much;
I feared my love could not remain unmoved;
Indeed, I even wished I'd never loved.
Alas! my lord, for his and for our weal,   *1015*
He is too well-informed of how we feel.
Once more, I beg you, shun his sight, away:
My heart will tell you more some happier day.
A thousand little secrets it will beat.

BRITANNICUS

This is too much to hear, my lady sweet,   *1020*
My happiness, your goodness and my crime!

To make for me this sacrifice sublime!
Ah, let me at your feet all expiate!

JUNIA

What are you doing? Nero! Ah, harsh fate!

SCENE VIII

Enter NERO

NERO

Pray keep on, Prince, with your delightful pranks.[13]   *1025*
I well conceive your favours from his thanks,
My lady: I surprise him at your knees;
But he must thank me also if you please:
This palace favours him. I hold you here
Easier to make for him such converse dear!   *1030*

BRITANNICUS

I may put at her feet my joy or pain
Wherever to receive me she may deign;
And I have no cause to feel out of place
Within this palace—her gaol, by your grace.

NERO

And what is there, not warning you, quite clear,   *1035*
I have to be obeyed, respected, here?

BRITANNICUS

These walls did not raise us from infancy,
Me to obey you, you to browbeat me;
And when they saw us born they dared not say
Domitius[14] would my master be some day!   *1040*

---

[13] Literally "fervour."
[14] Both Tacitus and Suetonius record this contemptuous reference to Nero by Britannicus.

NERO

Our hopes are often star-crossed in this way.
Then I had to obey, now you obey.
If you do not know how to behave you ought,
You are still young—and may perhaps be taught.

BRITANNICUS

And who will teach me?

NERO

The Empire and the State.   *1045*

BRITANNICUS

And in your numerous rights does the Empire rate
All that is cruel in injustice, force,
Imprisonments, abduction and divorce?

NERO

The Empire casts no curious glances, Sir,
Into the secrets that I hide from her.   *1050*
Follow her respect.

BRITANNICUS

Her respect is hollow.

NERO

She holds her tongue at least: her silence follow!

BRITANNICUS

Nero begins thus to grow out of reach.

NERO

Nero begins to weary of your speech.

BRITANNICUS

His subjects were to bless his happy reign!   *1055*

NERO

Happy or not, enough if fear constrain.

BRITANNICUS

I know ill Junia if you think such views
Will win her smiles and make her Nero choose.

NERO

If I do not know how to win her heart,
At least I know to make my rival smart.   *1060*

BRITANNICUS

Yet, in whatever danger I am thrown,
I would be frightened by her hate alone.

NERO

Desire it; that is all I can express.

BRITANNICUS

Her love enshrines my only happiness.

NERO

She'll love you still, she swore it by her honour.   *1065*

BRITANNICUS

At least I do not know to spy upon her.
I let her freely roam her thoughts among
And do not hide myself to seal her tongue.

NERO

I understand you. Guards!

JUNIA

                            What are you doing?
He is your brother. Ah! a jealous lover!   *1070*
My lord, a thousand ills afflict his life.
Must you be envious of his happiness?
To tie once more the knots that bound your hearts,
I'll run away from you and flee from him.
My flight will put an end to your dread discords;   *1075*
My lord, I will become a Vestal Virgin.

You need no longer wrest my hapless love;
It will be offered to the Gods alone.

NERO

Madam, this is a strange and sudden plan.
Guards, take back Junia to her own apartments: *1080*
And guard Britannicus in his sister's suite.

BRITANNICUS

So this is Nero's way of making love.

JUNIA

Do not excite him, bend before the storm.

NERO

Guards, obey at once; do not dally longer.

Exeunt JUNIA *and* BRITANNICUS *with the* GUARDS

SCENE IX

Enter BURRHUS

BURRHUS

Heavens! What's this?

NERO (*Without seeing* BURRHUS)
                    Their love is thus intenser.   *1085*
I recognise the hand that made them one.
To see me, Agrippina came anon
And stretched her converse out to such a length
Merely to play this odious trick on me.
See, if my mother's still within the palace!   *1090*
Burrhus, within the palace see she's kept,
And that she has my guard instead of hers.

BURRHUS

What, Sire? A mother? Without hearing?

NERO

                Stop!
Burrhus, I do not know what you are after;
But, for some days, whatever's in my mind   *1095*
Must in you a censorious critic find.
Take charge of her, I say; if you refuse,
Others will take charge of her and Burrhus.

ACT IV

SCENE I

AGRIPPINA, BURRHUS

BURRHUS

You may at leisure here defend yourself,
My lady; Caesar has agreed to listen.   *1100*
If he has ordered you to be detained,
It is perhaps on purpose to see you.
However that may be, if I may say so,
No more remember he has done you wrong;
Be ready, rather, to stretch out your arms;   *1105*
Defend yourself without accusing him.
As you have seen, the Court obeys but him.
Although he is your son, indeed your creature,
He's still your Emperor. You are just like us,
A subject of the sovereignty you fashioned;   *1110*
According as he frowns, or fondles you,
The Court around you either flees or fawns;
It is his ear they seek in seeking yours.
But here the Emperor comes.

AGRIPPINA

Leave me with him.

Exit BURRHUS

SCENE II

Enter NERO

AGRIPPINA (*Sitting down*)

Nero come here, and take your seat beside me.   *1115*
I have, they say, to clear up your suspicions.
I do not know with what crime I've been blackened:
I'm going to tell you all those I have done.
You reign. You know how very far your birth
Had put you from the summit of the Empire.   *1120*
Even my ancestors' claims, Rome-revered,
Would have been useless props without my aid.
Upon Britannicus's mother's[15] doom,
Which left the bed of Claudius in dispute,
Among so many, vying for the honour,   *1125*
Who begged, importunate, his freedmen's aid,
I sought his hand, obsessed with but one thought,
To leave you on the throne where I should sit.
I curbed my pride and begged the aid of Pallas.
His master, daily fondled in my arms,   *1130*
Insensibly caught, in his niece's eyes,
The love to which I hoped to lead his fondness.
But this consanguine tie which joined us both
Forbade to Claudius an incestuous bed.
He did not dare to wed his brother's daughter.   *1135*
The Senate was seduced: a laxer law
Put Claudius in my bed, Rome at my feet.
I had come far, but you were nowhere still.
Like me, I knit you close to his own flesh:
I picked on you to give his daughter's hand.   *1140*
Silanus, who loved her, by her forsaken,
Sealed with his suicide that fatal day.

[15] Britannicus's mother was the notorious Messalina, whose orgies (Tacitus, XI) resulted in her execution, an episode in which Narcissus, in his "palmy days," (line 1447) was the chief prosecutor.

All this was nothing yet. Could you imagine
Claudius one day would choose you, not his son?
Once more I begged the aid of this same Pallas: *1145*
Claudius, convinced by him, adopted you,
And called you Nero, and himself desired
To invest you in advance, with power supreme.
Then it was everyone, raking the past,
Uncovered all my quick-maturing plans;   *1150*
That poor Britannicus's future doom
Aroused the murmur of his father's friends.
The eyes of some were dazzled by my offers;
And exile rid me of the most rebellious;
Claudius himself, exhausted by my clamour,   *1155*
Sequestered from his son all those whose zeal,
Committed too long to his destiny,
Might still once more have championed his succession.
Further, I myself chose from out my suite,
Those whom I wished to be his guides and mentors;   *1160*
On the other hand, I took good care to find
To tutor you men high esteemed by Rome.
Deaf to intrigue, I sought out worth alone.
From exile I recalled and from the army,
This very Seneca and this same Burrhus,   *1165*
Who since . . . Rome then esteemed their worth—
The while, I lavished on all sides the wealth
Of Claudius, in your name, without restraint.
The alluring bait of entertainments, presents,   *1170*
Drew you the people's and the soldiers' hearts,
Who, mindful once more of their former love,
Preferred in you Germanicus, my father.
Now Claudius, meanwhile was about to die.
His eyes, long blinded, opened in the end!
He recognised his error. In his fear,   *1175a*
He cried out in concern for his own son,
And wished, but too late, to collect his friends.
His guards, his house, his bed, were in my power.
I let him spend his love in fruitless moan;
And of his last breath made myself the mistress.   *1180*
On pretext of not causing Claudius pain,

I hid his son's tears from his dying eyes.
He died. A thousand rumours point my shame.
I still kept secret news about his death;
And, furtively, whilst Burrhus set about   *1185*
Procuring the Army's loyalty to you,
Whilst you were led to camp beneath my name,
In Rome, the altars smoked with sacrifice;
The populace, spurred on by my false orders,
Sought anxious news of their dead Emperor's health.   *1190*
At last, when the allegiance of the Guard
Had firm established your imperial power,
Claudius was seen; and the astonished people
Learnt of your reign and of his death together.
This is the avowal that I wished to make.   *1195*
Those are my crimes and here is my reward.
You had scarce six months tasted the sweet fruits
Of all my cares, when failed your gratitude,
When, weary of a deference that irked you,
You went about as though ignoring me.   *1200*
I've seen Burrhus and Seneca souring you,
Giving you lessons in ingratitude,
Delighted to be outshone in the art.
I've seen you favour with your confidence
Otho, Senecio, young voluptuaries,   *1205*
Who pander shamelessly to all your pleasures;
And when, moved to remonstrance by your scorn,
I've asked you to explain so many insults,
—Last refuge of a wretch who's put to shame—
You have replied to me with fresh affronts.   *1210*
Today I promise Junia to your brother;
Both are delighted with your mother's choice:
And you? Junia, abducted to the Court,
Becomes at once the object of your passion;
I see Octavia, from your heart erased,   *1215*
Ready to quit the bed where I had placed her;
Pallas banished, Britannicus arrested;
Indeed you even dare lay hands on me!
Burrhus has had the impudence to guard me.
And when, convicted of such perfidies,   *1220*

You should, at sight of me, fall on your knees,
You order me instead, defend myself!

NERO

I shall remember always that I owe
The Empire to you. No need to repeat it.
Your goodness, Mother, could with confidence   *1225*
Rely upon my grateful memories.
Therefore these doubts and all these constant cries
Have made all those who've heard them firm believe,
You previously—if I dare plainly speak—
Have only worked, in my name, for yourself.   *1230*
"Are all these honours, all this deference,
But scant rewards," they'd say, "for her deserts?
What crime has her contemnèd son committed?
Has she then crowned him only to obey?
And is he but the casket of her power?"   *1235*
Not that, if I could fall in with your wishes
Even so far, I would not gladly yield you
This power your cries seemed ever calling back.
But Rome demands a master, not a mistress.
You heard the rumours springing from my weakness: *1240*
The Senate and the people, still annoyed
To hear your orders spoken through my voice,
Would daily bruit abroad, the dying Claudius
Had, with his power, bequeathed me his obedience!
You've often seen our disaffected soldiers   *1245*
Bearing before you their unwilling eagles;
Ashamed, by this unworthy use, to sully
The heroes whose great image they yet bear.
All others would have yielded to their pain;
But if you do not reign you still complain.   *1250*
Allied against me with Britannicus,
You wish to strengthen him with Junia's hand—
And Pallas' cunning fingers spin these plots;
And when, against my will, I guard my safety,
You are obsessed with anger and with hate.   *1255*
You wish to lead my rival to the Army;
The rumour has already reached the camp.

AGRIPPINA

I make him Emperor, wretch? Could you believe it?
What would my purpose be? What could I hope?
What honours, rank, could I expect from him?   *1260*
Ah! if when you rule I am nothing spared,
If my accusers watch my every step,
If they pursue the mother of their Emperor,
How would I fare amid an alien Court?
They would accuse me, not of heedless cries,   *1265*
Of dim designs no sooner born than dead,
But crimes for you, committed in your sight,
And of which all too soon I'd be convicted.
You cannot gull me, I see all your tricks.
You are a thankless knave and always were one.   *1270*
Right from your infancy my love and care
Have but extracted feigned caresses from you.
Nothing could move you and your stony heart
Should in its course have stayed my lovingkindness.
Unhappy that I am! By what mischance   *1275*
Must I, despite my acts, remain unwanted?
I have but one son. Heaven, that hearest me,
Have I, except for him, asked aught of thee?
Nothing could daunt me, remorse, dangers, lies;
His scorn I swallowed and I shut my eyes   *1280*
To the dread horror then foretold to me;
I've done my all. You reign. So let it be!
My freedom you have taken. End this strife,
If you desire it, also take my life;
So long as all the people do not tear   *1285*
From you in outrage what cost me so dear!

NERO

Well, tell me what you want me now to do.

AGRIPPINA

Punish the impudence of my accusers.
Appease the anger of Britannicus,
Let Junia give her hand to whom she will,   *1290*

Let both of them be freed, let Pallas stay,
Let me have access to you night and day—
And lastly, let not Burrhus any more—
See here he comes—dare halt me at your door.

Enter BURRHUS

NERO

My lady, yes. I want my gratitude   *1295*
Henceforth to carve your power in every heart;
And I already bless this happy coldness
That ends in the rekindling of our love.
What Pallas may have done, I will forget;   *1300*
I will befriend Britannicus once more;
And as regards this love that has estranged us,
I'll make you arbiter and you shall judge.
Go then and take this good news to my brother.
Guards, see my mother's orders are obeyed.

Exit AGRIPPINA

SCENE III

BURRHUS

My lord, how charming is this tender sight   *1305*
Of warm embraces and domestic peace!
You know if ever I desired to cross her,
If I desired to kill your love for her,
If ever I deserved her unjust anger.

NERO

I will not hide it, I complained of you,   *1310*
Burrhus; I thought you acted both in concert;
But her hostility restores my faith.
Burrhus, she thinks too soon to mother him.
I'll hug my rival, but to smother him.

BURRHUS

What, my lord?

NERO

        It is too much. His death must   *1315*
Deliver me for ever from her madness.
While he still breathes, I cannot fully live.
She maddened me with mention of his name;
And I'll not stomach her outrageous crime
Of offering him my place, a second time.   *1320*

BURRHUS

Is she then soon to mourn Britannicus?

NERO

I'll fear him no more ere the set of sun.

BURRHUS

And what is it that prompts you to the knife?

NERO

My fame, my love, my safety and my life.

BURRHUS

Whatever you may say, this horror dread   *1325*
Was never, Sire, conceived within your head.

NERO

Burrhus!

BURRHUS

      O heavens! Can your mouth utter it?
Could you yourself hear it without a shudder?
Ah! have you thought in whose blood you'll be wading?
Is Nero tired of reigning in all hearts?
What will they say of you? What are you thinking?   *1330*

NERO

What? Must I ever, chained by my past fame,
Retain before my eyes some nameless love
That Chance gives us and takes away in one day?
Slave to their wishes, tyrant of my own,   *1335*
Merely to please them do I wear the crown?

BURRHUS

And is it not enough for your desires
The public weal should be your highest good?
It is for you to choose, you are still master.
Virtuous till now, you may be ever virtuous: *1340*
The path is marked, there's nothing more to stop you;
You need but stride from virtue on to virtue.
But if you hearken to your flatterers,
You'll have, my lord, to run from crime to crime,
Support your harsh deeds with fresh cruelties   *1345*
And wash your blood-stained arms in thicker blood.
Britannicus in dying will incite
His friends, all ready, burning to avenge him;
These, in their turn, will foster new defenders,
Who even as they die will raise successors: *1350*
You'll light a flame that cannot be extinguished.
Feared by the whole world, you will fear each man,
Will ever punish, ever trembling plan,
And as your foe your every subject scan.
Ah, does your first years' sweet experience   *1355*
Render your goodness odious, my lord?
Have you thought of the happiness that marked them?
In what deep peace, O Heaven, have they not passed!
What joy to think and to yourself attest:
"At this hour, everywhere, I'm loved, I'm blest.   *1360*
The people are not frightened at my name;
If they should weep, I'm not the one to blame;
They do not shun my face, as mark of woe;
Hearts fly to greet me everywhere I go!"
Such were your pleasures. What a change, O Gods!   *1365*
The meanest blood was precious then to you.

One day, the Senate, justly, I recall,
Pressed you to sign a guilty man's death warrant;
You fought, my lord, against their strict demand:
Your heart was fearful lest it be too cruel;   *1370*
And full of pity for an Emperor's plight,
"I wish," you said, "I did not know to write."[16]
No, either you shall hear me, or my death
Will save me from this horror's sight and grief.
You shall not see me long survive your honour.   *1375*
If you will perpetrate so black a deed,

(*He falls on his knees*)

See, I am ready, Sire: before you go,
Strike through my heart that cannot let you do this;
Call back the cruel men who have seduced you;
Let them try out their unsure hands on me.   *1380*
But I see my tears have touched my Emperor;
I see his goodness shuddering at their evil.
Waste no time: name to me the faithless scoundrels
Who dare to give this murderous advice.
Call back your brother. In his arms forget . . .   *1385*

NERO

What are you asking?

BURRHUS

                        No, he does not hate you,
Sire; he's betrayed: I know he's innocent;
I'll guarantee his loyalty to you.
I'll run to him to speed this happy meeting.

NERO

Let him, with you, await me in my chamber.   *1390*

Exit BURRHUS

[16] Both Seneca (*De Clementia*, II, 1) and Suetonius (*The Twelve Caesars*, Nero, X) record this incident about the early Nero, although Suetonius might seem to hint that it was said for effect—not so Seneca.

SCENE IV

Enter NARCISSUS

NARCISSUS

I've made all preparations for his death,
My lord. The poison's ready and Locusta
Has made assurance doubly sure for me:
She put a slave to death before my eyes;[17]
The knife is not so quick to end a life   *1395*
As the new poison she has handed me.

NERO

Enough, Narcissus. Thank you for your pains.
I do not wish you to pursue the plan.

NARCISSUS

What? Has your hatred of Britannicus
Dwindled to stop me . . .

NERO

We must mend our quarrel.   *1400*

NARCISSUS

Far be it from me to dissuade you, Sire;
But he is smarting still from his arrest:
This insult will long rankle in his breast.
There are no secrets, not revealed by time:
He'll learn I was to perpetrate the crime   *1405*
Of poisoning him under the Emperor's orders.
The Gods forbid he execute this plot!
But he perhaps will do what you dare not.

---

[17] Racine heightens the horror by substituting "a slave" for the goat and pig
mentioned by Suetonius as experimental victims (Nero, XXXIII).

NERO

They guarantee his heart; I'll conquer mine.

NARCISSUS

And will the hand of Junia be the tie?   *1410*
You'll make this further sacrifice, my lord?

NERO

You speak too much. However that may be,
I count him no more as my enemy.

NARCISSUS

Sire, Agrippina swore she could achieve this:
She has resumed her sovereign sway upon you.   *1415*

NERO

What's that? What did she say? What is your meaning?

NARCISSUS

My lord, she made a public boast of this.

NERO

Of what?

NARCISSUS

That she had but to see you once:
That we should see a modest silence follow
On all this angry, independent show;   *1420*
That you would be the first to sue for peace,
Delighted she should deign to pardon you.

NERO

Narcissus, tell me, what am I to do?
I am all poised to punish her effrontery;
And did I heed my urge, her blurting triumph   *1425*
Would soon be followed by eternal anguish.
But then, how will the babbling world regard it?

Do you insist I choose the tyrant's path,[18]
That Rome, erasing all marks of esteem,
Should leave me but the name of poisoner?   *1430*
My vengeance they will brand as fratricide.

NARCISSUS

And must you take their whims, my lord, for guide?
Do you fancy they will always hold their tongues?
Is it for you to listen to their chatter?
Will you forget the prick of your desires?   *1435*
And will you be the only one denied?
But Sire, you do not know the Romans yet.
No, no, they're much more prudent in their speech.
So much precaution undermines your reign;
They'll deem themselves deserving to be dreaded.   *1440*
For long they've been adapted to the yoke;
They kiss the hand that gives their back the stroke.
To fawn at you, you'll find them ever eager.
Tiberius wearied of their servitude.
Why, I myself, though clothed with borrowed power,   *1445*
That I received from Claudius with my freedom,
Have, in my palmy days, a hundred times
Tempted their patience, quite without exhaustion!
You fear the evil of a poisoning?
Sentence the brother and renounce the sister;   *1450*
Rome, lavishing her victims on her altars,
Will find them guilty, were they innocent;
You'll see them list, as inauspicious days,
The birthdays of the sister and the brother!

NERO

Narcissus, once more, I cannot do it.   *1455*
I promised Burrhus; I just had to yield.
I wish no more to break my word to him
And gave his virtue arms against myself.
Against his arguments my courage sticks,

---

[18] Racine with consummate art brings us with this verse almost to the brink of sympathy for the young Nero, at the mercy of Narcissus' evil genius.

And when he speaks to me my conscience pricks.   *1460*

NARCISSUS

Burrhus, does not believe, Sire, all he says.
To raise his power he draws upon his virtue;
Or, rather, all of them have but one thought:
They fear this blow will end their influence;
You would be free then, Sire, and these proud masters   *1465*
Would have, like us, to bend the knee to you.
What? Are you unaware of all they whisper?
"Nero," they hint, "was not born to the Throne;
He only says and does what he is told,
His mind controlled by Seneca, his heart   *1470*
By Burrhus. His highest aim, his noblest part
Is to excel as Rome's first charioteer,
To strive for prizes that may raise a cheer,
But are unworthy of a Caesar. How
He loves before the mobs to be on show,
To spend his life before the public gaze,   *1475a*
To sing his songs he wants the world to praise,
The while his soldiers move, if he should pause,
Among the crowd to snatch him some applause."
Ah! will you not compel them to be dumb?

NERO

Let's see what we must do. Narcissus, come.   *1480*

ACT V

SCENE I

BRITANNICUS, JUNIA

BRITANNICUS

Yes, lady, who would have imagined Nero
Awaits me in his chamber to embrace me?
He is inviting all the young patricians.
He wants the merry splendour of a feast
To ratify our pledges in their sight,   *1485*
And to ignite the warmth of our embrace.
He quells his love, the cause of so much hate;
And makes you sovereign mistress of my fate.
And as for me, though banished from the throne,
Whereon he sits wearing my father's crown,   *1490*
Since he no longer stands against my love
And yields to me the crown of pleasing you,
My heart in secret, I admit, forgives,
And lets him have the rest with less regret.
What? I'll no more be parted from your sweetness?   *1495*
What? I may even now look without fear
Into your eyes, unmoved by threat or tear,
That for my sake, have sacrificed the Empire?
Dearest princess! What fresh timidity
Holds back your joy amid my ecstasy?   *1500*
Why, as you hear me, do your sweet, sad eyes
Gaze far away from me into the skies?
What do you fear?

JUNIA

I do not know myself,
But I do fear.

BRITANNICUS

You love me?

JUNIA

How I love!

BRITANNICUS

Nero no longer mars our happiness.   *1505*

JUNIA

But can you be so sure of his good faith?

BRITANNICUS

Do you suspect him of a hidden hate?

JUNIA

Nero loved me but now and swore your ruin.
He shuns me, seeks you. Can such change of tune,
My lord, my dearest lord, occur so soon?   *1510*

BRITANNICUS

My lady, this is Agrippina's stroke:
She felt my ruin would her fall provoke.
Thanks to her nature, jealous, overwrought,
Our greatest enemies for us have fought.
I place reliance on her obvious joy;   *1515*
On Burrhus I rely; even on his master.
Like me, he cannot have foul play in store,
Either he open hates or hates no more.

JUNIA

Ah! do not judge his heart, my lord, by yours:
You walk on different paths the two of you.   *1520*
I know the Court and Nero but one day;
But in this Court alas! I dare to say
How far is what one says from what one thinks!
Between the mouth and heart how few the links!

With what alacrity one breaks one's word! 1525
A strange abode for you and me, my lord!

BRITANNICUS

But whether true or false his friendship be,
If you fear Nero, must he not fear me?
No, no, he dare not, by a cowardly blow,
Become the people's and the Senate's foe. 1530
Indeed, his wrong he has to recognise;
His shame stood out, even in Narcissus' eyes.[19]
If my Princess had heard how far and knew—

JUNIA

But are you sure Narcissus is still true?

BRITANNICUS

Why should you wish distrust in me to wake? 1535

JUNIA

I do not know. But, Sir, your life's at stake.
I find all suspect; fear their treachery;
I fear Nero; fear my fixed misery.
Obsessed by dark forebodings of affright,
I hate to let you wander from my sight. 1540
Woe, if this peace, that you think ends the strife,
Should hide a trap to compass your dear life;
If Nero, furious at our changeless love,
Had picked the night to veil some desperate move!
If he were now preparing some dark brew! 1545
If, for the last time, I were seeing you!
Ah! Prince.

BRITANNICUS

You're weeping! Ah, my sweet Princess,
Must your dear heart so deep its love express?
What? In a single day when, full of glory,
Nero hoped dazzle with his splendour's story, 1550

[19] Among many examples of the eloquent use of "eyes" throughout Racine's tragedies, this is perhaps the most telling. Britannicus, in his innocence, mistakes the shiftiness in the murderous Narcissus' eyes as reflecting Nero's remorse!

Where all shun me and all to him resort,
Prefer my wretchedness to his great Court?
What? On this same day and at this same place,
Reject an Empire, weep before my face!
But please, my lady, stay your precious tears: *1555*
My quick return will soon dispel your fears.
Longer delay might his suspicions move;
Farewell. I go, my heart full of my love,
In the blind din of youth's convivial press
To see, to dream alone of my Princess.   *1560*
Farewell.

JUNIA

Prince . . .

BRITANNICUS

They are waiting. I must go . . .

JUNIA

But wait at least until they tell you so.

SCENE II

Enter AGRIPPINA

AGRIPPINA

Why are you dallying, Prince? Be off, at once:
The impatient Nero murmurs at your absence.
The joy and pleasure of the company   *1565*
To reach their climax wait for your embrace.
Do not allow their ardent zeal to cool . . .
Then go. And, Madam, let us see Octavia.

BRITANNICUS

Go, lovely Junia; with a happy mind
Haste to embrace my sister who awaits you.   *1570*

As soon as I am able I shall follow,
My lady, and thank you for all your pains.

Exit BRITANNICUS

SCENE III

AGRIPPINA

Unless I am mistaken, your eyes tell me
You have been weeping, taking leave of him.
May I enquire what cloud is troubling you?   *1575*
Do you doubt a peace I've made my handiwork?

JUNIA

With all the anguish that this day has cost
How can I calm my agitated heart?
I cannot fully grasp this wonder yet.
Were I to fear some check even to your goodness,   *1580*
It is because a Court is full of change;
And Fear must still as Love's companion range.

AGRIPPINA

Enough, I've spoken; all is different now.
My pains for your mistrust no room allow.
I'll answer for a peace that's sworn to me: *1585*
Nero has given me his guarantee.
If you had only seen with what caresses
He pledged to me his earnest faith afresh!
With what embraces he has just detained me!
He could not take his arms away from me;   *1590*
With patent goodness, shining in his face,
He told me, first of all, the smallest secrets.
He was my darling son who came to rest
His proud head on my broad, forgiving breast.
But soon, resuming the imperial air   *1595*
Of Caesar taking counsel of his mother,
He asked my aid in great affairs of State

On which depends the universe's fate.
No, I must, to his credit, here confess
His heart is free of any wickedness.   *1600*
It is our foes alone who spoil his goodness
By taking mean advantage of his kindness.
But now, at last, their power is on the wane;
Rome soon will know her Agrippina again!
Already they're enraptured at my favour.   *1605*
But let us not stay here until it's dark.
Let's go and give Octavia all the news
Of a day as happy as I feared it fatal.
But what is that I hear? What din confused?
What can it be?

JUNIA

Heavens! Save Britannicus!   *1610*

SCENE IV

Enter BURRHUS

AGRIPPINA

Where are you running, Burrhus? Stop. What means . . .

BURRHUS

The end has come, Britannicus is dying.

JUNIA

Ah, my Prince!

AGRIPPINA

Dying?

BURRHUS

Rather, he is dead.

JUNIA

My lady, pardon me my desolation.
I run to save him, if I can, or die.   *1615*

Exit JUNIA

SCENE V

AGRIPPINA

Whose crime was it?

BURRHUS

                    I cannot longer live,
My lady; I must leave the Court and Emperor.

AGRIPPINA

Did he not shrink even from his brother's blood?

BURRHUS

This deed was shrouded in more mystery.
As soon as Nero saw his brother come,   *1620*
He rose and kissed him. All stood silent, then
The first to raise his cup the Emperor said:
"To see this day in better omen ends,
My hand the promise of this cup extends;
Ye Gods, who witness this effusion,   *1625*
Come, deign to favour our reunion."
With the same oath Britannicus then pledged;
Narcissus poured the wine into his cup;
But hardly had his young lips touched the rim—
Steel cannot kill so suddenly, my lady—   *1630*
The poison drained the lustre from his eyes.
He fell upon his couch, all cold and dead.
You may imagine how all shook with terror;
Half of them left the room with cries of horror;

But those with greater knowledge of the Court   *1635*
Stayed in their seats, eyes fixed on Caesar's eyes.
Through all this, on his couch he still reclined
And did not seem to show the least surprise.
"This ill, you fear," he said, "has, since his childhood,
Often attacked him sharply without danger."   *1640*
In vain Narcissus tried to show concern,
His wicked joy broke loose in spite of him:
And even should the Emperor punish me,
I had to leave the hateful, crowded Court;
And, crushed by this base murder, I was going   *1645*
To mourn Britannicus and Nero's Rome.

AGRIPPINA

Here he comes. You will see if I inspire him.

SCENE VI[20]

Enter NERO *and* NARCISSUS

NERO (*Seeing* AGRIPPINA)

Gods!

AGRIPPINA

Nero, stop. There's something I must tell you.
Britannicus is dead. I've traced the blows;
I know the murderer.

NERO

Who, my lady?

AGRIPPINA

You.   *1650*

[20] In the edition of 1670 there was a scene (before the present Scene VI) between Nero and Junia, which Racine later suppressed.

NERO

I! Such are the suspicions of your mind.
There is no crime of which I am not guilty;
And if one were, my lady, to believe you,
It was my hand that cut short Claudius' life.
You loved his son. His death may have upset you: *1655*
But, for the blows of Fate I cannot answer.

AGRIPPINA

No, no. Britannicus was killed by poison.
Narcissus did it. And you ordered it.

NERO

Who, Madam, can have told you such a tale?

NARCISSUS

My lord, is this suspicion so accusing?   *1660*
Britannicus had secret plans, my lady,
That would have given you better cause for grief.
His aim was higher than the hand of Junia.
He would have punished you for your own kindness.
He was deceiving you; full of resentment,   *1665*
He hoped some day to disinter the past.
Then whether Fate has rescued you, despite you,
Or whether, knowing of the plot against him,
Caesar relied on me to deal with it,
Leave tears, my lady, to your foes alone.   *1670*
Let them regard this doom as sinister,
But you . . .

AGRIPPINA

      Go on with such a minister.
By glorious deeds you'll mark your glorious reign.
Go on. You have not done this deed in vain.
Your murderous hand, beginning with your brother,   *1675*
Will, I foresee, reach even to your mother.
Within your inmost heart I sense your hate;
You'll want to snap our bond and seal my fate.

But I wish my very death to burn your breast.
Do not think, dying, I shall let you rest.   *1680*
Our Rome, this sky, this light I gave to you,
Shall always, everywhere, thrust me in view.
Remorse shall rend you, like the raging Furies,[21]
That you'll appease with fresh barbarities;
Your frenzy, ever growing as it goes,   *1685*
Shall see, as each day dawns, some fresh blood flows.
But I hope, at last, Heaven, weary of your breath,
Will add to all your victims your own death;
That after weltering in their blood and mine,
You'll have to shed your own, in moan and whine: *1690*
And to the basest tyrants shall your name
Through all the ages spell the basest shame:
And that is what my heart forbodes for you.
Farewell. You may be off.

NERO

Narcissus, come.

Exeunt NERO *and* NARCISSUS

SCENE VII

AGRIPPINA

Ah, Heavens! How my suspicions were unjust!   *1695*
Burrhus I scorned, in Narcissus put my trust.
Ah, Burrhus, did you see what looks of hell
Nero, in parting, left me in farewell?
The end has come. He's broken loose from all.
Upon my head the blow foretold shall fall.   *1700*
He will, alas, crush you too in your turn.

[21] Suetonius (*Nero*, XXXIV) depicts Nero pursued by the Furies for the murder of his mother. Agrippina in this speech reaches for a moment the moral stature of a prophet.

BURRHUS

My lady, I have lived a day too long.
Ah, would to Heaven his hand, more happily,
Had aimed at me his first essay in madness;
That, through this blow, he had not given me   *1705*
A certain gauge of Rome's catastrophe.
His crime alone is not what shatters me;
His jealous love could make him kill his brother;
But, if I must make clear why I am crying,
Nero turned not a hair as he lay dying.   *1710*
His listless eyes already have the hardness
Of a tyrant raised in crime from infancy.
My lady, let him make an end and sentence
An irksome minister who cannot bear him.
Ah! far from seeking his vile mood to flee,   *1715*
The speediest death would be most dear to me.

LAST SCENE

Enter ALBINA

ALBINA

My lord, my lady, run to save the Emperor:
Come, rescue Caesar from his own mad temper.
He has for ever been cut off from Junia.

AGRIPPINA

What's that? Has Junia taken her own life?   *1720*

ALBINA

To crush the Emperor with eternal anguish,
My lady, though alive, she's dead to him.
You know how she rushed out from this apartment:
She made pretence of visiting Octavia;
But soon, by devious paths, she took her way,   *1725*

While, with my eyes, I traced her hurried steps.
She left the palace gates as though demented.
Seeing the statue of Augustus there,
She washed with tears the marble of his feet,
Which she held tightly in her frightened arms: *1730*
"Prince, by these knees," she said, "that I embrace,
Protect now the last remnant of your race.
Rome, in your palace, has just murdered seen
Your sole descendant who like you has been.
They want me, now he's dead, falsely to act;   *1735*
But I, to keep for him my faith intact,
Myself a Virgin of the Gods declare
Whose altars your great virtues made you share."
The people, meanwhile, wondering at this sight,
Run up in throngs from all sides and surround her,   *1740*
Touched by her tears; and pitying her pain,
With one accord they take her in protection.
They lead her to the temple where, so long,
Our Virgins, destined to the altars cult,
Guard faithfully the precious sanctuary   *1745*
Of the flame kept ever burning for our Gods.
Caesar sees them but dares not interrupt.
Narcissus, bolder, presses on to please him.
He makes for Junia and, quite unafraid,
Tries to arrest her with a hand profane.   *1750*
A thousand blows his shameless daring end,
His false blood spurting over Junia.
Caesar, sudden dismayed by all these sights,
Leaves him to them who had surrounded him
And comes back. All avoid his savage silence.   *1755*
The one word 'Junia' escapes his lips.
Aimless, he walks and his unsteady eyes
Dare not turn heavenward their distracted looks;
And it is dreaded, if the lonely night
Sharpens the violence of his despair,   *1760*
If you will leave him longer without help,
His grief may move him soon to end his life.
Run, time is short; for in his present plight,
Madam, he'll kill himself.

AGRIPPINA

　　　　　'Twill serve him right.
But let us see how far his passions range;　　　*1765*
Let's see if his remorse will make him change
And wiser counsels will prevail with time.

BURRHUS

Pray Heaven this were his one and only crime!

THE END

BERENICE

A Tragedy

To Monseigneur Colbert,* Secretary of State,
    Controller-General of Finance,
    Superintendent of Public Works;
    Grand-Treasurer of the Orders of the King,
    Marquis of Seignelay, etc.

Your Lordship,

*However justified my mistrust of myself and of my works may
be, I venture to hope that you will not condemn the liberty I
take to dedicate this tragedy to you. You have not deemed it
altogether unworthy of your approval. But what constitutes its
greatest merit in your eyes, is, your Lordship, that you have
witnessed its good fortune of not displeasing His Majesty.
It is well-known that the least trifles become important to you
in so far as they further, however little, his fame or his
pleasure. And this is what, in the midst of so many weighty
preoccupations, to which you are perpetually tied by your
monarch's zeal and the public welfare, makes you not disdain to
descend sometimes to us to ask us to account for our leisure.
I would have here a fine opportunity to enlarge on your
praises, if you would allow me to praise you. And what would I
not say about so many rare qualities which have brought you the
admiration of all France, about that deep insight which nothing
can escape, about that vast intellect which embraces, executes
at the same time, so many great projects, about that spirit
which nothing can daunt nor weary?
But, your Lordship, one must be more restrained in speaking
to you about yourself, and I would fear by embarrassing praise
to risk making you regret the favourable attention with which*

* Racine's good relations with Colbert were maintained to the extent that
Colbert was a witness to Racine's marriage contract in 1677.

*you have honoured me. It is better for me to think of earning it
by some fresh work. This, indeed, is the most palatable thanks
one can give you.*

> *I am with profound respect,*
> *Your Lordship.*
>> *Your very humble and
>> very obedient servant,*
>> RACINE

Preface

Titus reginam Berenicen, cui etiam nuptias pollicitus ferebatur, statim ab Urbe dimisit invitus invitam. *

That is to say, "Titus, who loved Berenice passionately, and who even, as was believed, had promised to marry her, sent her away from Rome, against his will and against hers, in the first days of his reign." This action is very famous in history; and I I have found it very suitable for the stage, on account of the depth of the passions that it could arouse. Indeed, we have nothing more moving in all the poets except for the separation of Aeneas and Dido in Virgil. And who can doubt that what could furnish enough matter for a whole book of an epic, in which the action lasts several days, may not suffice for the subject of a tragedy of which the span can only be a few hours? It is true that I have not pushed Berenice to the point of killing herself like Dido, because Berenice, not having had in my play the ultimate union with Titus which Dido had with Aeneas, is not obliged like her to give up her life. Short of that, the last farewell she bids Titus, and her struggle to part from him is not the least tragic moment of the play, and I make bold to say that it renews pretty effectively in the audience's hearts the emotion the rest of the play had succeeded in arousing. It is by no means essential that there should be blood and corpses in a tragedy; it is enough that its action should be great and its actors heroic, that passions should be aroused, and that everything in it should breathe that majestic sadness in which all the pleasure of tragedy resides.

I believed I could find all these ingredients in my subject. But what pleased me more about it is that I found it extremely simple.

* Suetonius (*Twelve Caesars*, Titus, Chap. VII).

For a long time I have been wanting to see whether I could construct a tragedy with that simplicity of action so greatly to the taste of the Ancients. For it is one of the first precepts they have left us. "Let whatever you do," says Horace, "be ever simple and one whole."* They have admired the *Ajax* of Sophocles, which is nothing else than Ajax killing himself for grief, because of the rage into which he had sunk after being refused the arms of Achilles. They have admired his *Philoctetes*, the whole subject of which is Ulysses coming to filch the arrows of Hercules. His *Oedipus* itself, although full of recognitions, is less burdened with matter than the simplest tragedy of our days. Finally we see that the supporters of Terence, who rightly put him above all comic poets for the elegance of his diction and the verisimilitude of his manners, cannot help admitting that Plautus has a great advantage over him on account of the simplicity of most of Plautus' subjects. And it is doubtless this marvellous simplicity which has won him all the praises the Ancients showered on him. How much simpler still was Menander, since Terence is obliged to take two comedies of that poet to make one of his own!

And one must not imagine that this rule is based only on the caprice of those who have made it. Only what is probable can move us in a tragedy. And what is there probable about a multitude of things happening in one day which could hardly happen in several weeks? There are some who think that this simplicity is a sign of lack of invention. They do not reflect that on the contrary all invention consists in making something out of nothing, and that all that multiplicity of incidents has always been the refuge of poets who did not feel in their own genius either enough fertility or enough strength to hold their audience through five Acts, by a simple plot, sustained by the depth of the passions, by the beauty of the sentiments and by the elegance of the expression.† I am very far from imagining that all these qualities are found in my work; but I also cannot imagine that the public will bear me a grudge for having given it a tragedy honoured by so many tears and the thirtieth performance of which has been followed with as much attention as the first.

* Horace, *Ars Poetica*, line 23.
† Doubtless a thrust at Corneille, whose *Tite et Bérénice* on the same subject was first performed by Molière's company, a week after Racine's had appeared at the Hôtel de Bourgogne.

It is not as though some people had not reproached me for this very simplicity for which I have striven so carefully. They believed that a tragedy so little burdened with intrigues could not be in accordance with the rules of drama. I enquired whether they complained that it had bored them. I was told they all confessed that it did not bore them at all, that it had even moved them in several places, and that they would see it again with pleasure. What more do they want? I beg them to have a good enough opinion of themselves not to believe that a play which moves them and gives them pleasure can be altogether against the rules. The chief rule is to please and to move. All the others are laid down in order to achieve this first one. But all these rules are full of details about which I advise them not to bother themselves. They have more important business. Let them place on our shoulders the burden of interpreting the difficulties of the *Poetics* of Aristotle; let them keep for themselves the pleasure of weeping and being touched; and let them allow me to say to them what a musician once said to Philip, King of Macedon, who asserted that a song was not according to the rules: "God forbid, my lord, that you ever be so unfortunate as to know these things better than I!"*

That is all I have to say to those persons whom I shall always aspire to please. For as regards the libel made against me†, I believe my readers will spare me gladly from replying to it. And what would I reply to a man who cannot think properly and who cannot even shape what he does think? He speaks of "protasis" as though he understood the word and insists that this first of the four parts of a tragedy be always next to the last, which is the catastrophe. He complains that his profound knowledge of the rules prevents him from enjoying himself at the theatre. Certainly, to judge by his dissertation, never was complaint less well-founded. It seems clear that he has never read Sophocles, whom he very wrongly praises "for a great multiplicity of incidents," and that he has never read even anything of the *Poetics* except in the prefaces of some tragedies. But I forgive him for not knowing the rules of drama, since happily for the public he does not set himself

---

* Plutarch's treatise, "How to distinguish a flatterer from a friend."
† The *Criticism of Bérénice*, by the Abbé de Villars. In spite of his resentment, Racine made certain modifications in the light of De Villars' criticism, which was even more cutting when dealing with Corneille's *Tite et Bérénice*.

to write for this medium. What I do not forgive him, is to know so ill the rules of polite jesting, him who does not wish to utter a word without jesting. Does he imagine he can greatly amuse men of breeding by his "pocket alases!" his, "my ladies, the rules," and a heap of other squalid affectations, which he will find condemned by all good authors, if he ever takes the trouble to read them?

All these criticisms are the handiwork of four or five wretched little authors, who have never been able, of themselves, to arouse the interest of the public. They always lie in wait for some work which is a success in order to decry it. Not indeed out of jealousy. For on what ground could they possibly be jealous? But in the hope that someone will trouble to reply to them and thus rescue them from the obscurity where their own works would have left them throughout their lives.

BERENICE

First performed at the Hôtel de Bourgogne on Friday, November 21, 1670; first edition, 1671.

CHARACTERS

TITUS	*Emperor of Rome*
BERENICE[1]	*Queen of Palestine*
ANTIOCHUS	*King of Commagene*
PAULINUS	*Lord-in-waiting to Titus*
ARSACES	*Lord-in-waiting to Antiochus*
PHENICE	*Lady-in-waiting to Berenice*
RUTILIUS	*A Roman*

Attendants of Titus

The scene is at Rome, in a vestibule between the apartment of Titus and that of Berenice.

[1] Pronounced in three syllables, rather like the French, and not in four syllables as is often done in English, after the Greek.

ACT I

SCENE I

ANTIOCHUS

Let's stay awhile. Arsaces, I can see
The splendour of this place is new to you.
Within this grand secluded chamber Titus
Often unburdens his most secret thoughts.
Here it is sometimes, stealing from his Court,   5
He comes to whisper to the Queen his love.
This door gives access to his private chamber
And that door opens on the Queen's apartment.
Go to her now, with my apologies,
And say I want a private interview.   10

ARSACES

Apologies, my lord? From you, her friend,
Who ever loyally defends her interests?
From you, Antiochus, her former suitor?
From you, one of the Orient's greatest kings?
Does she believe, already wed to Titus,   15
She has the Empress' right to keep her distance?

ANTIOCHUS

Go now I say, and without more ado
See, if I soon may speak to her alone.

Exit ARSACES

SCENE II

ANTIOCHUS (*Alone*)

Antiochus, my friend, are you the same?
May I tell her 'I love you' without trembling?   20
Already, ah, I tremble. My torn heart
Mistrusts this moment much as I desired it.
Long since, she put an end to all my hopes
And bade me never utter more my love.
For five years I kept silent; till today   25
I hid my passion under friendship's veil.
Can I believe, upon the Empire's brink
She'll hear me better than in Palestine?
Titus will wed her. Is this then the time
For me to come to her to tell my love?   30
What shall I profit from this rash avowal?
Since I must go, why go, annoying her?
Let me withdraw, depart, without a word,
And far away let me forget or die.
What? Must she never know the pangs I suffer?   35
And must I always weep and gulp my tears?
Why fear her anger, when I'm losing her?
My lovely queen, why should you be offended?
Am I demanding you should leave the Emperor?
That you should love me? I come but to say   40
That having for a long time hoped my rival
Would find a fatal bar to his desires,
Today when he is master and would wed you,
I, sad example of long constancy,
After five years of love and luckless longing,   45
Depart, still loyal, when my hope is dead.
Far from being angry, she may pity me.
So let me speak; I've held my tongue enough.
Alas! What can a hopeless lover fear
Who is resolved to see her nevermore?   50

SCENE III

Re-enter ARSACES

ANTIOCHUS

Shall we go in?

ARSACES

    My lord, I've seen the Queen;
But just to reach her it was pretty hard
To breast my way through the oncoming waves
Of a fawning mob drawn by her dawning greatness.
After a week of stern seclusion, Titus   55
No longer mourns Vespasian his father.
Once more he turns to prosecute his love;
And if we credit what the Court is saying,
Perhaps, before night falls, blest Berenice
Will change the name of Queen for that of Empress. 60

ANTIOCHUS

Alas!

ARSACES

What, can this happy news upset you?

ANTIOCHUS

Then may I not converse with her alone?

ARSACES

You may, my lord. The Queen has been apprised
You wish a private interview with her.
She indicated by a gracious nod   65
Her willingness to grant your urgent plea;
And doubtless she awaits a proper moment
To steal away from the oppressive throng.

ANTIOCHUS

Enough. Meanwhile, I hope you have complied
With all the weighty orders I have given.   70

ARSACES

My lord, you know my prompt obedience;
In Ostia our vessels lie equipped,
All ready to depart at any hour,
Awaiting only your command to sail.
But whom are you sending to Commagene?[2]   75

ANTIOCHUS

We must depart when I have seen the Queen.

ARSACES

Who must?

ANTIOCHUS

                I.

ARSACES

            You?

ANTIOCHUS

                Yes, when I leave this palace,
I leave Rome, and, Arsaces, leave forever.

ARSACES

My lord, this is indeed surprising news.
To think that Berenice should have so long   80
Drawn you so far away from your dominions;
For three years she has held you here in Rome;
And when the Queen, as surety of her triumph,
Expects you as her ceremonial witness;
When her belovèd Titus, as her consort,   85
Gives her a splendour that will flash on you. . .

[2] Lying to the northeast of Syria, it became a Roman province in the reign of
Domitian, Titus' brother and successor.

ANTIOCHUS

Arsaces, let her savour her good fortune,
And end, I say, this tedious conversation.

ARSACES

I understand, my lord. Her new found rank
Has rendered her unmindful of your favours;   *90*
And hatred follows your regard betrayed.

ANTIOCHUS

Arsaces, she was never hated less.

ARSACES

What is it then? Has the new emperor
In overweening greatness scorned your worth?
Some inkling of his coldness causes you   *95*
Far, far away from Rome to shun his presence?

ANTIOCHUS

Titus has not shown less esteem for me.
I would be wrong to murmur.

ARSACES

                    Then why go?
What whim makes you your own worst enemy?
Heaven puts upon the throne a Prince who loves you,   *100*
A Prince, himself a witness of your feats,
Who saw you by his side seek death and fame;
Whose valour, with your aid, at last prevailed
In conquering rebellious Judaea.
Can he forget that tragic, glorious day   *105*
That clinched the fate of a long, shifting siege?
Upon their triple ramparts our foes calmly
Looked down upon our vain assaults unscathed;
Our battering ram stood there, a useless threat.
You only, only you, seizing a ladder,[3]   *110*

[3] Josephus lends some support to this account, which Racine has embellished
to enhance the stature of Antiochus.

Threw death and dire destruction on their walls.
That day blazed almost your own funeral:
Titus embraced you, dying in my arms,
And the whole camp mourned your victorious death.
Now is the time, my lord, you may expect   *115*
The fruit of so much blood they've seen you shed.
If, anxious to return to your own realms,
You tire of living where you do not reign,
Unhonoured must Euphrates welcome you?
Let Caesar send you home in triumph laden   *120*
With sovereign dignities, those farewell gifts
Endowing kings who are the friends of Rome.
My lord, can nothing turn you from your course?
You are still silent.

ANTIOCHUS

              What more can I say?
I only wish to speak to Berenice.   *125*

ARSACES

And then, my lord?

ANTIOCHUS

           Her fate will settle mine.

ARSACES

How so?

ANTIOCHUS

           I want to hear about her marriage.
If by her lips the rumour is confirmed,
If it is true she mounts the imperial throne;
If Titus marries her, I take my leave.   *130*

ARSACES

What makes this marriage fatal in your sight?

ANTIOCHUS

I'll tell you all when we are on our way.

ARSACES

What doubts, my lord, you cast into my mind!

ANTIOCHUS

I see the Queen. Farewell. Do all I ordered.

Exit ARSACES

SCENE IV

Enter BERENICE *and* PHENICE

BERENICE

At last I've stolen away from all these new   *135*
Friends, my good fortune sends me with their chatter;
I have escaped their tedious respects
To seek a friend who ever speaks his mind.
Let me not mince the truth. My just impatience
Already blamed you for neglecting me.   *140*
What? I complained, Antiochus, whose kindness
All Rome and all the Orient have seen;
Who in my travails ever faithful proved,
Following with steady step my varied fortunes;
Today when Heaven seems presaging for me   *145*
An honour, I intend to share with you,
This same Antiochus, avoiding me,
Leaves me alone amid an alien throng?

ANTIOCHUS

Then it is true, my lady, and you are
About to crown your timeless love with marriage?   *150*

BERENICE

I would, my lord, confide to you my fears.
These last few days my eyes have filled with tears:
This mourning Titus laid upon his court

Included the suspension of his love.
No longer did I have his warm attentions   *155*
That made him spell-bound pass the days with me.
Silent and troubled and with tearful eyes,
He only greeted me with sad "good-byes."
Imagine then my grief, as you well can,
When my whole heart loves in him but the man,   *160*
And far from all the grandeur of his birth
Would choose his heart alone and seek his worth.

ANTIOCHUS

He has resumed his former tenderness?

BERENICE

You saw, yourself, the spectacle last night,
When, setting seal on his religious rites,   *165*
The Senate raised his father to the gods.
His filial duty, justly satisfied,
Left him the right to care for his beloved;
And at this moment, without telling me,
He's in the Senate, meeting at his order.   *170*
There he extends the bounds of Palestine,
Adding to it Arabia and all Syria,
And if I heed the gossip of his friends,
Or heed his vows a thousand times repeated,
He makes me sovereign of these many realms,   *175*
To crown my titles with the name of Empress.
He is to come to tell me so himself.

ANTIOCHUS

Then I have come to say good-bye forever.

BERENICE

What's that? What are you saying? What good-bye?
Why, you are agitated and change colour.   *180*

ANTIOCHUS

My lady, I must go.

BERENICE

May I not know. . .?

ANTIOCHUS

I should have gone instead of seeing her.

BERENICE

What do you fear? Speak, you are too long silent.
My lord, what is behind this quick departure?

ANTIOCHUS

At least remember I'm obeying you,   *185*
And for the last time you are hearing me.
If in your high degree of pomp and power
You bring to mind the country of your birth,
You will, my lady, bring to mind, my heart
Was the first victim of your lovely eyes.   *190*
I fell in love, your brother gave consent
And spoke to you: you were perhaps about
To let me woo you, when to my mischance
Your Titus came, and saw and conquered you.
He stood before you, clothed in all the splendour   *195*
Of one who bears Rome's vengeance in his hands.
Judaea paled; and sad Antiochus
Became the first of all his numerous victims.
Your eyes soon read the reason for my gloom;
Your lips commanded mine to hold their peace.   *200*
For long I struggled, made my eyes my lips,
My tears and sighs pursued you everywhere;
But then at last your firmness won the day,
Imposing on me silence or else exile.
I had to promise, indeed, swear it you.   *205*
But since I now feel free to speak my mind,
The moment you extorted this fell promise,
My heart took oath to love you and forever.

BERENICE

What are you saying?

ANTIOCHUS

                    Five years I've held my tongue,
And go away to hold it longer still.   *210*
I was comrade in arms of happy Titus.
I hoped to shed my blood as I shed tears;
Or that, at least, a thousand exploits should
Make my name speak to you, if not my lips.
Heaven seemed to grant an end to my distress: *215*
You mourned my death. Alas, too premature!
My dangers were in vain. How ill I reckoned!
The worth of Titus far surpassed my fire.
I must give credit to his lionheart;
Though heir, my lady, to the throne of Rome,   *220*
Admired by all the world and loved by you,
He seemed to draw each blow upon himself,
Whilst, void of hope or love or wish to live,
His hapless rival seemed but following him.
I see your heart is secretly applauding;   *225*
I see you listen now with less distaste,
And most attentive to my mournful tale,
For Titus' praise you pardon all the rest.
After a siege as long as it was cruel,[4]
At last he crushed the rebels—sad, pale remnant   *230*
Of famine, flames and intestinal fury—
And left their ramparts buried in the ruins.
Rome welcomed his return, along with you.
How wearisome became the empty Orient!
I lingered roaming long in Caesarea[5]   *235*
Through those delightful haunts where I had loved you,
My plaintive sighs re-echoed through your realms
And with my tears I watered all your footprints.
At last, a prey to my despair, I turned
My melancholy steps to Italy.   *240*
There Fate reserved for me its final blow.
In greeting me, Titus brought me to you;
Our veil of friendship led you both astray

---

[4] The siege of Jerusalem, ending with the destruction of the Temple in 70 A.D.
[5] On the Mediterranean coast of Palestine, where Racine placed the capital of Berenice's realm.

And my love proved the privy of your love.
A secret hope, however, soothed my cares: *245*
Rome and Vespasian frowned upon your love;
Titus perhaps would yield, despite his struggling.
Vespasian dies and Titus is now lord.
Why did I not flee then? I wished to know
The way his first few days of rule would go.   *250*
My fate is settled. Soon you will be crowned.
Witness enough without me will be found
To give to all your bliss their claps and cheers;
For me who could have added only tears,
Poor, faithful victim, who have loved too well,   *255*
Happy in my unhappiness to tell
My blameless tale to her who caused my fever,
I take my leave, more deep in love than ever.

BERENICE

I could not, Sir, imagine any man
Would dare, upon the same day Caesar weds me,   *260*
To come before me with impunity
And make confession of his love for me.
In pledge of friendship I shall hold my tongue,
And shall forget the outrageous avowal.
I did not shorten its offensive flow;   *265*
Indeed, I say I'm sad to see you go.
Heaven knows, in all the happiness it showers
On me, I wanted only you as witness.
With all the world I honoured your great heart.
Titus esteemed you and you cherished Titus.   *270*
A hundred times I've found the greatest joy
In seeing Titus in his other self.

ANTIOCHUS

Just that I flee. But too late now I shun
Those cruel talks where I'm the other one.
Titus I flee; I flee this name that riles,   *275*
The name your mouth's repeating all the while.
What shall I say? Your absent eyes I flee,

That ever seeing me, never see me.
Farewell: I go, my heart too full of you,
In love, to wait till death brings me my due.   280
Above all, do not fear, in sorrow blind,
I'll fill with moans the ears of all mankind;
Only when sweet news of my death arrives
Will you remember I was still alive.
Farewell.

Exit ANTIOCHUS

SCENE V

PHENICE

How I pity him! Such loyalty   285
Deserved, my lady, better to succeed.
Do you not pity him?

BERENICE

This quick retreat,
I must confess, leaves me a secret pang.

PHENICE

I would have kept him here.

BERENICE

I keep him here?
I should forget his very memory.   290
You wish me then to fan a senseless passion?

PHENICE

Titus has not yet clearly told his mind,
Rome looks upon you with a jealous eye,
And for your sake her stringent laws appal me.
In Rome a man may only wed a Roman;   295
Rome hates all Kings and Berenice is Queen.

BERENICE

The time for fear, Phenice, is long since past.
Titus, all powerful, loves: he need but speak.
He'll see the Senate bringing me its homage,
The people crown with flowers his every image;   *300*
Have you not seen the splendour of last night?
Did not his greatness captivate your sight?
The night of crackling flames, the pyre, the torches,
The eagles, fasces, people, soldiers, arches,
The consuls, senators, the crowd of kings,   *305*
Whose brilliance all from my beloved springs;
The gold and purple, glittering with his glory,
The laurels witness to his triumph's story;
The myriad eyes you saw from every side
Gazing their fill at him, unsatisfied;   *310*
His royal stance, his fascinating airs;
With what respect, what reverential stares
Did all in secret pledge their loyalty!
Speak; who that saw him would not think like me,
However humble might have been his birth,   *315*
He would be hailed her master by the earth?
But where's this magic memory wafting me?
Yet at this very moment, Italy
Prays for Titus; with sacrifices they
Are hallowing the first fruits of his reign.   *320*
Why are we dallying? For his empire's weal
To guardian Heaven come let us, too, appeal.
No further need we wait. Immediately
I'll come to seek him, both at long last free
To tell each other all that lovers tell   *325*
When unrestrained at last their passions swell.

ACT II

SCENE I

TITUS, PAULINUS, ATTENDANTS

TITUS

Who went to tell the King of Commagene?
Is he aware I want him?

PAULINUS

    I saw the Queen.
The Prince had just been visiting her chamber.
He had already left when I arrived;   *330*
I bade them tell him, Sire, you wished to see him.

TITUS

Enough. And what is Berenice now doing?

PAULINUS

The Queen at present, mindful of your boons,
Is praying to Heaven for your prosperity.
She was about to leave.

TITUS

    Enchanting Queen!   *335*
Alas!

PAULINUS

 My lord, what makes you sad for her?
Her rule will now extend to half the Orient.
You pity her?

TITUS

Paulinus, you remain.

Exeunt ATTENDANTS

SCENE II

TITUS

I am aware Rome, doubtful of my plans,
Still waits to hear the fate of Berenice,   *340*
And that the secrets of her heart and mine
Have now become the gossip of the world.
The time has come for me to make pronouncement.
What do they say about the Queen and me?
Speak: what do you hear?

PAULINUS

          I hear everywhere,   *345*
My lord, your virtues and her beauty praised.

TITUS

What do they say of my desire for her?
How do they think our faithful love will end?

PAULINUS

You are all powerful. Love or cease to love,
The Court will always side with what you wish.   *350*

TITUS

And I have also seen this shallow Court,
Too ready always to obey its masters,
Approving Nero's most revolting crimes;
I've seen them praise his madness on their knees:
I will not take these sycophants as judge,   *355*
Paulinus. I desire a nobler audience;
And without listening to the voice of flatterers,
I wish your mouth to speak for every heart.

You've promised it to me. Respect and fear
Shut off from me the passage of complaint;   *360*
Better to see, better to hear, Paulinus,
I have required from you your eyes and ears.
I made this a condition of my friendship;
I wished you to interpret every heart;
And that, in face of flattery, your frankness   *365*
Would still ensure I duly heard the truth.
Then speak and say what Berenice may hope:
Will Rome be gracious or be harsh to her?
Am I to think so beautiful a Queen
Would still offend upon the imperial throne?   *370*

PAULINUS

You may be sure of it: be it right or wrong,
Rome does not wish to see her as her Empress.
They know her spell; and such exquisite hands
Seem made to hold dominion over men.
She even has, they say, a Roman heart;   *375*
She has a thousand virtues, but is Queen.
Rome, by an ancient law, that brooks no change,
To her blood will admit no foreign blood,
Will recognise no lawless progeny
Sprung from a marriage counter to her code.   *380*
Besides, you know, in banishing her Kings,
Rome to that title, once so high and holy,
Attached a deep and everlasting hate;
And though she's firmly loyal to her Caesars,
This hate, my lord, as symbol of her pride,   *385*
Lives on in every heart, though free no more.
Julius, the first to bend her to his power,
Who silenced law amid the alarms of war,
For Cleopatra pined and, undeclared,
Left her alone to languish in the Orient: *390*
While Antony, who loved her to idolatry
And on her breast forgot fame, fatherland,
Yet did not dare to take the name of husband.
Rome sent to bring him to his very knees,
And did not stay her all-avenging wrath   *395*

Till she destroyed both lover and his mistress.
Since then, my lord, Caligula and Nero,
Monsters, whose names I mention with regret,
And who, retaining but a man's appearance,
Trampled on all the sacred laws of Rome,   *400*
Feared this one law and did not dare to light
A nuptial torch abhorrent in our eyes.
You've ordered me, above all, to be frank.
We've seen the brother of the freedman Pallas,[6]
Felix, still bearing marks of Claudius' chains,   *405*
Become, my lord, the husband of two queens,
And if I must obey you to the end,
These two queens were of Berenice's blood;
And yet you think you may, without offence,
Conduct a queen into our Caesar's bed,   *410*
While the Orient sees its queenly beds defiled
By slaves, but lately freed from Roman chains?
This then is Rome's opinion of your love;
And it may well be before set of sun,
The Senate, bearing all the Empire's prayer,   *415*
Will come to tell you here what I've just said,
And with the senators Rome, at your feet,
Will beg a choice that's worthy of you both.
My lord, you may prepare your answer now.

TITUS

How deep the love they want me to renounce!   *420*

PAULINUS

One must admit the ardour of your love.

TITUS

A thousand times more ardent than you think,
Paulinus. It has been my daily joy
To make a point of seeing, pleasing her.
Much more—I have no secrets from your eyes—   *425*

---

[6] Pallas and Felix were both freedmen of Claudius. Pallas is mentioned several times in *Britannicus*.

For her a hundred times I've thanked the gods
Who chose my father from far Idumea,
And ranged behind him Orient and army,
And, rousing the remainder of the world,
Restored to bleeding Rome peace with his reign.   430
I've even wished to fill my father's place,
Paulinus, I, who would a hundred times,
Have given my life to stretch my father's days,
Had kinder fate deigned to extend his span:
All this (how ill a lover knows his will!)   435
Hoping to crown my Berenice as Empress,
As recognition of her love and faith,
And at her feet to see the world with me.
In spite of all my love and all her beauty,
After a thousand tear-supported vows,   440
Now that I can crown her enchanting brow,
Now that I love her even more than ever
And a sweet marriage binding me to her
Can set seal on my five years' hopes at last,
I'm going . . . gods! Ah, how can I asseverate . . . ?   445

PAULINUS

What, Sire?

TITUS

                    I'm going to part from her forever.
I have not only just abandoned hope.
I made you speak, I listened to your words,
So that your zeal might secretly succeed
In countering my love that still would speak.   450
Victory for long was poised towards Berenice,
And, if at last my honour wins the palm,
Be sure the battle to defeat such love
Will leave my heart to bleed for many a day.
I loved and sighed for her when all was peace;   455
Another ruled the empire of the world;
Captain of my fate, and still free to love
I was accountable to me alone.
But hardly had the gods recalled my sire,

As soon as my sad hand had closed his eyes,   460
I clearly saw how hopeless my desire!
I felt the burden that had fallen on me;
Far from belonging to my love, I knew
I had now to renounce my very self;
And that Heaven's choice, contrary to my love,   465
Gave to the world all my remaining days.
Rome closely scans today my every act.
What shame for me, for her what premonition,
If from the first, transgressing all her rights,
I built my bliss on the ruins of her laws!   470
Resolved to make this cruel sacrifice,
I wished to break it gently to my queen;
But where to begin? Twenty times this week
I wished to broach the subject in her presence;
Yet from the first word my embarrassed tongue   475
Within my mouth stayed frozen twenty times.
I hoped at least my troubled air and grief
Would hint to her our common misery:
All unsuspecting, feeling I am troubled,
She lends her hand to wipe away my tears,   480
Not dreaming for a moment that my vagueness
Spells sentence to a love so rich deserved.
At last today I summoned my resolve.
Paulinus, I must see her and must speak.
I'm waiting for Antiochus to entrust   485
To him this precious charge I cannot keep.
I want him to escort her to the Orient.
Tomorrow Rome shall see the Queen depart.
She shall soon be informed of it by me,
And for the last time I shall speak to her.   490

PAULINUS

I looked for nothing less from your deep love
Of honour, that brought victory everywhere.
Judaea conquered and her smoking ramparts,
Eternal monuments of your great zeal,
Made me feel certain your magnanimous heart   495
Would not, my lord, destroy your handiwork;

And that the conquering hero of the nations
Would soon or late know how to conquer self.

TITUS

Beneath fine names, how cruel is my honour!
Ah, how much finer would my sad eyes find it,   *500*
If it were to confront me but with death!
Indeed this very passion for my honour
Was planted in my breast by Berenice.
You know it well. This shining fame was not
From the beginning broidered with my name: *505*
Raised at the court of Nero in my youth,[7]
By bad example I was led astray
And still pursued the slippery slope of pleasure.
I fell in love with Berenice. To impress her
And gain her love, I did my very best;   *510*
My blood I lavished, taking all by storm.
Triumphant, I returned; but blood and tears
Were not sufficient to subdue her heart:
I strove to make a thousand wretches glad,
And my beneficence spread all around.   *515*
Happy! and happier far than you imagine,
When I could come before her beaming eyes,
Bearing a thousand hearts won by my boons!
I owe her all, Paulinus. Harsh reward!
All that I owe her is to crash on her.   *520*
As price of all my fame and all her virtue,
I'll say to her "Depart, see me no more".

PAULINUS

How so, my lord, how so? These generous gifts
That to Euphrates will extend her sway,
These piled up honours that surprised the Senate,   *525*
Can scarce convict you of ingratitude.
She rules a hundred new domains tomorrow.

---

[7] Suetonius recounts how Titus, present at the poisoning of Britannicus, his
bosom friend, was so overcome with grief that he drained the poisoned glass and
became dangerously ill. (Titus, *Twelve Caesars*, Chap. II.)

TITUS

Hollow diversions for so great a sorrow!
I know the Queen; am certain from the start
Her heart has wanted nothing but my heart.   530
I loved her and she loved me. Since that day
(Fatal, or fortunate, am I to say?)
In loving, having only love as goal,
In Rome a stranger, knowing not a soul,
She passes all her days with scarce a smile,   535
Happy only if I see her awhile:
And sometimes if, detained by cares of State,
I go to visit her a little late,
I'm sure to find with tears her fair face stained:
My hand in drying them is long detained.   540
In short the strongest bonds that Love may fashion,
Reproaches sweet and ever surging passion,
An artless spell, with ever bubbling fear,
Fame, virtue, beauty, all I find in her.
I've seen her every day for five whole years,   545
And ever for the first time it appears.
Enough, Paulinus, come. The more I think,
The more my fortitude begins to sink.
Ah, gods! What cruel news I'm going to break!
Come, think no more, or my resolve will shake;   550
I know my duty, let me do it now;
I do not care if I survive the blow.

SCENE III

Enter RUTILIUS

RUTILIUS

My lord, Queen Berenice would speak with you.

TITUS

Paulinus!

PAULINUS

What, already you withdraw?
Bring back to mind, my lord, your noble plans.   *555*
Now is the time.

TITUS

Well then, let her approach.

Exit RUTILIUS

SCENE IV

Enter BERENICE *and* PHENICE

BERENICE

Pray, pardon me if, too importunate,
I dare intrude upon your privacy.
While all around me your assembled Court
Proclaim aloud your multitudinous gifts,   *560*
Sire, is it fitting at this moment, I
Alone should pine in dumb ingratitude?
But see, my lord, (I know your loyal friend
Is privy to the secrets of our hearts)
Your mourning now is over, nothing stops you,   *565*
You are at last alone and do not seek me.
I hear you're offering me another crown
And yet I may not hear you speak yourself.
Alas! give me more peace and fewer honours.
Can you not show your love but in the Senate?   *570*
Ah, Titus! for love after all breaks loose
From all those names that awe and fear impose,
What is the care that presses on your love?
Are realms the only presents it can give?
Since when do you believe I prize my greatness?   *575*
A sigh, a look, a word from your dear mouth,
Is all the ambition of a heart like mine.

See me more often, give me nothing more.
Is all your time devoted to the State?
After a week, you've nothing more to say?   580
How one small word could banish all my fears!
But were you speaking of me when I came!
Did all your secret talk include my name,
Sire? Was I present in your thoughts at least?

TITUS

You may be sure. The high gods I attest,   585
Berenice is ever present in my eyes.
Nor time, nor absence, I will swear once more,
Can wipe you from my ever loving heart.

BERENICE

An everlasting love you swear to me,
And yet with such frigidity you swear it?   590
And why invoke the name of Heaven itself!
Need you dispel my fears by dint of oaths?
My heart would never dream of doubting you
And, to convince me, just one sigh would do.

TITUS

My lady . . .

BERENICE

                Well, my lord? You still say nothing   595
And turn your eyes away and seem confused.
Must you still show to me a stricken face?
And must your father's death obsess your mind?
Can nothing charm away your gnawing pain?

TITUS

Ah, would to Heaven my father were alive!   600
How happy I should be!

BERENICE

                Your sorrows prove
How deep and tender was your filial love;

Your tears have done full honour to his name:
Now you must look to Rome and to your fame.
I do not dare to speak of my affairs.   605
Once Berenice could waft away your cares;
How eagerly you heeded all I said!
Tormented for your sake by ills I dread,
For your one word I've offered many a tear!
You mourn a father: lesser grief to bear!   610
And I—I shudder at the thought once more—
They wished to tear me from all I adore;
Me, who you know must ever weep and moan
When but a moment you leave me alone;
Me, who would die upon the very day   615
That they forbade . . .

                          TITUS

                What have you come to say?
At what a time! Please stop, I beg of you!
On one unworthy do not heap your boons.

                          BERENICE

On one unworthy? Are you such a one?
My boons perhaps to bore you have begun?   620

                          TITUS

No, Lady, no. Ah! never, I must say,
Has my desire been deeper than today.
But . . .

                          BERENICE

          Go on.

                          TITUS

          Alas!

                          BERENICE

          Speak.

                          TITUS

                The Empire . . . Rome . . .

BERENICE

Well?

TITUS

I can say no more: Paulinus, come.

Exeunt TITUS *and* PAULINUS

SCENE V

BERENICE

To leave me thus, so soon, and tell me nothing?   625
Phenice, alas, what a disastrous meeting!
What have I done? He seemed upon the brink . . .

PHENICE

Like you I'm in the dark the more I think.
But is there nothing you can call to mind
That may explain why the Emperor seems unkind?   630
Think carefully.

BERENICE

       Ah! you may believe me:
The more I call the past to memory,
From the time I saw him first to this sad time,
Too great a love has been my only crime.
But you heard everything. Tell me, my friend,   635
Have I said anything that might offend?
Who knows? Perhaps I have with too great heat
Dispraised his gifts and scolded his retreat.
Perhaps he dreads the hate in Rome he's seen.
He fears perhaps, he fears to wed a queen.   640
If it were true! But no, repeatedly
Against their harsh laws he gave guarantee.
Repeatedly . . . Let him explain so rude
A silence: I'm choked by incertitude.

How could I live, Phenice, if I thought he   645
Neglected me or I'd offended him!
Let's go to him. But when I think again,
I feel I see the reason for my pain;
He must have known all that has taken place!
Antiochus' love lost me his grace.   650
They tell me he is waiting for the king.
This is the sole cause of my suffering.
Of course, his gloom that caused me so much dread
Is but a slight suspicion easily shed.
I am not proud of my poor victory, dear,   655
Ah, would to Heaven (leaving your fame clear)
Some stronger rival came to test my troth,
With greater realms than yours to shake my oath,
And at my feet placed every pomp and power,
That you had nothing but your soul as dower!   660
Then only Titus, only then you'd see
Your heart, victorious, ah! how dear to me!
Come Phenice, just one word will make it plain.
Take comfort, heart, he loves me once again.
My haste to be unhappy this disproves—   665
If Titus can be jealous, Titus loves.

ACT III

SCENE I

TITUS

You were about to leave? What sudden cause
Speeds your departure, not to say your flight?
Were you about to flee without good-byes?
Are you withdrawing like some enemy?   670
What will the Court, Rome and the Empire say?
But as your firm friend what can I not say?
Of what do you accuse me? Have I merged
You hitherto with all the crowd of kings?
You had my open heart while father lived.   675
It was the one gift I could make to you.
And now, when with my heart my hand may shower
On you my ready benefits, you flee?
Do you believe, forgetful of my past,
I fix my thoughts upon my greatness only,   680
Keeping my distance from my dearest friends,
As strangers whom I no more need? Indeed,
You, Prince, who wished to steal away from me,
Are to me more than ever necessary.

ANTIOCHUS

I, my lord?

TITUS

You.

ANTIOCHUS

What could my lord expect   685
From an unhappy prince except good wishes?

TITUS

I've not forgotten, Prince, my victory
Owed half its glory to your noble deeds,
That in my triumph Rome saw thousands pass
Who wore the fetters of Antiochus;   690
That in the Capitol she sees displayed
The spoils of the Jews captured by your hands.
I want no further bloody deeds from you,
I only want to ask of you your voice.
I know how Berenice, who owes you much,   695
Believes she has in you a loyal friend—
She sees and hears in Rome no one but you;
We look upon you as our heart and soul.
For friendship's sake, so noble and so true,
Draw on the influence you have on her.   700
See her on my behalf.

ANTIOCHUS

I? Go before her?
I've taken my eternal leave of her.

TITUS

Prince, you must speak to her, for me, once more.

ANTIOCHUS

You speak to her, my lord. She worships you.
Why, at this moment, do you wish to miss   705
The joy of making her your own avowal?
Impatiently, my lord, she waits to hear it.
I'll vouch for her consent, as I depart.
She even said to me, resolved to wed her,
You'd only see her now to win acceptance.   710

TITUS

Ah! how I should have loved this sweet avowal!
How happy I should be if I could make it!
I hoped today to give my passion play;
And yet I must abandon her today.

ANTIOCHUS

Abandon her, my lord?

TITUS

            Such is my fate.   *715*
From Titus, Berenice must separate.
With marriage hopes in vain I lulled my heart.
Tomorrow, Prince, with you she must depart.

ANTIOCHUS

Do I hear right?

TITUS

         Pity my irksome greatness.
As master of the world, I rule its fate: *720*
Kings I may make and I may unmake kings,
And yet I am not free to give my heart.
Rome, with her hate inveterate for kings,
Disdains a queen, however choice she be.
Her sparkling crown and hundred royal fathers   *725*
Sully my love, offending every eye.
Free otherwise, my heart could darkly burn
And not fear to provoke the slightest murmur;
And Rome would gladly welcome as her Empress
The lowliest beauty suckled at her breast.   *730*
Julius himself drew back when faced by the flood
Engulfing me. Tomorrow if the people
Do not see the Queen leave, she will tomorrow
Hear their wild clamour for her prompt departure.
Let's spare my name and hers from such affront;   *735*

And since we must yield, let's to honour yield.
My glances and my lips, mute for a week,
Will have prepared her for this sad recital,
And at this very moment anxious, urgent,
She seeks an explanation face to face.   *740*
Please mitigate a stricken lover's pain;
And spare my heart this cruel explanation;
Then go to her and tell my troubled silence.
Explain, above all, I must not see her.
Be the sole witness of her tears and mine;   *745*
Bid her farewell from me and bring me hers.
Let us both flee, the tragic meeting flee
That would overwhelm our feeble constancy.
If knowing she alone is my soul's mate
Can serve to soothe the harshness of her fate,   *750*
Prince, swear to her that ever loyally
Moaning at Court and banished more than she,
Bearing unto the grave her lover's name,
My reign will drag—an exile without aim,
If avid Heaven, robbing me of wife,   *755*
Wills further to afflict me with long life.
You, bound to her only by friendly care,
Do not forsake her, Prince, in her despair.
Let Orient see you hand in hand alight;
Let it become a triumph, not a flight;   *760*
Let your sweet friendship last eternally—
In all your converse ever mention me.
To make sure your domains are side by side,
Euphrates shall your empires now divide.
I know the Senate, ringing with your name,   *765*
Will ratify this present with acclaim.
I add Cilicia[8] to your Commagene.
Farewell: never leave my princess, my queen,
All that my heart could ever sanctify,
All I shall ever love until I die.   *770*

Exit TITUS

---

[8] Contiguous west of Commagene.

SCENE II

ARSACES

So Heaven at last begins to do you justice.
You'll leave, my lord, but leave with Berenice.
Instead of snatching her, he yields her to you.

ANTIOCHUS

Arsaces, give me time to breathe a little;
The change is great and I am thunderstruck.   775
Titus entrusts in my hands all he loves?
Should I believe, great gods, what I've just heard?
And if I do believe, should I rejoice?

ARSACES

But in my turn, Sir, what am I to think?
What hindrance to your happiness remains?   780
Were you deceiving me when you left here,
Still agitated by your last good-byes,
Your heart tense with the daring declaration
Of all its love that you recounted to me?
You fled a marriage that was shaking you.   785
This marriage now is off. Why worry more?
Give passionate rein to your enticing love.

ANTIOCHUS

Arsaces, I'm entrusted with her charge;
I'll have with her long, precious colloquies,
Her eyes too may become attuned to mine;   790
Perhaps her heart will read the difference
Between Titus' coldness and my constancy:
I'm crushed here by the weight of Titus' greatness;
In Rome all pales before his gorgeous splendour;
But though the Orient's full of his exploits,   795
There Berenice shall see my glory's signs.

ARSACES

Be sure, my lord, your wishes all shall prosper.

ANTIOCHUS

Ah! how we both love to deceive ourselves!

ARSACES

Deceive ourselves?

ANTIOCHUS

       You think she would accept me?
Would Berenice no more reject my love?   *800*
Would Berenice console me with one word?
Do you a moment fancy, in her grief,
Even if the whole world spurned her loveliness,
The wretch would let me shed a tear for her,
Or that she'd stoop to welcome sweet attentions   *805*
She would believe were prompted by my love?

ARSACES

Who can console her better in her plight,
My lord, than you? Her fortune will now alter.
Titus abandons her.

ANTIOCHUS

       From this great change,
Alas, I shall be but afresh tormented   *810*
To fathom from her tears how much she loves him.
I'll see her moan. Myself, I'll pity her.
As fruit of all my love I'll have the pain
Of garnering tears that are not shed for me.

ARSACES

Must you delight in torturing yourself?   *815*
Was ever such a mighty heart so weak?
Open your eyes, my lord. Think carefully.
How many reasons give you Berenice.
Since Titus from today claims her no more,
She has no choice except to marry you.   *820*

ANTIOCHUS

No choice?

ARSACES

Allow her tears a few days' grace;
Let her first lamentations run their course.
Then all shall speak for you; her spite, her vengeance,
Titus' absence, the flow of time, your presence,
Three sceptres that she cannot hold alone,   825
Your neighbouring realms that seek to be made one.
Everything binds you, interest, reason, friendship.

ANTIOCHUS

Once more I breathe, Arsaces, you revive me.
I joyfully accept so sweet a prospect.
Then why delay? Let me fulfil my task.   830
Let's go to Berenice and, as commanded,
Announce to her Titus abandons her.
But rather let us stay. Is it for me
To play the part of harsh emissary?
Be it virtue, be it love, my heart takes fright.   835
The lovely Berenice learning her plight
From my mouth! Queen, whoever might have thought,
Such news to you could ever have been brought!

ARSACES

On Titus all her hate is sure to fall;
My lord, if you speak, it is at his call.   840

ANTIOCHUS

No, let us not see her. Respect her sorrow.
Others will flock to tell her all, tomorrow.
And is not her misfortune harsh enough
To learn of his humiliating sentence
Without this further fatal provocation   845
Of learning it from his own rival's lips?
Once more, let's flee: before it is too late,
Let's not with such news earn her lasting hate.

ARSACES

Ah, here she comes, my lord. Make up your mind.

ANTIOCHUS

Gods!

SCENE III

Enter BERENICE *and* PHENICE

BERENICE

What, my lord, you have not yet departed?   *850*

ANTIOCHUS

Your disappointment, Madam, is clear to see;
Your eyes were seeking Caesar here, not me.
Yet blame but him, if after my good-byes
My further presence here offends your eyes.
I might now well have been in Ostia's port,   *855*
Had he not ordered, not to leave his Court.

BERENICE

You, only you, he seeks. He shuns our view.

ANTIOCHUS

He has detained me but to speak of you.

BERENICE

Of me, Prince?

ANTIOCHUS

Yes.

BERENICE

And what, pray, was discussed?

ANTIOCHUS

Others, not I, may tell you, if they must.   *860*

BERENICE

What, Sir, may they tell?

ANTIOCHUS

Restrain your wrath,
Please. Others, far from keeping silent now,
Would gloat perhaps and full of confidence
Would gladly yield to your impatient urge.
But I, still timid, I, as you well know,   865
To whom your peace is dearer than my own,
Not to disturb it, risk your deep displeasure,
Fearing far more your misery than your anger.
You'll know I'm right before the end of day.
Lady, farewell.

BERENICE

Heavens! What do I hear? Stay.   870
My near despair I'll not attempt to screen.
You now behold a half-demented Queen,
Who, meditating death, must ask you this:
You fear, you tell me, to disturb my peace;
Yet your refusals, far from sparing me,   875
Arouse my anger, hate and misery.
Prince, if my peace is truly dear to you,
If I was ever precious in your view,
Throw light into my soul's obscurity.
What did Titus say?

ANTIOCHUS

Ah! Lady, pity . . .   880

BERENICE

What? You are not afraid to disobey?

ANTIOCHUS

I only have to speak to win your hate.

BERENICE

I must insist you speak.

ANTIOCHUS

What vehemence!
Once more, my lady, you will praise my silence.

BERENICE

Prince, satisfy my wishes instantly,   *885*
Or be assured forever of my hate.

ANTIOCHUS

Well, after this, I'll hold my tongue no longer.
Since you insist, you shall be satisfied:
But have no false hopes. You shall now receive
News of misfortunes that you daren't conceive.   *890*
You must expect, for I can read your heart,
I shall be striking at its tenderest part.
Titus has ordered . . .

BERENICE

What?

ANTIOCHUS

To tell you straight,
That he and you must ever separate.

BERENICE

Separate? Me? Who? What, Berenice from Titus!   *895*

ANTIOCHUS

Before you it is fair, I do him justice.
Whatever horror love's despair can pour
Into a heart that's generous and sore,
I've seen in his. He weeps, he worships you,
But what's the use of all his love for you?   *900*
A queen is suspect on the throne of Rome,
You two must separate and you sail home.

BERENICE

Must separate! Phenice!

PHENICE

Do not grieve so;
The greatness of your soul you now must show.
Of course the blow is hard, you must be dazed.   905

BERENICE

After such vows, that Titus should betray!
Titus who swore . . . I can't believe he'd break . . .
He cannot leave me, his honour is at stake.
He's innocent. Why turn me against Titus?
This trap is set only to disunite us.   910
Titus loves me. He would not see me die.
Let's go to him: I must speak instantly.
Let's go.

ANTIOCHUS

What's this? You think I could deceive you . . .

BERENICE

You wish it too much for me to believe you.
You cannot persuade me. In any case,   915
Take care you nevermore show me your face.

(*To* PHENICE)

Do not forsake me in my sad surprise.
Alas! I do my best to shut my eyes.

Exeunt BERENICE *and* PHENICE

SCENE IV

ANTIOCHUS

Did I hear right? Did my ears not deceive me?
Not show my face! She never will receive me!   920
I'll take good care of that. Would I have stayed,
Had Titus not, despite me, barred my way?
Let's leave at once. Arsaces, come with me.
She thinks I'm hurt, her hatred sets me free.

Just now you saw me, restless, sick at heart,   925
In jealous love's despair set to depart,
And now, Arsaces, after all her scorn,
I shall depart perhaps with unconcern.

ARSACES

Now more than ever here you must remain.

ANTIOCHUS

I? Shall I stay to see her hard disdain?   930
For Titus' cruelty am I to blame?
Must I be punished if he's not the same?
With what injustice and indignity
She dared to question my integrity!
Titus loves her, she says, and I've betrayed her.   935
The jade! to charge me with such base behaviour!
And when indeed? Why, at the very time
My rival's tears I painted as sublime,
And, to console her, lauded in her view
His steadfast love, more than perhaps is true.[9]   940

ARSACES

Why plague yourself, my lord? I beg you stay,
Allow this torrent time to pass away.
It needs perhaps a week or month to flow.
Only remain.

ANTIOCHUS

Arsaces, I must go.
Her pain—to pity her—might move my heart.   945
My honour, peace, all spur me to depart.
Let's go; and stay so far away from her
That news of her could scarcely reach my ear.
Yet some light's left before we need depart.
I'll linger in my palace. Till we start,   950
Go, see how far in grief she'll mourn and chafe.
Run. Let us leave, assured her life is safe.

[9] A splendid psychological stroke, typical of Racine.

ACT IV

SCENE I

BERENICE (*Alone*)

Will Phenice never come? O cruel moments,
How slow to my impatient need you seem!
Restless I run, in anguish all cast down;   955
Forsaken by my strength and killed by rest.
Will Phenice never come? How her delay
Affrights my heart with fatal premonitions!
Phenice will have no answer to my prayer.
Titus, the ungrateful Titus, would not hear her: 960
He flees, he hides himself from my just rage.

SCENE II

Enter PHENICE

BERENICE

Well, Phenice, have you seen the Emperor?
What did he say? Will he come?

PHENICE

                    I have seen him,
And clearly painted all your soul's distress.
I saw the tears flow that he tried to check.   965

BERENICE

Will he come?

PHENICE

Yes, you may be sure he will.
But how can you be seen in such disorder?
My lady, calm yourself and gain control:
Let me re-do these veils that slip from you,
And these loose tresses that conceal your eyes;   970
Let me repair the havoc of your tears.

BERENICE

Leave it alone, he'll see his handiwork.
What more do these vain ornaments avail?[10]
If all my faith and tears, my moans and sighs—
Do I say tears? if all my anguished cries,   975
My imminent death, do not bring him to me,
Tell me, what use will your attentions be,
And all this feeble charm that leaves him cold?

PHENICE

My lady, why this undeserved reproaching?
I hear some noise. The Emperor is approaching.   980
Come, shun the crowd and make a quick retreat.
Alone in your own chamber you should meet.

Exeunt BERENICE *and* PHENICE

SCENE III

Enter TITUS, PAULINUS *and* ATTENDANTS

TITUS

Paulinus, calm the Queen's anxiety.
I'm going to see her. Leave me now alone.
I wish to think.

[10] Contrast the movement at the beginning of Act I, Scene 3, of *Phèdre*, where Racine's love-stricken Phaedra longs to disarray the careful toilette that oppresses her, following a hint given by Euripides' Phaedra.

PAULINUS

Heavens! how I fear this struggle! 985
Great Gods, save Titus' name and the Empire's fame!
Let's see the Queen.

Exeunt PAULINUS *and* ATTENDANTS

SCENE IV

TITUS (*Alone*)

What, Titus, will you do?
Berenice awaits you. Where are you going,
Rash man? Are all your farewells ready? Do
You know your mind? And have you steeled your 990
  heart?
For be assured in the impending struggle
Firmness is not enough, you must be brutal.
Shall I resist those lovely, languid eyes
That find so well their way into my heart?
And when I see them flaming in their beauty, 995
Gazing at mine and crushing me with tears,
Shall I remember then my dreary duty?
Can I then say: "I wish no more to see you?"
I come to break a loving heart I worship.
And why break it? Who orders? Only I. 1000
For Rome has not yet given voice to doubts.
Around the palace have we heard her shouts?
Do I see the Empire tottering on the edge?
Can I not save it but by this sacrilege?
There's not a sound; too soon to agitate, 1005
Ills I may stem must I anticipate?
And who knows, conscious of her worth as woman,
If Rome might not wish to proclaim her Roman!
Rome by her choice may vindicate my choice.
No, no, once more, come let us keep our poise. 1010

Let Rome put in the scales against her laws
The whole weight of our tears, our love, our longing:
She'll side with us . . . Titus, open your eyes!
What air do you breathe? Are you not in that place
Where neither fear nor love can ever staunch   *1015*
The hate for Kings, suckled with mother's milk.
Rome judged your Queen when sentencing her Kings,
Have you not heard this voice since you were born?
And have you not heard also your renown
Bid you your duty even in your army?   *1020*
And when your Berenice arrived in Rome,
Did you not hear what Romans thought of her?
Must you have it repeated all the time?
Ah coward! make love and yield the reins of Empire.
Go, run and hide at the other end of the world,   *1025*
Make room for hearts more worthy of the throne.
Are these then all my grand and glorious plans
That were to consecrate my memory?
I've reigned a week. My deeds till now will prove
I've nothing done for honour, all for love.   *1030*
How to account for precious time deflected?
Where is the happy epoch men expected?
What tears have I dried? In what beaming eyes
Have I seen fruit of my fine enterprise?
Is there a change in the world's destiny?   *1035*
Do I know the sum of days Heaven's sanctioned me?
And of this little span, won at such cost,
How many, wretch, have I already lost![11]
No longer dally, do as honour bids,
Break the sole bond . . .

[11] Suetonius, in Chap. VIII of his Titus (*Twelve Caesars*), recounts Titus'
memorable words, when a day passed without his having done some good deed:
"My friends, I have wasted a day."

Has Rome condemned me not to see you more?
Do you begrudge me even the air you breathe?

TITUS

Alas, you may do what you will. Stay, Lady: *1130*
I do not counter it, but feel my weakness:
Forever I should have to fight and fear you,
Forever strain to hold my footsteps back
The magnet of your charm would still keep drawing.
Why, at this moment, my distracted heart   *1135*
Remembers only how it loves you still.

BERENICE

Sire, even so, what harm can come of that?
Do you see the Romans rising in revolt?

TITUS

And who knows how they will regard this insult?
If they protest, if cries succeed their murmurs,   *1140*
Must I then justify my choice with blood?
If they keep silent, selling me their laws,
To what will you expose me? What compliance
Must I yield some day to requite their patience?
What might they not then dare to ask of me?   *1145*
Shall I uphold the laws I cannot keep?

BERENICE

You count for nothing Berenice's tears.

TITUS

I count them nothing? Ah, gods! how unjust!

BERENICE

How so? For unjust laws that you may change,
You plunge yourself in everlasting woe?   *1150*
Rome has her rights, my lord; have you then none?
Her interests are more sacred than our own?
Say, speak.

SCENE V

Enter BERENICE

BERENICE (*Coming out*)

      Let me alone, I say.   *1040*
In vain you wish to hold me back from him.
I must see him. My lord, ah! here you are.
It is then true Titus abandons me?
We have to separate? And he who orders it?

TITUS

My lady, do not crush a hapless Prince.   *1045*
We both must pledge ourselves now not to weaken.
I'm torn and tossed enough by cruel cares
Without the precious torment of your tears.
Rather recall your courage that so often
Has made me recognise my duty's voice.   *1050*
Now is the time. Compel your love to silence,
And moved alone by reason and by honour,
Regard my duty in its awful strictness.
I beg you fortify my heart against you,
And help me dam its weakness, if I can,   *1055*
And hold back tears that spring continually;
Or if we are not master of our tears,
Let honour then at least sustain our sorrows,
And let by all the world be clearly seen
An Emperor's tears and the tears of a Queen.[12]   *1060*
For, my Princess, we have to separate.

[12] Racine has sometimes been criticized for excessive lachrymosity in this play. For his English translator this raises a peculiar difficulty, for whereas the French have two words for "tears" (*larmes* and *pleurs*), in English we have only the one. It is, however, significant that Racine, in this speech of Titus, has used for "tears" the same word *pleurs* five times, glistening like pearls with masterly effect.

BERENICE

Ah, cruel man, why say such things so late?
What have you done? I thought myself beloved.
My soul used to the joy of seeing you
Lives but for you. Did you not know your laws   1065
When for the first time I confessed my heart?
Why did you lead me on to love so well?
Why did you not say then, "Hapless Princess,
Think, what ties you are seeking, what your hope?
Ah! do not give a heart I may not take."   1070
Did you not take it, only to return it,
When you alone were all my heart could love?
The Empire has conspired against our marriage
So many times, why not leave me before?
A thousand reasons then could comfort me: 1075
I could accuse your father of my death,
The Roman people, Senate, all the land,
The whole world, rather than so dear a hand.
Long since against me voiced aloud, their hate
Would long since have prepared me for my fate.   1080
I'd not have had a blow as harsh as this
The moment when I looked for lasting bliss;
Now when your happy love may win its prize,
When Rome is quiet, when your father dies,
When at your feet the world brings you your due,   1085
When I at last have none to fear but you.

TITUS

And I alone too could destroy myself.
Then, I could live in all too sweet illusion.
My heart took care not to provoke the future,
To look for what some day might separate us.   1090
I wanted nothing to withstand my wish.
I hardly thought at all, hoping against hope.
Who knows, perhaps? I hoped to die for you
Before I'd have to face this harsh adieu.
All obstacles seemed but to fan my flame.   1095
The Empire spoke, but Reputation, Madam,

Had not yet in my heart assumed the tone
With which she speaks in an emperor's heart alone.
I know the agony my choice will give;
I feel without you I may no more live;
That my own heart will shrivel in its pain;
But living no more matters, I must reign.

BERENICE

Well, reign then! Satisfy your reputation.
An end to argument. I but awaited
A sentence from those lips, which a thousand times
Have sworn eternally to bind our loves,
A sentence from those lips, now clearly false,
Condemning me to everlasting absence.
I wished myself to hear you in this place.
I'll hear no more; and so farewell forever.
Forever! Ah, my lord, are you aware
How stark these cruel words to lovers are?
In a month, a year, how great our pain will be,
With all those seas still parting you from me!
The sun shall rise and set and rise again
While Titus seeks his Berenice in vain,
And Berenice in vain her Titus seeks!
But how I am mistaken! My heart speaks
Too soon. Already quit of all his pain,
He bids my absent days untold remain?
These days so slow for me, will fly pell-mell
For him!

TITUS

I'll not have many days to tell.[13]
My hope is very soon my sad renown
Will force you to admit you were beloved.
You'll see how Titus could not without dying . . .

BERENICE

If it is true, my lord, why should we part?
I speak no more of an auspicious marriage.

[13] Titus died two years later.

TITUS

How you are tearing me to shreds!

BERENICE

My lord, you are the Emperor and you weep![14]

TITUS

Yes, Lady, it is true, I weep, I sigh,   *1155*
I tremble; and yet when I claimed the Empire,
Rome made me promise to uphold her laws:
And I must now uphold them. More than once
Rome put to test her rulers' constancy.
Ah, if you were to go back to her birth,   *1160*
You'd find them all submissive to her laws.
One, jealous of his word,[15] goes to her foes
To seek, in death, his ready punishment;
Another puts to death a conquering son;[16]
A third, with dry and almost callous eyes,   *1165*
Sees two sons draw their last breath at his order.[17]
Unhappy men! but always with the Romans
Their country and their honour win the day.
I know in leaving you, the wretched Titus
Surpasses all their high austerity,   *1170*
That cannot equal my great sacrifice.
But, Lady, do you think I am unworthy
Of leaving future ages an example
That none may emulate without great effort?

BERENICE

I think all's easy to your savagery.   *1175*
I think you worthy, wretch, of killing me;

[14] This line recalls Marie Mancini (Mazarin's niece) in a similar situation, renouncing her hopes of Louis XIV's hand with the words, "You love me, you are King, and I go."

[15] Regulus. But it was in obedience to his conscience, not the laws of Rome.

[16] Manlius Torquatus, who put his son to death for fighting, contrary to his orders.

[17] Brutus, after the expulsion of the Tarquins.

And all your feelings I see clearly through.
I speak no more of staying here with you.
Who? I? Should I have wished, in sad disgrace,
To be the mock of Rome that hates my race?   *1180*
I wanted from your lips your 'no' to hear.
All's over now, soon, no more need you fear.
Do not expect to hear abuses flow,
With cries to Heaven, every perjurer's foe.
No, if my tears may still Heaven's pity gain,   *1185*
I pray, in dying, it forget my pain.
If arms I seek against your cruelties,
If, facing death, the mournful Berenice
Wants vengeance for her end to make you smart,
I'll seek no further than within your heart.   *1190*
I know so great a love must leave some traces,
That all my present grief, my past embraces,
My blood that through this palace I shall strew,
Are enemies enough I leave to you;
And unrepentant persevering, I   *1195*
On them for all my vengeance will rely.
Farewell.

Exit BERENICE

SCENE VI

Enter PAULINUS

PAULINUS

What was her mind in parting now,
My lord? Has she at last agreed to go?

TITUS

Paulinus, I am lost, I cannot live.
The Queen is bent on dying. We must follow   *1200*
And rush to save her.

PAULINUS

Have you not, my lord,
Commanded that a watch be kept on her?
Her ladies, all solicitous, around her,
Will take care to deflect her sombre thoughts.
You need fear nothing. You have passed the worst,   *1205*
My lord; continue, victory is yours.
I know you had to hear her with compassion.
Myself, at sight of her could not withold it.
But look beyond; think, in your deep distress,
What fame will follow but a moment's pain,   *1210*
What plaudits all the world prepares for you,
What future rank.

TITUS

No, I'm a savage brute.
I loathe myself. Even the hateful Nero
Never drove his cruelty so far.
I will not suffer Berenice to die.   *1215*
Let Rome say what she will. I shall defy
Her.

PAULINUS

What, Sire?

TITUS

I do not know what I'm saying.
My spirit's broken by my utter grief.

PAULINUS

Do not disturb the course of your renown:
The news of your farewells has reached the town.   *1220*
Rome, fearful once, rejoices in your fame;
Smoke rises from all temples in your name;
The crowd, shouting your virtues to the air,
With laurels crown your statues everywhere.

TITUS

Ah, Rome! Ah, Berenice! Ah, Gods above!   *1225*
Why am I Emperor? Why am I in love?

SCENE VII

Enter ANTIOCHUS *and* ARSACES

ANTIOCHUS

What have you done, Sire? Lovely Berenice
May well be dying in Phenice's arms.
Nor tears, nor prayers, nor reason will she heed;
She begs aloud a dagger or a poison.   *1230*
Alone you may deflect her from this course,
The mention of your name alone revives her.
Her eyes, forever turned towards your chamber,
Seem in their anguish to be calling you.
I cannot bear it. The sight is killing me.   *1235*
Ah! why delay? Pray, hasten to her side.
Save all this sum of virtue, grace and beauty,
Or give up, Sire, all claim to human kindness.
Say something.

TITUS

              Ah, what am I to reply?
Do I myself know if I live or die?   *1240*

SCENE VIII

Enter RUTILIUS

RUTILIUS

My lord, the tribunes, consuls and the Senate
Have come to see you in the name of Rome.
A great crowd follows them impatiently
Awaiting your arrival in your chamber.

TITUS

I understand, great Gods! This is your way   *1245*
To save my heart about to go astray!

PAULINUS

Come, my lord, enter the adjoining chamber
And see the Senate.

ANTIOCHUS

Hasten to the Queen.

PAULINUS

Could you, my lord, by this indignity,
Trample in dust the Empire's majesty?   *1250*
Rome . . .

TITUS

Ah! enough, Paulinus, we will hear them.
This is a duty, Prince, I cannot shun.
You see the Queen. On my return I'll prove
She'll have no reason more to doubt my love.[18]

[18] The act in the first edition (1671) ended with a Scene 9, in which Antiochus somewhat mawkishly bewailed his amorous frustration to Arsaces, lending some substance to the Abbé de Villars' criticisms. Racine wisely suppressed it, thereby strengthening Antiochus' character.

ACT V

SCENE I

ARSACES (*Alone*)

Where shall I find my ever-faithful prince?   *1255*
O Heaven, help me and lead me where he is.
Ordain I may at once impart to him
This happy news perhaps he dared not dream.

SCENE II

Enter ANTIOCHUS

ARSACES

Sir, what a stroke of luck has led you back
To me?

ANTIOCHUS

       If my return brings you some joy,   *1260*
You may give thanks to my despair alone.

ARSACES

The Queen departs.

ANTIOCHUS

       Departs?

ARSACES

           This very evening.
Her orders have been given. She is angry
Titus has left her to her tears so long.
A grand disdain has followed on her raving;   *1265*

And Berenice renounces Rome and Emperor.
She even wants to leave before Rome learns this
And sees her grief and relishes her flight.
She writes to Caesar.

ANTIOCHUS

Who would have believed it!
And Titus?

ARSACES

Titus has not come to her.   *1270*
With joy the people halt and circle him,
Applauding all the names the Senate gives him;
And all these names, these courtesies and these plaudits,
Have now become so many bonds for Titus,
That, fettering him with honourable chains,   *1275*
In spite of all his sighs and all his tears,
Attach his shifting wishes to his duty.
All's over now. Perhaps no more he'll see her.

ANTIOCHUS

Arsaces, I confess, I sense some hope!
But fortune has so long made me its plaything,   *1280*
So often have my plans all crashed in failure,
That I, with fear, listen to all you say;
And, with a pressing sense of doom, my heart
Feels even hoping may envenom fortune.
But what is this? Titus approaches us.   *1285*
What does he want?

SCENE III

Enter TITUS

TITUS (*On entering*)
Stay: no one else need follow.
At last I come, Prince, to fulfil my promise.
Berenice preoccupies and tortures me.

I come, my heart touched by your tears and hers,
To calm less cruel torments than my own.   *1290*
Come, Prince, come. Before you I will prove
For the last time whether or not I love.

Exit TITUS

SCENE IV

ANTIOCHUS

There goes the hope that you had given me;
And you behold the bliss I had expected.
The angry Berenice was just departing!   *1295*
Titus had left her, not to see her more!
What have I done, great Gods? What fatal course
Have you predestined for my wretched life?
Throughout my days I'm being forever tossed
From fear to hope, from hope to desperation.   *1300*
Must I still live? What? Berenice and Titus!
O cruel Gods! You shall not mock me more.

Exeunt ANTIOCHUS *and* ARSACES

SCENE V

Enter TITUS, BERENICE *and* PHENICE

BERENICE

I will not listen. I am quite resolved;
I wish to leave. Why show yourself to me?
Why come to deepen further my despair?   *1305*
Are you not satisfied? I will not see you more.

TITUS

But listen, please.

BERENICE

It is too late.

TITUS

My lady,

Just one word.

BERENICE

No.

TITUS

How she torments my soul!
My Princess, what has brought this sudden change?

BERENICE

All's over. You want me to leave tomorrow;   *1310*
And I've resolved to leave this very instant;
And I am leaving.

TITUS

Stay.

BERENICE

You tell me stay!
For what? To hear the insults of the crowd
That all around shout my deep pain aloud?
Do you not hear their glee, their savage tone,   *1315*
While in my tears I drown myself alone?
What crime, what wrong provoked their hideous knell?
What have I done, alas, but loved too well?

TITUS

Why do you listen to a senseless mob?

BERENICE

I can see nothing here that does not wound me.   *1320*
This very chamber, furnished as you planned,
This place, that saw so long my love expand,

That seemed to guarantee your own forever;
These festoons, with our twin names nought could sever,
Encountering my sad eyes everywhere,   *1325*
Are all impostors that I cannot bear.
Phenice, let's go.

TITUS

Oh, how unjust you are!

BERENICE

Return, my lord, return to your high Senate
Who come here to applaud your cruelty.
Well, were you captivated by their speeches?   *1330*
Have you quite satisfied your reputation?
And pledged them to forget me faithfully?
But this were scant atonement for your love:
Have you pledged them eternal hate for me?

TITUS

I have pledged nothing. That I'd ever hate you!   *1335*
That I could ever forget Berenice!
Ah Gods! At what a time her unjust taunts
Afflict my heart with all their cruel doubts!
Then know me, Lady, and for full five years
Think back on all the moments, all the days   *1340*
When I, by dint of passion and of sighs,
Expressed to you the surgings of my heart.
Today crowns all. Never, I must avow,
Were you so dear to me as you are now;
And never . . .

BERENICE

You still love me, so you say,   *1345*
Yet, at your order, I depart today!
Is my despair so ravishing to you
That you're afraid my tears might prove too few?
Of your returning heart what use to make?
Ah, wretch, show me less love, for pity's sake!   *1350*
Do not recall the sweet dreams of my heart,

And let me, at the least, convinced depart
That secretly, despite his outward show,
I leave a man who's glad to see me go.

(*He snatches and reads a letter*)

You've snatched from me what I have just been   *1355*
    writing.
And that is all I'm asking of your love.
Read it, ungrateful man, and let me go.

TITUS

You shall not go. I cannot give consent.
Your going then was but a strategem?
You seek to die? And but your sad remains   *1360*
Would represent the memory of my love!
Go, find Antiochus and bring him here.

(BERENICE *sinks down on a seat*)

Exit PHENICE

SCENE VI

TITUS

My lady, I must tell you all my heart.
When I foreshadowed first the dreadful moment,
When, beaten by the laws of my strict duty,   *1365*
I should be forced to give you up for ever:
When I foresaw this sad farewell approach,
My struggles, fears and your reproachful tears,
I steeled my soul to all the misery
That ultimate misfortune might arouse;   *1370*
But not my deepest dread could have conceived
A fraction of the torment I endure.
I thought my resolution less unsteady
And I'm ashamed to see it prove so weak.
I saw before me massed the whole of Rome;   *1375*

The Senate spoke, while my afflicted spirit
Listened but did not hear, and in reply
To all their zeal returned a frozen silence.
Rome's still uncertain of your destiny.
And all the time myself I scarce recall   *1380*
If I am Emperor or I am Roman.
I came to see you, unsure of my course,
Drawn by my love; I came perhaps to seek
Myself in you with knowledge of myself.
What have I found? Death painted in your eyes;   *1385*
You, leaving Rome, only to seek out death!
It is too much. This tragic sight at last
Has made my sorrow burst its farthest bounds.
I feel the last extremity of grief.
I also see the way to find relief.   *1390*
Do not expect, exhausted by my fears,
Through happy wedlock I shall dry your tears.
However far you may have pushed my pain,
Implacable my fame must still remain;
To my numbed soul it ceaselessly portrays   *1395*
Your marriage incompatible with my reign,
And bids, with all my bright and high endeavour,
My duty is to wed you less than ever.
And less than ever, Madam, may I say,
I will for your sake throw my throne away   *1400*
And to earth's farthest borders with you fly,
And slavishly in amorous dalliance sigh.
You would yourself my cowardly course disdain
And see with sorrow, marching in your train,
A shabby Emperor, empireless and powerless,   *1405*
Base spectacle to men of all love's weakness.
To end the pain to which my soul is prey,
There is, as you know well, a nobler way;
And, Lady, this stern path I have been taught
By many a hero, many a Prince distraught: *1410*
When multitudinous ills have sapped their might,
They all explained the unremitting spite
That ruthless Fate upon their heads would pour,
As secret orders to resist no more.

If further now your tears offend my eye,   *1415*
If I behold you still resolved to die,
If I must ever tremble for your days,
If you'll not swear to cherish them always,
Crueller sorrows crueller tears will bring:
In my despair I may dare anything,   *1420*
And cannot answer if before your eyes
I'll breathe to you my bloody last good-bye.

BERENICE

Alas!

TITUS

No, there is nothing I mayn't dare.
The balance of my days is in your care.
Think well, my lady, if I'm dear to you . . .   *1425*

LAST SCENE

Enter ANTIOCHUS

TITUS

Come, Antiochus, come, I sent for you.
I want you here to witness all my weakness,
See if my love for her lacks tenderness.
Judge.

ANTIOCHUS

I believe all, I know both of you.
But you yourself know now a hapless Prince;   *1430*
My lord, you've honoured me with your esteem:
And in my turn, as blameless I may swear,
I've striven to be thought your dearest friend:
I've striven for this even with my blood.
Despite me, you have both confided in me,   *1435*
The Queen, her love, and you, my lord, your own.

The Queen, who hears, is free to contradict:
She's seen me always ardent in your praise,
Repaying with my service your great trust.
You may believe you owe me thanks for this;   *1440*
But could you have believed, at this high moment,
That I, your friend most faithful, was your rival?

TITUS

My rival!

ANTIOCHUS

    It is time I told you all.
Yes, Sire, I've always worshipped Berenice.
A hundred times I've fought to love no more: *1445*
Forget I could not. Silence I could keep.
The fond illusion of your changing mind
Had sometimes given me some feeble hope:
But this, my hope, the Queen's tears have extinguished.
Her eyes, all bathed in tears, asked but for you.   *1450*
Myself, my lord, I came to summon you.
You now have come. You love her, she loves you.
You've given in. I never doubted it.
For the last time I've searched my inmost heart;
A last communion with myself I've made;   *1455*
I have just mustered all my powers of reason
And never have I felt more deep in love.
I must find other means to break such bonds.
The only way to snap them is by dying.
Gladly I die. I wished to tell you this.   *1460*
Yes, Lady, I have called him back to you.
I have succeeded, and do not regret it.
May Heaven on all your years incessant shower
A thousand bounties in continuous flower!
Or if it keep some little wrath in store,   *1465*
I beg the Gods to wipe out from their score
The ills in your fine life, they might think due,
Against the days I sacrifice for you.

BERENICE (*Rising*)

Stop, stop, my most magnanimous princes.
To what a pass you've brought me, both of you!   *1470*
Whether I look at you or gaze on him,
Everywhere I find the image of despair.
I see but tears and hear but mention made
Of horrors, woes and blood about to flow.

(*To* TITUS)

My heart is known to you, my lord, and I   *1475*
May say, for the Empire never did it sigh.
Not glorious Rome, nor Caesar's majesty
Has ever, as you know, attracted me.
I loved, my lord, I loved. I wanted love.
Today, I must confess, fear almost drove   *1480*
Me mad. I thought your love about to die.
I know my error, and your loyalty.
Your heart was torn, I saw your flowing tears.
Berenice, my lord, scarce merits all these fears,
Or that your love should rob the hapless world,   *1485*
When all its hopes in Titus are unfurled
And it begins to taste your virtuous might,
At one stroke of its love and its delight.[19]
For five long years until this very day
I've loved you only, I can truly say.   *1490*
This is not all. I will, in my despair,
By one last effort crown the whole affair.
I shall live, I shall follow your command.
Farewell and reign, my lord. Give me your hand.

(*To* ANTIOCHUS)

Prince, after this farewell, you surely know   *1495*
I cannot leave the man I love to go
Away from Rome and hear another's plea.
Live, you too prove your magnanimity.
Pattern your course on Titus and on me.
Titus loves and forsakes: I love and flee.   *1500*

[19] Suetonius, in his opening chapter on Titus (*Twelve Caesars*), refers to him as "the love and delight of the human race."

Your sighs and bonds take from me far away.
Farewell. Let us—all three of us—portray
To all the world the sweetest, saddest love,
Whose painful tale it ever will preserve.
All's ready. They await me. Let me pass.   *1505*

(To TITUS)

For the last time, farewell, my lord.

ANTIOCHUS

Alas!

THE END

✸✷✸

About the Translator

SAMUEL SOLOMON was educated at Clifton College, Bristol, and at King's College, Cambridge, where he graduated in the Modern Language Tripos. His first publication, *Poems from East and West,* included translations from the French and German. After spending twenty years in the Indian Civil Service, Mr. Solomon returned to England to devote his full time to literary and political activity. He ran for the House of Commons as a Liberal candidate in 1959 and 1964.

The author began his version of Racine's *Théâtre Complet* in 1949 and finished it in 1961. The publication of these plays in English, as well as Racine's prefaces to the plays, is the second translation of all of the plays into English, and the first complete translation of Racine's dramatic works in the twentieth century. These two volumes contain the only English translations of the *Théâtre Complet* with both plays and prefaces.

Mr. Solomon has also translated *Seven Plays of Corneille,* and the Austrian playwright Grillparzer's Greek plays.

The Best of the World's Best Books
COMPLETE LIST OF TITLES IN
THE MODERN LIBRARY

A series of handsome, cloth-bound books, formerly available only in expensive editions.

MISCELLANEOUS

MODERN LIBRARY GIANTS

A series of sturdily bound and handsomely printed, full-sized library editions of books formerly available only in expensive sets. These volumes contain from 600 to 1,400 pages each.

THE MODERN LIBRARY GIANTS REPRESENT A SELECTION OF THE WORLD'S GREATEST BOOKS